The French Revolution and British Popular Politics

The French Revolution and British Popular Politics

Edited by

Mark Philp

Fellow of Oriel College, Oxford

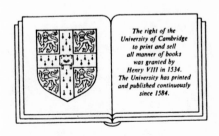

The right of the
University of Cambridge
to print and sell
all manner of books
was granted by
Henry VIII in 1534.
The University has printed
and published continuously
since 1584.

Cambridge University Press

Cambridge
New York   *Port Chester*
Melbourne   *Sydney*

PUBLISHED BY THE PRESS SYNDICATE OF THE UNIVERSITY OF CAMBRIDGE
The Pitt Building, Trumpington Street, Cambridge, United Kingdom

CAMBRIDGE UNIVERSITY PRESS
The Edinburgh Building, Cambridge CB2 2RU, UK
40 West 20th Street, New York NY 10011–4211, USA
477 Williamstown Road, Port Melbourne, VIC 3207, Australia
Ruiz de Alarcón 13, 28014 Madrid, Spain
Dock House, The Waterfront, Cape Town 8001, South Africa

http://www.cambridge.org

© Cambridge University Press 1991

First published 1991
First paperback edition 2002

A catalogue record for this book is available from the British Library

Library of Congress Cataloguing in Publication data
The French Revolution and British popular politics / edited by Mark
Philp.
      p.   cm.
Outgrowth of a conference held at the Maison Française in April
1989.
Includes index.
ISBN 0 521 39123 7 (hardback)
1. Great Britain – Politics and government – 1789–1820.   2. France –
History – Revolution, 1789–1799 – Influence.   4. Great
Britain – Civilization – French influences.   5. Great Britain – Foreign
relations 1789–1820.   6. Great Britain – Foreign relations – France.
7. France – Foreign relations – Great Britain.   8. France – Foreign
relations – 1789–1815.   9. Public opinion – Great Britain – History.
I. Philp, Mark.
DA520.F724   1991
941.07′3–dc20   90-24263   CIP

ISBN 0 521 39123 7   hardback
ISBN 0 521 89093 4   paperback

In memoriam
John Dinwiddy
(1939–1990)

The nine essays in this collection focus on the dynamics of British popular politics in the 1790s and on the impact of the French Revolution and the subsequent war with France. Leading scholars in the field explore the nature and origins of the ideological conflicts between reformers and loyalists, the impact of the war with France on the organisation of the British state and on its relations with its people, and the extent of the threat of revolution on both British and colonial territory.

These essays challenge a narrow reading of the 'debate on France', they reassess the respective roles of rhetoric and political principles in the writing of the period, and they explore the intellectual and practical contexts which shaped the ideologies and strategies of reformers and loyalists. They provide comparative studies of French and British ideological traditions and of the impact which organising for war had on both countries, together with an assessment of the key factors influencing the fortunes of the revolts in Ireland and the West Indies. In addition, they provide contrasting perspectives on the question of how close Britain came to revolution in the 1790s.

The French Revolution and British Popular Politics makes an unusually integrated and coherent collection of essays, substantially advancing knowledge in this controversial area and bringing together important new work by senior figures in the field.

Contents

Acknowledgements

In the summer of 1987, at the invitation of Madame Monica Charlot, the then Director of the Maison Française in Oxford, and initially in partnership with Alan Ryan, who shortly after moved to a chair at Princeton, I organised a conference on Britain and the French Revolution at the Maison Française held in April 1989. This collection has grown out of that event. In planning the conference, arranging the practical details, ensuring the smooth functioning of the event itself, and in the time since the event, I incurred many debts for which this acknowledgement is scant repayment. The French Government, the Maison Française and the British Academy each contributed financially to the conference costs. Moreover, Madame Charlot and the Maison Française were generous enough to host a seminar for the contributors to this volume in March 1990, which allowed us to debate further a number of points of disagreement before producing final drafts of the papers. While working on the conference programme I received invaluable advice from John Dinwiddy, Martin Fitzpatrick, Iain Hampsher-Monk, Colin Lucas, Alan Ryan and John Walsh. Martin Fitzpatrick and Harry Dickinson helped chair the conference sessions and John Brims, Marianne Elliot, Jenny Graham, Suzi Halimi, Iain Hampsher-Monk, Brian Rigby and John Rule also read papers. Thanks are also due to Jonathan Clark for behind-the-scenes assistance. Subsequent to the conference I have been greatly assisted by my collaborators in the 1790s seminar in Oxford, David Eastwood and Jon Mee, by Harry Dickinson, Jo Innes, Sarah Turvey and Marcus Wood, and by Austin Gee who compiled the index.

This collection of essays is dedicated to the memory of John Dinwiddy who died in May 1990. For those involved in this project, as for the many scholars and students who knew him, John's intellectual integrity, his willingness to advise and assist all who came to him, and his seemingly unfailing good humour, made him an exemplary colleague.

Introduction

Mark Philp

The history of the French Revolution is more than usually subject to the vagaries of intellectual fashion and remains a vehemently contested field for research. Indeed, this has been the case since the first days of the Revolution. Although less subject to historical fashions, the precise nature of the British response to France has also been hotly disputed territory ever since news of events in France first crossed the Channel. It is not difficult to see why this should be so. The French Revolution, following hard on the heels of the American, raised questions for contemporaries, as for later generations, about the legitimacy of Britain's '*ancien régime*' and the degree and sources of its stability. It also led many to believe that substantial parliamentary reform was both necessary and inevitable, and this gave rise to a number of organisations dedicated to making the inevitable actual. The period from 1791 to 1803 is seen by many historians as the first major opportunity (and for some also the last) for a radical, popular, democratic reform of the British social and political order. One indication of its significance is Alfred Cobban's description of the pamphlet debate which followed the publication of Burke's *Reflections on the Revolution in France* in November 1790 as, 'perhaps the last real discussion of fundamentals of politics in this country...Issues as great have been raised in our day, but it cannot be pretended that they have evoked a political discussion on the intellectual level of that inspired by the French Revolution'.[1] The intellectual debate, however, is only one dimension of events in Britain in the 1790s. By the end of 1792, it had largely been displaced by the development of reforming and loyalist organisations which played a major role in shaping Britain's domestic politics in the decade, and which carried the debate over into a practical struggle for and against parliamentary reform. Moreover, it is in 1792 that the first democratic organisations for political reform with memberships drawn predominantly from the artisan and working classes enter British

---

[1] Cited by Marilyn Butler, *Burke, Paine, Godwin and the Revolution Controversy* (Cambridge, 1984), p. 1.

1

politics.[2] By the end of the 1790s these organisations, after a series of conflicts and confrontations with the government, had been driven underground and, in association with similar groups from Ireland, sought to achieve their initially reformist objectives through insurrectionary action.[3] What was triggered by events in France culminated in fugitive attempts to use French arms to emulate her revolution, with a French raid in Wales and with landings in Ireland (but too late to aid the rebellion there) in 1797–8, and with acute crises on mainland Britain in 1797–8 and 1801–2.

The connection between domestic political concerns and events in France was signalled as early as Price's sermon, *A Discourse on the Love of our Country*, given in November 1789, which provided Burke with one of his principal targets in his *Reflections*. Price's ostensible purpose was to celebrate the benefits of the Glorious Revolution of 1688, although he also used the occasion as an opportunity for pointing to remaining shortcomings in the British constitution. But he concluded by reminding his audience of 'the favourableness of the present times to all exertions in the cause of public liberty':

I have lived to see a diffusion of knowledge, which has undermined superstition and error – I have lived to see the rights of men better understood than ever; and nations panting for liberty, which seemed to have lost the idea of it. – I have lived to see THIRTY MILLIONS of people, indignant and resolute, spurning at slavery, and demanding liberty with an irresistible voice; their king led in triumph, and an arbitrary monarch surrendering himself to his subjects. – After sharing in the benefits of one Revolution, I have been spared to be a witness to two other Revolutions, both glorious. – And now, methinks, I see the ardour for liberty catching and spreading; a general amendment beginning in human affairs; the dominion of kings changed for the dominion of laws, and the dominion of priests giving way to the dominion of reason and conscience.

Tremble all ye oppressors of the world! Take warning all ye supporters of slavish governments, and slavish hierarchies! Call no more (absurdly and wickedly) REFORMATION, innovation. You cannot now hold the world in darkness. Struggle no longer against increasing light and liberality. Restore to mankind their rights; and consent to the correction of abuses, before they and you are destroyed together.[4]

Price's sermon encapsulates three aspects of the early response to the

[2] Cf. Mary Thale (ed.), *Selections from the Papers of the London Corresponding Society 1792–1799* (Cambridge, 1983); Albert Goodwin, *The Friends of Liberty: The English Democratic Movement in the Age of the French Revolution* (London, 1979); E. P. Thompson, *The Making of the English Working Class* (Harmondsworth, 1968); Gwyn. A. Williams, *Artisans and Sans-Culottes: Popular Movements in France and Britain during the French Revolution*, 2nd edn (London, 1989); and many others.

[3] Roger Wells, *Insurrection: The British Experience, 1795–1803* (Gloucester, 1983); Marianne Elliot, *Partners in Revolution: The United Irishmen in France* (New Haven, Conn., 1982).

[4] R. Price, *Discourse on the Love of our Country* (London, 1789), pp. 50–1.

French Revolution. He unashamedly joins the general enthusiasm for events, and the approbation of the ambitions of the French, but there is not much attempt to understand the French on their own terms. Many people on this side of the Channel saw events in France as mirroring the British Revolution of 1688, and expected the establishment of a limited monarchy alongside representative institutions. Few early commentators were initially critical, and few grasped or made much attempt to grasp the complex set of forces which made up the Revolution.[5]

Price's sermon also links together British and French affairs, not simply by seeing French events as emulating British achievements, but also in identifying the cause of reform in France with that in Britain and in the use of French affairs to make domestic political points. Charles James Fox, the opposition Whig leader, welcomed the fall of the Bastille with a degree of hyperbole which was later to cause him problems ('How much the greatest event that has happened in the history of the world, and how much the best'), and he succumbed to the common tendency to interpret French events in English terms, seeing the Revolution as 'a good stout blow against the influence of the crown'.[6] This process of reading French events through domestic political concerns and domestic traditions of political controversy, is often combined with attempts to use the example of France to stimulate the activities of organisations and party factions in Britain. The example of France comes to act first as a beacon for, but later as a warning against reformist ambitions in the decade. Three groups in particular tried to use French affairs to further their domestic political ambitions, and later found themselves tarnished by their connections: the Society for Constitutional Information (SCI), which had been in eclipse since the demise of the Yorkshire movement for political reform of the early 1780s; the Protestant Dissenters, whose attempts to repeal the Test and Corporation Acts in 1787, 1789 and 1790 had failed; and the opposition Whigs, whose cause was in disarray following the debacle over the Rockingham administration and subsequently the Regency crisis. Each found in France a cause with which they could identify, but each also came to find their attachment to France a more costly association than they had initially assumed, especially after the declaration of war between France and Britain in February 1793.

The sermon also indicates a third aspect of the subsequent debate and

[5] Burke first showed evidence of hostility in the September of 1789 – Burke to Windham, 27 September 1789, in T. W. Copeland (ed.), *The Correspondence of Edmund Burke* (Cambridge, 1958–78), vol. VI, p. 25. Derek Jarrett's recent *Three Faces of Revolution: Paris, London and New York in 1789* (London, 1989), gives a shrewd account of the variety and confusion of response to the early events of the Revolution. On the early response, see Robert Hole's discussion below, ch. 1.

[6] Cited in John Derry, 'The opposition Whigs and the French Revolution 1789–1815' in H. T. Dickinson (ed.), *Britain and the French Revolution 1789–1815* (London, 1989), p. 40.

of the terms in which it was conducted. Out of the particular affairs of the French nation, commentators began to draw lessons and see signs of more universal import. As Major John Cartwright, one of the mainstays of the earlier days of the SCI, put it: 'The French, Sir, are not only asserting their own rights, but they are advancing the general liberties of mankind.'[7] This universalisation of particular to general liberties is also found in Price's sense of the 'light' of reform 'setting AMERICA free, reflected to FRANCE, and there kindled into a blaze that lays despotism in ashes, and warms and illuminates EUROPE!'[8] It is also evident in the emphasis on the progress of reason and opinion insistently reiterated in the works of reformers such as Paine, Godwin, Priestley, Thelwall and others. Indeed, in Priestley's work, as in others, there is also a distinct millenarian streak, in which the French Revolution is assigned a role in the inauguration of the thousand year rule of Christ.[9] In each case, a little local difficulty becomes a sign of a broader march of principle which inevitably has implications for British politics.

Burke, in his vehement denunciation of the Revolution and its English sympathisers – most obviously Price and Lansdowne, but also implicitly his erstwhile Whig friends, like Fox – poured derision on this attempt to translate political practices and principles from one country to another by appealing to reason and truth. Against principle, Burke set accumulated wisdom and experience; against reason, he set precedent, prescription and property. British enthusiasts for France used an inheritance of common-wealthman and country party thought as a basis for constructing their understanding of the implications of French events, but they often interpreted these traditions in more universalist terms than their predecessors. In contrast, Burke seized on the more parochial aspects of this inheritance and sought to establish an opposition between the Englishman's legacy of particular rights and duties, set within a hierarchical social, political and economic order, and the wild fanaticism of those who thought it possible thoroughly to reform a society whilst preserving the blessings of culture and civilisation which derived from the old order. Burke's initial responses were seen as exaggerated hyperbole by most of his contemporaries, but as time passed and affairs in France became more bloody and threatening, the *Reflections* came to be seen as

---

[7] J. Cartwright, cited in H. T. Dickinson, *British Radicalism and the French Revolution 1789–1815* (Oxford, 1985), p. 7.

[8] Price, *Discourse on the Love of Our Country*, p. 51.

[9] Clark Garrett, *Respectable Folly: Millenarians and the French Revolution in France and England* (Baltimore, Md., 1975), pp. 126–43, on Priestley. See also chs 7–9, on the English dimension of Millenarianism more generally. On Irish Millenarianism, see David W. Miller, 'Presbyterianism and "modernization" in Ulster', *Past and Present*, 80 (1978), especially pp. 80–4.

prescient, and the stark choice it offered between the status quo and chaos seemed more appropriate.[10]

This sense of appropriateness was enhanced for those now growing increasingly hostile to France by developments on the British scene arising out of the pamphlet debate which the *Reflections* sparked. The pamphlet debate has considerable significance as a watershed in the development of British liberal and conservative political thought, and it is also an important moment in the growth of a popular press and the evolution of a popular political literary style. But it also had a more intensely practical significance in terms of the sheer scale of the exchanges. Burke's *Reflections* sold some 30,000 copies in the first two years after its publication, and it drew over a hundred replies, and probably over two hundred works in support.[11] But the volume of items is over-shadowed by the extent of circulation achieved by some of the contributions. Paine's *Rights of Man*, on the most conservative estimate, probably sold between 100,000 and 200,000 copies in the first three years after its publication, and with the procedures available to ensure multiple readerships and the 'bridging mechanisms' which brought the text even to illiterate and semi-literate people, it seems likely that a substantial proportion of all classes would have had some acquaintance with Paine. The innovative character of many works in the debate, their rhetorical inventiveness and power, their sheer volume and their mass circulation, ensured that the debate, in some form or other, penetrated through British society. This 'mass', popular character to the debate is picked up by and reinforced first by reformers and subsequently by loyalists, and plays a critical role in shifting the focus of events from France to Britain.[12]

[10] Cf. Leslie Mitchell's editorial 'Introduction' to *The Writings and Speeches of Edmund Burke: The French Revolution 1790–1794*, vol. VIII (Oxford, 1990).

[11] This is probably a low estimate. See Gayle Trusdel Pendleton, 'Towards a bibliography of the *Reflections* and *Rights of Man* controversy', *Bulletin of Research in the Humanities*, 85 (1982), pp. 65–103, and Gregory Claeys, 'The French Revolution and British political thought', *History of Political Thought*, 11, 1 (1990), pp. 59–80. There are obviously many ways to count publications as contributing to the debate – are, for example, the critical reviews to be seen as contributions to it? But even on the relatively tight criteria used by Pendleton and Claeys, it is possible to find items which are not included. For example, Pendleton does not include many of the songs and ballads which can plausibly be claimed to be commentaries on Burke and Paine. Moreover, by focusing on the *Reflections* and *Rights of Man*, much of the broader reform literature, including newspapers and periodicals, such as Thomas Spence's *Pig's Meat, or Lessons for the Swinish Multitude* (London, 1793–5), and Daniel Eaton's *Hog's Wash or a Salmagundi for swine/Politics for the People* (London, 1793–5), is necessarily excluded. While this is legitimate given Pendleton's limited project, it would be dangerous to rest generalisations about the balance of radical and loyalist publications on this basis.

[12] On the loyalist side, in addition to Butler, *Burke, Paine, Godwin*, see S. Pedersen, 'Hannah More meets Simple Simon: tracts, chapbooks, and popular culture in late eighteenth century England', *Journal of British Studies*, 25 (1986), pp. 84–113; also, more generally on the publication of loyalist material which by 1795 was, in the form of the Cheap

The pamphlet war led reformers to attempt to strengthen their case for reform by widening their base of support, and they did this by seeking the maximum possible proliferation of radical and reforming publications. In doing so, they helped encourage artisan and working-class involvement in the extra-parliamentary reform movement. The vehicles for the dissemination of political literature were the metropolitan and provincial corresponding societies which sprang into life (or, for some, back into life) in the first two or three years of the decade. Manchester's society was formed in 1790, and the London-based Society for Constitutional Information, and London Revolution Society, were in action from this time. But the real spate of activity occurred later: eight societies were formed in and around Sheffield at the end of 1791 and the beginning of 1792; and societies were also formed in Liverpool, Stockport, Warrington, Leeds, Wakefield, Halifax, Newcastle-upon-Tyne, Cambridge, Norwich, Great Yarmouth, Ipswich, Chester, Derby, Belper, Birmingham, Walsall, Coventry and Wolverhampton. Smaller groups also appeared throughout the south and south-west, and a crop of new organisations sprang up in London.[13] The newest phenomenon in all this is the London Corresponding Society, founded by Thomas Hardy, which catered specifically for the working man and which, consequently, marked a major departure from the older societies which were dominated by minor gentry and professional men.[14] But perhaps equally worrying to the government at this stage was the formation of the Whig Association of the Friends of the People, whose attempts to secure reform were at least partly aimed to pre-

Repository Tracts, far outstripping reformist publications, see Robert Hole, 'British counter-revolutionary popular propaganda in the 1790s' in Colin Jones (ed.), *Britain and Revolutionary France: Conflict, Subversion and Propaganda* (Exeter, 1983), and n.19, below.

[13] Albert Goodwin, *The Friends of Liberty* (London, 1979), chs. 5 and 7; Dickinson, *British Radicalism and the French Revolution*, pp. 9–13. As with the parameters of the pamphlet debate, so with radical organisations – the boundaries are not easily drawn. One little explored area of political activity, which falls short of a formal organisation for parliamentary reform, but which would none the less have had a major role in extending the controversy is the debating societies. Mary Thale's 'London debating societies in the 1790s', *Historical Journal*, 32, 1 (1989), pp. 57–86, has helped open up this field of research for the metropolis, but many of the less formally organised discussion groups are difficult to trace such as the Cannonians, mentioned by Holcroft's friend Shield (cited in E. Colby, *The Life of Thomas Holcroft* (London, 1925), vol. I, p. 209), or the even more informal open-house dinners, such as those given by Horne Tooke at his house in Wimbledon. The problem for the historian is not simply to trace these informal debating contexts, but also to assess how far such activity is in any way different in the 1790s. Unfortunately our evidence for Horne Tooke, for example, is limited to the 1790s, but Tooke's entertaining of men and (less often) women from a range of social classes does seem to have been in part a consequence of his involvement in the radical societies, and might well have been a phenomenon distinctive to the 1790s (the data on his contacts is drawn from Godwin's diary, Bodleian Library (Bod. Lib.), Abinger MS,.

[14] See in particular, Thale, *Selections from the Papers of the London Corresponding Society*; Williams, *Artisans and Sans-Culottes*, ch. 4; and Thompson, *Making of the English Working Class*, ch. 5.

empt more widespread extra-parliamentary activity, but who were nonetheless seen by the government as encouraging the reform movement and thereby as posing a threat to the established order.[15]

It was partly to alienate the more conservative Whigs from their reforming allies that the Royal Proclamation against Seditious Writings and Publications was issued in May 1792; but the move was also prompted by the rapid spread of Paine's work and the burgeoning of the radical presses in both the metropolis and provinces which led to a proliferation of handbills, chapbooks, poems, songs and squibs in support of the radical cause. This spate of radical activity was associated by many, including the government, with the growing number of food riots, and the confidence of the political elite was not helped by the often fierce rhetoric which peppered the societies' correspondence with France, expressing support and admiration for their revolution, and sometimes the wish to emulate it. Local magistrates also found evidence of potential insurgence in handbills and verses, dissenting sermons and casual conversations, strikes, riots, murmurings in the army and, finally, in rumours of the wholesale production of arms.[16] To add to government concern, the situation in both Scotland and Ireland seemed even worse. Scotland greeted each new French victory in its war with the Counter-Revolutionary Coalition with toasts, bells and lighted windows; Dundas, the Home Secretary, was regularly burnt in effigy; there was a spate of violent rioting towards the end of the year; and in December a general convention of reformers was held in Edinburgh. Ireland had corn riots from the summer of 1792, a swelling of republican agitation in the north, and there was the prospect of further attempts to remove the disabilities of the Catholics at the end of the year.

Two aspects of all this activity were especially alarming. A major concern for those in government circles was the extent of the communication between corresponding societies, which bridged both geographical and social distances, and which raised the spectre of mass, organised and centrally directed political activity. Moreover, this occurred against a background of growing international tension. With domestic radicalism rife, the prospects of maintaining internal security in the event of a war with France might not have looked good, and the enthusiasm for fraternal exchanges between the reform societies and the National Assembly could only have added to government fears of subversion and

---

[15] See Goodwin, *Friends of Liberty*, p. 206, which mentions Pitt's view that because certain prominent members of the association were 'concerned' with others who harboured a 'direct hostility to the very form of our government ... this afforded suspicion, that the motion for a reform was nothing more than the preliminary to the overthrow of the whole system of our present government'.

[16] Cf. John Ehrman, *The Younger Pitt: The Reluctant Transition*, vol. II (London, 1983), chs. 4 and 5.

domestic revolution.[17] In December 1792 the government seemed to believe that insurrection was imminent and in response embodied the militia, fortified the Tower, brought hundreds of troops into London and issued a further Proclamation against Seditious Writings.[18]

The end of 1792, however, brought some consolation for the government with the formation in November of the Association for the Preservation of Liberty and Property against Republicans and Levellers. Several hundred provincial associations followed Reeves's London example and by early 1793 there may have been as many as two thousand such organisations spread throughout the country.[19] The active members were drawn predominantly from men of property, but they did attract participation from the lower orders by public meetings and other loyalist demonstrations, such as processions, bonfires, Paine burnings, and so on. In more practical ways the loyalists orchestrated a campaign against reform organisations by putting pressure on publicans to refuse to rent rooms to the societies and by harassing known sympathisers with France and reform. Moreover, in an attempt to stem the spread of Painite principles, the associations financed the publication of a range of loyalist works, from pamphlets to chapbooks, broadsides and songs.[20]

By the time war broke out with France in February 1793, popular politics in Britain had been deeply affected by the example of France. The British government faced widespread, organised pressure for parliamentary reform, and a public which had been so encouraged to flirt with republicanism by Paine's works, that the social and political elite had felt

[17] Although there might also be some sense, as some reformers pointed out, that a war might force reform off the political agenda in a way which could command public support. See, for example, Godwin's commentary on the declaration of war with France, Bod. Lib., Abinger MSS, dep. b. 227/1g.

[18] Clive Emsley, 'The London "Insurrection" of December 1792: fact, fiction or fantasy?', *Journal of British Studies*, 17, 2 (1978), pp. 68–86.

[19] H. T. Dickinson, 'Popular loyalism in the 1790s' in Eckhart Hellmuth (ed.), *The Transformation of Political Culture: England and Germany in the Late Eighteenth Century* (Oxford, 1990), p. 517–20. More generally, see A. Mitchell, 'The association movement of 1792–3', *Historical Journal*, 4, 1 (1961), pp. 56–77; D. E. Ginter, 'The loyalist association movement of 1792–3 and British public opinion', *Historical Journal*, 9, 2 (1966), pp. 179–90; E. C. Black, *The Association: British Extra-Parliamentary Organization 1769–1793* (Cambridge, Mass., 1963), ch. 7; R. R. Dozier, *For King, Constitution and Country: The English Loyalists and the French Revolution* (Lexington, Ky., 1983).

[20] To a greater extent than the radicals, a concerted attempt was made to disseminate loyalist songs written, for the most part, specifically for the occasion and using already well-known tunes. For example, 1792–3 saw the publication of two collections of the *AntiGallican Songster* and two of the *Anti-Levelling Songster*. No comparable collections exist for the radicals, and the radical songs from the period I have been able to trace are to be found either in Spence's *Pig's Meat*, Eaton's *Hog's Wash* or in loose-leaf broadsides (and these are in the minority). Although the loyalists devotion to the song as a means of confirming and eliciting support for their cause does not match that shown in 1803, when there were few radical competitors but where the invasion threat was clearly a stimulus to flights of poesy, it is still an impressive showing.

it necessary to organise to an unprecedented extent in defence of the status quo and the constitution. But, by this time, the example of France had come to play an increasingly complex role for people in Britain: many who had originally supported developments were now distressed by the increasing bloodshed and the increasing radicalism of the Revolution; others now looked to France as the way ahead. Interpretations of why France's Revolution had taken a bloody course were linked to changing senses of the prospects for radical change. If some found in her example reasons for becoming less politically adventurous, others found reasons for being more so; and still others found reasons for attempting to dissociate themselves from France, while insisting on the justice and necessity of reform at home. But for ten to fifteen years after 1793, British popular politics remained profoundly affected by the war with France and the changing state of French affairs. This is not to say, as we shall see, that popular politics was wholly, or even largely dependent on the impetus from France, so much as to insist that the Revolution and its course helped to establish an essential component of the background to the confrontation between reformism and loyalism which took place in British popular politics in the 1790s, and which at times seemed to threaten Britain with a similar degree of revolutionary change as France had experienced. The 'conventionism' of the reform societies in 1793 and 1794 and the sedition and treason trials in Scotland and in England to which they gave rise; the mass public meetings of 1795 and the 'Gagging Acts' which they elicited; the food and crimp riots of 1795–6 and the naval mutinies of 1797–8; the revolt in Ireland in 1798; the successive suspensions of habeas corpus after 1794 and the outlawing of the London Corresponding Society, the United Englishmen, United Britons, United Irishmen and United Scotsmen in 1799; the new spate of treason trials associated with the Irish revolt and with attempts to involve France in 1798; and the renewed rash of loyalist propaganda in 1803 in response to a further perceived threat of invasion by France – all these events, and the many others which chart the fortunes of the reformers and their loyalist opponents and which, for some, at times brought Britain close to revolution, are affected by the French Revolution, even if there are also strong, underlying domestic tensions and traditions providing some of the impetus. While it is appropriate to question the precise nature of the influence of French events, and while it is possible to doubt that the sources of ideological conflict and political tension in the two countries were wholly similar, it is not reasonable to doubt that events in France provided a central background condition for the confrontation in Britain in the 1790s especially, between the defenders of the status quo and a popular, extra-parliamentary movement for political (and, occasionally, social) reform.

In the analysis of the events in the 1790s and early 1800s there are many areas of disagreement, from which have emerged substantially different accounts of the period and of its significance in British history. There is controversy over how widespread was the enthusiastic response to events in France, how far radical and reformist views permeated down through the class structure, and to what extent they rendered uncertain the loyalties of the middling and lower orders of late eighteenth-century British society. There is dispute about the strength of the British state in the face of public demands for reform and for an end to the war in France, and on the depth of the commitment to the established regime on the part of the various sectors of the ruling elite. Also, it remains unsettled to what extent the government's prosecution of the war served to jeopardise the legitimacy and stability of the government by making enormous demands on the loyalty of British subjects at a time when food shortages and recruitment tactics were resulting in widespread rioting.

These issues, and a range of related concerns, have been the subject of a number of publications in recent years.[21] But there remain a series of substantial difficulties with the accounts which have been advanced thus far. These difficulties do not derive from a paucity of evidence, there has been a great deal of high-quality scholarship in this area which has done much to provide the basis for an adequate account of events. But problems remain, both because of the complexity of the flow of forces and events in the period – public mood is a far from stable commodity and is not easily measured at the best of times – and because the analysis of events in the decade lead us directly into important, but seemingly intractable, historical and sociological issues concerning the sources of order and disorder within the British state in the last decade of the eighteenth century. For example, to ask why Britain did not experience a revolution in the 1790s is a loaded question, if only because revolutions are not natural events, like thunderstorms, but social and political ones, the nature of which, and thus the conditions for which, necessarily change over time.[22] Political will must combine with circumstance, and both will and circumstance are profoundly affected by people's expectations and experience. That this is so makes questions of the sources of radical thought in Britain, of the exact nature of the reformers' intentions, and of

[21] In addition to those cited above by Dickinson, Dozier, Elliot, Ehrman, Emsley, Goodwin, Thale, Thompson, Wells and Williams, see also Ian R. Christie, *Stress and Stability in Late Eighteenth-Century Britain: Reflections on the British Avoidance of Revolution* (Oxford, 1984), and the bibliographies in Dickinson's edited collection, *Britain and the French Revolution*, and Gregory Claeys, *Thomas Paine: Social and Political Thought* (London, 1989).

[22] Theda Skocpol, *States and Social Revolutions* (Cambridge, 1979); but see also John Dunn, *Rethinking Modern Political Theory* (Cambridge, 1987), ch. 4, and *Modern Revolutions*, 2nd edn (Cambridge, 1989).

the extent to which their beliefs and aspirations were transformed as a consequence of Pitt's campaign against them, or as a result of events in France, central in estimating how close some Britons came to countenancing revolutionary action (or action which would have had a revolutionary outcome), and how close they brought the British state to revolution (and to what sort of revolution). Similarly, in the analysis of those who resisted the movements for reform, it is imperative to identify the sources of reaction, to examine the extent to which these were deeprooted among both the elite and the people of Britain, providing a reserve of instinctive loyalty to the British state, and to assess how far this loyalty could be pressed in times of war, famine and public unrest. This collection of essays does not pretend to solve all these problems nor, indeed, do the contributors agree in their interpretations of the events of the 1790s and their relative significance in securing or destabilising the status quo. We have, however, tried to clarify the points of disagreement and their implications; and although each essay focuses on different aspects of the period, each also draws out some of the broader implications of its analysis.

The literature on the period 1789–1803 revolves around two main issues: the first concerns the origins, nature and impact of the 'debate on France'; the second, the sources of order and disorder within the British state and the potential for revolution. This division is heuristically valuable, and divides the contributions to this volume into roughly equal groups but, as the chapters which follow demonstrate, the two sets of concerns are intimately and intrinsically connected. Political, social and religious ideologies are an essential component in sustaining or questioning the hegemony of elites and the legitimacy of states, and thus in preserving order or in initiating experimentation with insurrection. In addition, the French Revolution is not a single event, so much as a complex, evolving political and social process, and to speak of the 'debate on France' or the reaction to French affairs tends to underplay this dynamic character. The French Revolution is not something which can be endorsed or condemned once and for all, and its impact on Britain is also not once and for all. To take one instance, the war between Britain and France which arises from the Revolution, has a profound effect on Britain, at the very least in terms of making heavy demands on finances, equipment and personnel. Crimp riots, the naval mutinies and public anger at the cost of lives in the West Indies, all indicate ways in which popular unrest was exacerbated by the demands of the war. Moreover, once the Revolution controversy had changed its ground, a good deal of the pamphlet literature critical of Pitt's policies is directed primarily against the war, and attacks on the conduct of the war and on its objectives and cost are a central plank of the remaining parliamentary opposition of the period.[23] Just as the French Revolution is an evolving process, so is the ideological confrontation between government and opposition and loyalism and reform, and so too are the British government's attempts to win the war, to retain the allegiance of the political, social and financial elites, and to secure the compliance of the people of Britain. Moreover, each of these processes is affected by, and affects, each of the others. While there is heuristic value in distinguishing between issues associated with the debate and questions of the threat of insurrection, we should not think, as the chapters which follow show, that the issues can be, or ought to be, regarded as wholly distinct.

Although there has been a good deal of work on the intellectual debts of various contributors to the debate, and although an increasing amount of work has appeared on the language of the debate since Boulton's original work, it is true to say that our understanding of the sources of the debate on France, of its character, its multiple levels and its long-term impact, remains uncertain.[24] The period from 1770 to 1830 is one in which previous lines of ideological allegiance and adherence are broken up and reformed in ways which leave a substantially different ideological context for political action. The 'debate on France' plays a crucial, but as yet incompletely understood role in this transformation – one which the recent works of Dr J. C. D. Clark and Professor Pocock have further complicated.[25] It remains unclear how far the doctrines of radical reformers in the 1790s should be understood, as they were denounced, as part of a contagion of French principles, and how far they are indigenous to late eighteenth-century English political ideology. The same must also be said of the sources of reaction and of the complex role which religious

---

[23] J. E. Cookson, *The Friends of Peace: Anti-War Liberalism in England, 1793–1815* (Cambridge, 1982); also Clive Emsley, *British Society and the French Wars 1793–1815* (London, 1979), chs. 3–4.

[24] On the language of the debate see, James T. Boulton, *The Language of Politics in the Age of Wilkes and Burke* (London, 1963); Olivia Smith, *The Politics of Language 1791–1819* (Oxford 1984); Butler, *Burke, Paine, Godwin*; J. Turner, 'Burke, Paine, and the nature of language', *The Yearbook of English Studies*, 19 (1989), pp. 36–53. Butler's book gives an excellent bibliography for a range of the contributors to the controversy, but subsequent works of note include Malcom Chase, *The People's Farm: English Radical Agrarianism 1775–1840* (Oxford, 1989); Iain Hampsher-Monk, 'Rhetoric and opinion in the politics of Edmund Burke', *History of Political Thought*, 9, 3 (1988), pp. 455–84, and 'John Thelwall and the eighteenth century radical response to political economy', *Historical Journal*, 34 (1991); Claeys, *Thomas Paine*, and his 'The French Revolution debate'; and Nicholas Roe, *Wordsworth and Coleridge: The Radical Years* (Oxford, 1988).

[25] J. C. D. Clark, *English Society 1688–1832: Ideology, Social Structure and Political Practice during the Ancien Régime* (Cambridge, 1985); J. G. A. Pocock, *Virtue, Commerce, and History* (Cambridge, 1985), especially part 3. See also Claeys, 'The French Revolution debate'.

doctrine and theological disputation played in constructing the political positions and aspirations of the participants.[26]

What is clear, is that the period 1789–1803 is one in which the language of political debate undergoes a process of continual transformation. In this process, positions are polarised, terms become invested with value and meaning only to be subsequently abandoned, and the stakes of controversy become extraordinarily inflated. Faint-hearted reformers are denounced as Jacobin terrorists, well-meaning humanitarians become the enemy within, and the cautious critic of the status quo is accused of bringing the country to an inch of defeat. On the other side, the reformers are not above accusing their opponents of corruption and bribery, of war-mongering for profit, and of selling the birthright of liberty for the price of a place. Given this kind of response, viewing the period as involving a 'debate' on France becomes questionable. As Robert Hole's analysis of the development of reaction in the established church, John Dinwiddy's account of the anti-Jacobin's case, and my own discussion of the ideology of reform suggest, the term 'debate' needs to be handled with caution. Yet, one influential school of thought holds that the debate on France was in some sense 'won' by the defenders of the status quo – where the winning is being at least partially attributed to the force of the arguments used.[27] There are two ways of challenging this line of argument. The first claims that the best arguments were to be found with those challenging the status quo, and that their defeat is explicable in terms of the measures adopted by the government and its supporters to still the clatter of the radical presses and the tongues of its agitators.[28] The second, which can draw on a range of supports (such as the analysis of rhetorical styles and strategies)

---

[26] See Clark, *English Society*; T. P. Schofield, 'Conservative political thought in Britain in response to the French Revolution', *Historical Journal*, 29, 3 (1986), pp. 601–22; Robert Hole, *Pulpits, Politics and Public Order in England 1760–1832* (Cambridge, 1989), and his contribution to this volume.

[27] Cf. Dickinson, *British Radicalism and the French Revolution*; Christie, *Stress and Stability*. See John Dinwiddy's contribution below, ch. 2.

[28] For example, my *Godwin's Political Justice* (London, 1986), ch. 10; although, see Clive Emsley, 'An aspect of Pitt's "Terror": prosecutions for sedition during the 1790s', *Social History*, 6, 2 (1981), pp. 155–84, and 'Repression, "terror" and the rule of law in England during the decade of the French Revolution', *English Historical Review*, 100 (1985), pp. 801–27. Clive Emsley is surely right to say that in comparison with the French 'Terror' the radicals had little cause for complaint. This does not, however, mean that repression played no real role in the defeat of their cause. At the very least, by its willingness to resort to prosecution, to invoke the charge of treason in 1794, and to bring in new legislation in the second half of the decade, the government clearly signalled its unwillingness to negotiate with the extra-parliamentary movement. If we see this movement as predominantly pacific and reformist, it is not difficult to recognise that this message might have weakened significantly the movement's resolve – not because people necessarily feared prosecution, so much as because it would have been clear that the stakes had been raised in such a way as to make seeking reform tantamount to attempting the breakdown of the rule of law.

develops further the challenge to the very conception of a 'debate' – just who is trying to persuade whom, and of what? Given the delights to be found by the historian of ideas who has a smattering of political theory, in the literature of the 1790s, it is not surprising that much analysis sees the antagonists as locked in a battle of ideas. There are ideas a-plenty to be found; but it remains pertinent to ask how far they should be analysed for their intrinsic weight, and how far they should be assessed as epiphenomenal manifestations of a deeper, more practical struggle for and against the legitimacy of the status quo.[29]

An additional area of problems which further complicates the idea of a 'debate' concerns the variety of forms and media which are utilised. At its most narrowly defined, we are concerned with an exchange in pamphlets between Burke and others. At its broadest, we are concerned with the full range of literary and discursive forms within which men and women in the 1790s reflected on events in France, and increasingly turned to contemplate the prospect of reform at home – that is, from the *Prelude* to the broadsheet; from the pulpit to the pub; from the personal diary through to the filed reports of Dundas's network of spies.

In the first four chapters a wide range of issues concerning the debate on France are discussed, but their net effect is to force us to ask what it means to talk of a debate in the early years of the 1790s, and to encourage us to see such everyday artefacts of intellectual disagreement as, for example, propositions about human nature, more as the outcome of a complex range of forces than as simply a deduction from a set of self-evidently rational axioms. As these chapters show, fully to grasp the political thought of the period requires that we recognise that texts function in a variety of ways, that their meanings are shaped by forces beyond their authors' control, and that as the exchange of pamphlets blossoms into a full-blown struggle over the legitimacy of the British political system, the concept of a debate or controversy becomes increasingly misleading.

If fixing the parameters of the debate is a complex matter, then the analysis of how close Britain came to insurrection and revolution is certainly doubly so. Moreover, given that whole monographs have been devoted to this issue, it would be incautious to claim that this collection of essays can offer a complete analysis of the social and political order of Britain in the 1790s. However, the essays presented here do broach many of the broader questions which such an analysis must ask, concerning the character of the British state, its mechanisms of control, its regional variations, the extent of the demands which it placed upon its population, the impact of its military involvement with France, both directly across

[29] See below, ch. 3.

the Channel and in the West Indies, and the nature of the organisations which could help preserve order or make insurrection possible, such as the churches, reform societies and loyalist associations, trade unions and extra-parliamentary bodies.

As the chapters by Lottes, Emsley, Eastwood, Duffy, Christie and Wells show, we can only begin to understand the events of the period if we are prepared to engage in some 'middle-range' reflection on ideological, economic, social and political structures and an analysis of their weak points and areas of tension. While none of this can be done uncontentiously, these chapters make it clear that it can be done constructively; and despite their remaining disagreements, they considerably deepen our understanding of why Britain did not undergo radical or revolutionary change at the end of the eighteenth century. Answering such a question obviously calls for a comprehensive analysis of the social and political structure of Britain in the 1790s, of the form which Ian Christie has given us.[30] But as Roger Wells reminds us, it also requires a very careful analysis of events, in particular in the years 1799–1801. And to bridge the gap between these accounts, we require a careful assessment of the strengths and weaknesses of the institutions of the state, as given here by David Eastwood, together with some judicious counterfactual thinking of the kind which can be derived from comparative analysis – as is given in Günther Lottes's analysis of the respective ideological frameworks for political practice available to French and English reformers, Clive Emsley's discussion of the similarities and differences in the way the French and British states managed their populations during the war, and Michael Duffy's account of the variables affecting the different responses to the French Revolution in the Caribbean and Ireland. Moreover, to return to our first set of concerns, we also require an account of what the participants in events were trying to do – were reformers really revolutionaries? Was Pitt trying to prevent something which nobody was trying to bring about? And this in turn requires an account of the ideas, ideals, aspirations and fears of those who wrote and acted in the period which is firmly grounded in an understanding of the intellectual and ideological context within which events were interpreted and aspirations of fears formed. Although it is quite possible for someone to believe that they can bring about something which is not in fact politically possible, it is also true that what can be brought about does depend to some extent on what people think is possible. The structural and the ideological dimensions, the organisational and the individual, are inextricably interwoven, both in providing answers to our questions, and in helping us to decide which questions are in fact relevant.

[30] In his *Stress and Stability*, and in his contribution to this volume.

Moreover, as the chapters by David Eastwood and Clive Emsley in particular argue, we need to recognise the impact which the events of the 1790s have on the relationship between popular politics and the British state. A number of years ago Western argued that, prior to the 1790s,

> The stability of the regime did not primarily depend on the active support of public opinion mobilised by propaganda and mass movements. It was based more on the apathy and indifference of a nation which confined its political activity to incoherent protests at moments of crisis.[31]

Western's suggestion was that with the emergence of loyalism and of the Volunteer Movement in particular, we are witnessing some movement from an elite to a mass form of political activity. The rather dismissive attitude to the popular politics of the earlier eighteenth century has come under increasing criticism in recent years from scholars working on popular forms of protest and on electoral politics,[32] but it remains true that the 1790s see, in the development of a popular press, the mass circulation of political tracts, and the organisation and mobilisation of the people through democratic and loyalist associations and in the Volunteers, both the reformers and the British state seeking systematically to enlist popular opinion on their respective sides. As John Dinwiddy suggests, the 'people' as defined by Burke were probably more conservative than radical, but the same cannot be said of the other two-thirds of the population, particularly between 1795 and 1801. And even if the state sought from this broader body of the people their compliance rather than their consent, it remained imperative to harness the popular patriotism of the more educated and property-owning public. Nationalism and popular loyalism became important adjuncts of rule for the British state, even if they were resorted to with reluctance – as David Eastwood suggests, there is a tension between execrating democracy on the one hand and calling for mass support for and participation in the anti-revolutionary struggle on the other.[33] The net effect of these attempts is the creation of a mass public with an emerging national identity; but it is a mass public and a form of patriotism whose loyalty to the status quo could not be taken for granted: in so far as the 1790s see a mobilisation of the people through appeals to nationalism, popular patriotism and loyalty to the King, this remains

---

[31] J. R. Western, 'The Volunteer Movement as an anti-revolutionary force', *English Historical Review*, 71 (1956), p. 603.

[32] See, for example, Frank O'Gorman, *Voters, Patrons, and Parties: The Unreformed Electorate of Hanoverian England, 1734–1832* (Oxford, 1989); John Stevenson, *Popular Disturbances in England 1700–1870* (London, 1979); and John Bohstedt, *Riots and Community Politics in England and Wales 1790–1810* (Cambridge, Mass., 1983).

[33] See ch. 7, below, p. 160–4.

open to challenge from both the radical patriot tradition and the newer internationalist appeals of some reformers.[34]

The 1790s, then, play an important role in the emergence of a mass public and correspondingly new forms of popular mobilisation. Alongside and linked to this development, we can also recognise a changing language of political controversy, an expanding popular press, and a beginning transformation in the lines of ideological division within British politics. A good deal of this can be traced to antecedents in British traditions of political and religious thinking, but it is in the complex response of the popular politics of the 1790s to the outbreak of the French Revolution and subsequently to the war with France that these changes are initiated.

---

[34] In addition to the comments by Eastwood and Emsley, see Linda Colley's 'The apotheosis of George III: loyalty, royalty and the British nation 1760–1820', *Past and Present*, 102 (1984), pp. 94–129, and 'Whose nation? Class and national consciousness in Britain 1750–1830', *Past and Present*, 113 (1986), pp. 97–117; Hugh Cunningham, 'The language of patriotism: 1750–1914', *History Workshop*, 12 (1981), pp. 8–33; and John Dinwiddy, 'England' in Otto Dann and John Dinwiddy (eds.), *Nationalism in the Age of the French Revolution* (London, 1988), pp. 53–70.

1   English sermons and tracts as media of debate on the French Revolution 1789–99

Robert Hole

Readers of Parson Woodforde's *Diary* could be forgiven for thinking that the French Revolution made little impact upon the English pulpit.[1] The Fall of the Bastille was noted, on 24 July 1789, in just eight words, and the removal of the French Royal Family to Paris was recorded on 16 October 1789 almost as briefly, with the comment, 'Sad News from France all anarchy and Confusion'. By 14 July 1791, Woodforde was sufficiently uncertain to describe these events as having taken place 'last year'. Clearly, he felt no urge to reflect on French politics in his sermons. Woodforde's parish of Weston Longeville was, however, only a few miles from Norwich, a radical centre, where the Revolution was warmly greeted in the Baptist Chapel of St Paul's; and Woodforde's Bishop from June 1790 to January 1792 was a staunch supporter of royal government both in France and in Britain. The country parson's relative silence on these matters, however, cautions us not to assume that the political sermons considered in this chapter were universal, or even perhaps the norm.

That a number of clergymen did preach and publish their reflections on the implications of events in France, should not surprise us. The tradition of political sermons was a well-established one. Although a barrage of criticism was directed at the nature of the views expressed in Richard Price's *Discourse on the Love of Our Country*, at least one critic recognised that 'General truths in politics have indeed a dignity from their high importance to society, which may well permit them to be delivered even from the place where the gospel is usually expounded'.[2] Indeed, there were many occasions when a political sermon was expected. The Book of Common Prayer gave forms of service, with thanksgiving or fasting as appropriate, to commemorate the gunpowder treason, the execution of King Charles the Martyr, the restoration of the Royal Family, and the anniversaries of the King's accession. In the first two cases, the clergyman

---

[1] *The Diary of a Country Parson: The Reverend James Woodforde, 1758–1802*, ed. J. Beresford, 5 vols. (London, 1924–31), vol. III, p. 124: 'Very great Rebellion in France by the Papers.'

[2] *A Controversial Letter of a New Kind to the Rev. Dr. Price* (London, 1790), p. 7.

was instructed to read one of the homilies against disobedience and wilful rebellion, or encouraged to preach a sermon 'of his own composing upon the same argument'. In addition, fast days were appointed to pray for national needs and to reinforce these in the popular consciousness by appropriate sermons.[3] Sermons preached before the two Houses of Parliament, at the opening of Assizes, at gatherings of the militia and at the universities, were also frequently devoted to political themes, even in normal times. So, the sermon was a natural medium in which to discuss the French Revolution.

In October 1789, when Parson Woodforde was preoccupied with buying, selling and slaughtering pigs, coursing hares with his greyhounds and entertaining his friends, his fellow priest from a little further south in the diocese, William Jones, the perpetual curate of Nayland in Suffolk, was a guest at the Deanery in Canterbury where he was visiting his lifelong friend and patron, George Horne.[4] Here the news from France was eagerly discussed and much lamented. Horne and Jones were high church patriarchalists, who had consistently over the years argued the case for kingly government being of divine appointment.[5] They were among the first clergy in Britain publicly to denounce the Revolution, and they did so from the pulpit of Canterbury Cathedral.

When the news of the events of 5 and 6 October reached them, Jones dusted off an old sermon on *The Art of Tranquillity* he had preached in Norwich Cathedral the previous summer, and redelivered it on 13 October.[6] By the following Sunday, 20 October, he had composed a powerful piece on *Popular Commotions to Precede the End of the World*, which reflected his growing alarm over events in France. This sermon is remarkable chiefly for its date, for it developed themes which most churchmen did not take up until considerably later. By 1793 it would have been commonplace, but it was delivered at a time when most people were still welcoming the Revolution, and when senior clergy were recording their fears in private letters and diaries rather than in public forums.[7]

[3] See Helen Randall, 'The rise and fall of a martyrology: sermons on Charles I', *Huntingdon Library Quarterly*, 10 (1946–7), pp. 135–67, and Roland Bartel, 'The story of public fast days in England', *Anglican Theological Review*, 37 (1955), pp. 190–200.

[4] W. Jones, *Memoirs of the Life and Writings of the Right Reverend George Horne* (London, 1795), pp. 152–3.

[5] For example, G. Horne, *The Origin of Civil Government*, 2 March 1769, and *Restoration Day Sermon*, 1760, in G. Horne, *Works*, 4 vols (London, 1818), vol II, pp. 434–9, and vol III, pp. 115–36; and W. Jones, *The Fear of God and the Benefits of Civil Obedience: Two Sermons* (London, 1778).

[6] W. Jones, *The Theological, Philosophical and Miscellaneous Works*, 12 vols (London, 1801), vol. V, pp. 1–19.

[7] Lambeth Palace Library MS 2103 (Porteus Notebook 1786–1800), fos. 25, 27; MS 1767 (Horsley Letters and Papers), fos. 202–3.

The title Jones gave to the sermon implies a strong millenarian content. This was an approach he was to develop significantly in two later sermons in 1794. Here, however, he treated the chiliastic theme with much caution and was more concerned with placing the Revolution in the contexts of political theology and of the growth of infidelity over the preceding century. He began with a double assertion about the relationship of religion and government which he and George Horne had been stressing in sermons for the previous thirty years. First, that man is essentially a sinful creature whose 'turbulent passions' have to be restrained by religion and by government. Secondly, that government, and specifically royal government, has been explicitly ordained by God and that men are under a religious duty to submit to it. He made a crucial distinction between the power of government and the power of the people, 'for the power of government is ordained of God, and supported by his providence, to still that storm and prevent that confusion which the power of the people raises'. The French now mocked 'the doctrine of the divine authority of government' and took the power which belongs to God upon themselves; no greater calamity, he reflected, could happen to any nation.

Jones portrayed the state of affairs in France as arising from the growth of deism and infidelity and the development of 'natural religion'. He spoke with extreme distaste of the view that 'where government is concerned, man is born with a right to think and act as he pleases; that all authority in others is a dangerous imposition upon ourselves; and that the property of others belongs equally to us, if we can get it'. It was this 'wild spirit of independence' which had led to the rebellion in the American colonies, and this in turn set up 'a fatal precedent and encouragement to other wicked, discontented people'. The contagion had now spread to France, with the help of Lafayette, and had brought about the dreadful state of affairs from which they now suffered. Jones reflected:

While the laws are in force, a man's house is his castle, and his life, and fortune, and character, are secured to him: but when a lawless multitude is afloat, the best members of society are at the mercy of the worst. Every man is a convict, when his enemy is his accuser, judge, and executor. There are no rays of mercy from a throne to save the head of the unhappy victim from being made a spectacle upon a pole; no lawful force to protect his stores from being plundered, his lands laid waste, his buildings burned and demolished.[8]

Five days later, on Friday 25 October 1789, the anniversary of the King's accession, Dean Horne went into the pulpit of his cathedral church himself to preach on *Submission to Government*, an uncompromising statement of the doctrine of political obligation, which applied as

---

[8] Jones, *Popular Commotions to Precede the End of the World* in his *Works*, vol. VI, pp. 274–95.

powerfully to circumstances in Britain as to events in France. He examined the two scriptural texts most frequently cited in establishment political sermons, I Peter 2.13–17 and Romans 13.1–7, and insisted that 'the law of God enjoins obedience to every government settled according to the constitution of the country in which it subsists'. At birth man has an obligation of duty to his parents as a son and to his governors as a subject. This is an absolute duty of obedience. Christians should be as St Peter described them, not factious and turbulent, but 'quiet and peaceful, minding their own business, and knowing nothing more of politics than to obey their governors, and to pray for them;... to suffer rather than to rebel'. However bad government might be, men never had a right of rebellion. Government was the will of God and men must submit to it; if the governed were to seek to rule their governors, then chaos and civil war, invasion and slavery would ensue.[9]

While the overall anti-revolutionary tenor of this sermon is indisputable, Horne was a little more circumspect than Jones in his direct references to France. He acknowledged the view, popular at this time, that the French were seeking a constitution more like the British, and suggested that only time would discover whether these commotions would end like the opposition to Charles I in the seventeenth century. If one were to look merely at these two sermons, it would appear that the Dean was less extreme than his acolyte, but a consideration of their other writings shows that they were in almost complete agreement. Both sermons were denounced in the newspapers and Horne observed that were the Revolution to spread to England, they were both likely to be strung up to the same lamp-post.[10]

These sermons preceded the publication of Burke's *Reflections* by over a year. Although many churchmen applauded Burke's work, such sermons remained rare before the publication of Part One of Paine's *Rights of Man* in February 1791, and were not commonplace until after the publication of Part Two in February 1792. But this is not to suggest that such views were unpopular with the establishment. Indeed, Horne was rewarded in June 1790 by his elevation to the Bishopric of Norwich; he immediately appointed William Jones as Bishop's Chaplain. Horne's health had broken down prematurely in 1788 when he was only fifty-seven, and he relied greatly on Jones who, although four years his senior, remained in vigorous health.

When Woodforde attended the new Bishop's primary visitation in Norwich on 15 June 1791, he noted that Horne was absent in Bath 'having been very ill lately', and concentrated his attention on the visitation

---

[9] Horne, *Submission to Government* in his *Works*, vol. III, pp. 384–97.
[10] Jones, *Memoirs of Horne*, p. 153.

dinner when around thirty-four clergy sat down to 'Maccarel, Veal, Mutton, Green Goose, Ducklings, Peas &c. &c.'. He joyfully recorded that Bishop Horne provided the wine, 'one Bottle between two Clergymen', but omitted to mention that he also published the episcopal *Charge* he was too ill to deliver. In this *Charge*, the Bishop, feeling close to death, warned his clergy against the fashion for innovation which was especially dangerous when it led men to new opinions in religion and government. Wicked men lusted after power and claimed new rights which were inconsistent with the sense of subordination and right of possession which were essential to society. He explained:

Liberty of thought there must be in all men, good and bad, because it cannot be prevented; but the liberty of overt action, which is the only liberty that will please libertines, there cannot be, until the laws of God lose their force, and society itself is dissolved.

These issues were relevant to the clergy, not because they were politicians, but because they were 'concerned for the preservation of the divine laws, and the peace of the world in which we live'. Burke wrote to Horne on 9 December 1791 to congratulate him on this *Charge*, which he considered 'full of Wisdom, and piety, and of doctrine not only sound in itself, but for the time most seasonable'.[11]

The relationship between religion and the politics of revolution was more fully explored by William Jones in a sermon on 31 May 1791 at Bury St Edmunds, one of the other visitation centres, before the chancellor of the diocese and the clergy of that deanery. In this consideration of *The Difficulties and the Resources of the Christian Ministry in the Present Times*, he traced the origin of the French Revolution to a theological cause. He recalled that in his 1786 work on the figurative language of the Scriptures, he had argued that while the images and objects of the natural world were used to describe the invisible world, the distinction between them was always made clear. God is light, but the light is not God; the invisible world is the true reality, of which this material world is the shadow. But the arguments of Socinians, 'rational Christians', deists and infidels, made the natural world principle and took the creation for the Creator. He singled out for attack Hume and Voltaire for scoffing at grace and providence and disseminating irreligion: Hume, in his histories of Britain and the Roman Empire, attempted to explain events in purely material terms; while 'the Lucian of the Continent...the grand patriarch of modern infidelity' sought to pervert the young by his humour and

[11] G. Horne, *A Charge Intended to have been delivered to the Clergy of Norwich* (Norwich, 1791), pp. 3, 28–30; T. W. Copeland (ed.), *The Correspondence of Edmund Burke*, 10 vols. (Cambridge, 1958–78), vol. VI, p. 455.

lightness of touch. This materialism led to the destruction of manners and to the system of false principles set up by Paine. The restless desire for innovation and levelling principles was, Jones warned his fellow clergy, in danger of destroying the constitution in church and state in Britain, as it had in France. He vented his exasperation with the government's tactics as he perceived them:

Sedition, which used formerly to hide its trains of mischief in caverns under ground, now brandishes its torch in broad daylight: and the policy of the age (too deep for *me* to understand) leaves it to itself, and waits to see what it will do; and when the streets are in flames, tries to put out the fire as well as it can; and disperses a lawless multitude with blood and slaughter, which might have been restrained and saved by a timely execution of the laws.[12]

There can be little doubt that Jones was speaking with his Bishop's full approval.

George Horne would have found in his new diocese many clergy who shared this political outlook. Men like James Woodforde, despite their political passivity, were naturally inclined to a conservative view and lamented events over the Channel. Others were more active and expressed those views publicly, like Samuel Cooper, curate of Great Yarmouth, whose scholarly *First Principles of Civil and Ecclesiastical Government* (1791) supported Burke and attacked Priestley. In December 1792, Cooper used his position as a Justice of the Peace to instruct the local inn-holders and ale-house-keepers that they must not allow clubs and associations for reading libellous publications and holding seditious discussions to be set up on their premises.[13]

The Diocese of Norwich was, however, one in which the Old Dissenters were strongly represented and some of their ministers espoused the radical cause which received considerable popular support, at least in Norwich itself. One such minister was the Reverend Mark Wilks, a Baptist, and also a Norfolk farmer. On 14 July 1791, a day when Woodforde prayed that no 'bad Consequences' would come of the many meetings to be held in Norwich and elsewhere to commemorate the Revolution, Wilks preached two sermons in St Paul's chapel, Norwich, on *The Origin and Stability of the French Revolution*. These sermons are remarkable more for the intensity and sincerity of feeling they exhibit, than for the intellectual quality of their argument.

Opening his first sermon with the provocative words 'Jesus Christ was a Revolutionist', Wilks went on to argue that 'the French Revolution is

---

[12] W. Jones, *The Difficulties and Resources of the Christian Ministry in the Present Times* (Bury St Edmunds, 1791), pp.7–13.

[13] Samuel Cooper, *Notice to the Inn-Holders and Ale-House-Keepers in the Hundred of Mutford and Lothingland*, broadsheet [1792].

of God, and that no power exists or can exist, by which it can be overthrown'. He was not suggesting that it had been brought about supernaturally; indeed, such was the state of France that it would have taken a miracle to have prevented its outbreak. But he did detect the hand of divine providence at work in preserving the Revolution from its enemies. On this day, he remembered as especially providential the attack on the Bastille (which, he claimed, foiled Artois's plot to destroy the National Assembly) and, more recently, the failure of the King's attempted flight. If Englishmen were to regard the discovery of the Gunpowder Plot as providential, why, he asked, should the failure of counter-revolution in France not also be seen as the work of God?

Burke's *Reflections* was, of course, anathema to Wilks and was roundly condemned. The Baptist minister likened Burke's assertion that the National Assembly was made up of lawyers, physicians, merchants and farmers, to the common Anglican complaint that the nonconformist clergy were uneducated journeymen, tailors and shoemakers. Unlike Burke, he had no sympathy with the plight of the French church and quoted with delight the rhyme:

> The French, the French, they had a Church,
>   Which cost five million in a year;
> They left the Clergy in the lurch
>   And took the tythes their debt to clear.[14]

However, to suggest that Anglicans opposed the Revolution while non-conformists welcomed it would be true only in a general sense. Horne and Jones represented the extreme patriarchalist end of the spectrum of political opinion within the Church of England. At the other end, Richard Watson, Bishop of Llandaff, told his clergy in his 1791 *Charge* at his triennial visitation, that he could not 'but rejoice in the Emancipation of the French Nation from the Tyranny of Royal Despotism', but, because he detested the despotism of popular demagogues still more, he reserved his judgement on the Revolution until it was clear how it would develop. He was not to regret this caution. In his 1795 *Charge*, he denounced the French abandonment of religion, without which a state could not survive, and by 1798 his repudiation of the French was total and passionate.[15]

The Methodists (to whom Bishop Horne, an ex-Hutchinsonian, showed some sympathy) were staunch against the Revolution, but the Old Dissenters welcomed it in its early days. When, on 24 July 1791, following

---

[14] M. Wilks, *The Origin and Stability of the French Revolution*, 2nd edn (Norwich, 1791). See also Sarah Wilks, *Memoirs of the Rev. Mark Wilks, Late of Norwich* (London, 1821).

[15] Richard Watson, *A Charge Delivered to the Clergy of the Diocese of Llandaff June, 1791* (London, 1792), pp. 4–19; *Miscellaneous Tracts on Religious, Political and Agricultural Subjects*, 2 vols. (London, 1815), vol. I, pp. 90, 100–1, 126–50.

the Birmingham riots in which Priestley's house had been burned, John Clayton, the Independent minister at the Weigh-house Chapel in London, preached an anti-revolution sermon on *The Duty of Christians to Magistrates*, there were still plenty of Dissenters ready to condemn his betrayal.[16] Clayton had disapproved both of Priestley's theology and his politics. The Baptist minister Robert Hall, in *Christianity Consistent with a Love of Freedom* (1791), dissented from the Unitarian's theology, but approved his politics and his support for the Revolution.[17] Hall was later to regret this piece and to refuse to agree to its republication, and this was symptomatic of the Dissenters' gradual repudiation of the Revolution, and their retreat from radical politics in Britain. Mark Wilks was unusual in his continuing support; in April 1795 he preached in Norwich two collection sermons towards defraying the expenses of the defendants in the treason trials.[18]

For many, the change in their attitude to the Revolution came during the winter of 1792–3 when England appeared on the brink of revolution following the widespread dissemination of Part Two of Paine's *Rights of Man*. They were encouraged by a flood of anti-revolutionary pamphlets, many invoking religious arguments. Bishop Horne had died in Bath in January 1792, just a few weeks before the publication of Paine's second volume. Shortly before his death, he had been visited by his old friend Mrs Hannah More.[19] Later in the year she turned to tract writing to help counter the influence of Paine, as did Horne's old chaplain, William Jones. More produced only one tract at this time, the celebrated *Village Politics*;[20] the Cheap Repository Tracts were to follow between 1795 and 1798. In December 1792 and January 1793, Jones produced a series of letters from John Bull and members of his family.

The longer broadsheet version of the first of these, *One Pennyworth of Truth from Thomas Bull to his Brother John* (1792), not only denounced the violence of the French Revolution, but also characterised it as Godless; the French, 'massacre poor Priests; rob and plunder their country and their Church; put Kings and Queens in Prison; and they sing *ça Ira*, for Joy that *Hell is broke loose*! This theme of Godlessness recurs

16 *A Consolatory Letter to the Rev. John Clayton from Fidelia* (London, 1791); *Remarks on a Sermon Late Published by the Rev. John Clayton* (London, 1791).
17 Robert Hall, *Christianity Consistent with a Love of Freedom* in his *Works*, 6 vols. (London, 1832), vol. III, pp. 1–60, especially pp. 28–30.
18 M. Wilks, *Athaliah; or the Tocsin Sounded by Modern Alarmists* (Norwich, 1795).
19 Jones, *Memoirs of Horne*, p. 172. On the pamphlets see Robert Hole, 'British counter-revolutionary popular propaganda in the 1790s' in Colin Jones (ed.), *Britain and Revolutionary France: Conflict, Subversion and Propaganda* (Exeter, 1983).
20 *Village Politics Addressed to all Mechanics Journeymen and Day Labourers in Great Britain* (Canterbury, 1793).

throughout these letters. The women of the family, Moll and Bet Bull, are fearful lest the French repudiation of marriage should spread to England, and they lose their husbands.[21] John reports, in a letter dated 22 December 1792, on how their minister explained in a sermon why the French were being successful in the war against Germany; God was using bad people to punish others, and themselves, by the war.[22]

This Godlessness is most comprehensively examined in *John Bull's Answer to his Brother Thomas's Second Letter* of 28 December 1792, which explained in detail how the French had broken each one of the Ten Commandments. The revolutionaries were atheists or deists, but had taken the name of God in vain by swearing an oath to support nation, law and King, which they had since broken. Having driven out the clergy, the National Assembly met on a Sunday, like any other day. Far from honouring them, children sacrificed their parents; 'during the dreadful massacres, a young man cut off the heads of his own Father and Mother because they would not join in such proceedings, and bringing their heads in a basket, boasted of having done a good deed!' So far 28,000 had been murdered in cold blood, priests, men, women and children, and Marat was reported as saying that another 268,000 must be murdered before the Revolution would be complete. They sanctioned divorce and re-marriage which was nothing less than advocating adultery. The property of the King and nobles was stolen and that held by Englishmen in France was taken as well. They bore false witness, especially in the trials of 20 September, and ambition and avarice, the coveting of other men's goods, were the foundation of all their wickedness. Thus, each of the Ten Commandments had been breached.

Jones attributed to John Bull an experience which was common, but contrary to his own. At first, Bull claimed, he had had some sympathy with the French. They had not enjoyed the liberties of the English; they had no juries, could be imprisoned for long periods without appearing before the Assizes or Sessions. The revolutionaries claimed to be imitating the English, who alone in the world were free, and seemed to be setting up a constitutional monarchy. Louis XVI, 'a well-meaning, sweet-tempered Man' had already granted some reforms, and intended more, but this made the reformers over-bold and, instead of insisting on what they had a right to, they overturned everything.[23] He supposed they had no consciences at all, for if so, how could they reconcile them to their crimes:

The robbery of their Neighbours! Murder of their fellow Creatures! Treason to their King and Ruin to their Country! No Order! No Laws! No Honour! No

[21] *John Bull in Answer to his Brother Thomas*, broadsheet [December 1792].
[22] *Answer from John Bull to Thomas Bull*, broadsheet [22 December 1792].
[23] *Ibid.*

Justice! King! Religion! or God! – God forbid that *Englishmen* should follow such an Example![24]

Compared with Hannah More's tracts, William Jones's Bull family letters are crude propaganda, but perhaps no less effective for all that. More's greater literary sophistication led to her pieces being widely read and admired by the middle class, but Jones possibly had the greater impact in the streets in the three critical months of December 1792 to February 1793.

The alarm reached even Weston Longeville, and Parson Woodforde included more political references in his *Diary* in the months from November 1792 to January 1793 than in the rest of the forty-five years that the diary covered.[25] But there is no evidence to suggest that he discussed these concerns from his pulpit, though many clergy did in those days. Some of these sermons were delivered on obvious occasions for loyalist sentiment, as when Samuel Hayes preached before the members of the Association for Preserving Liberty and Property in St Margaret's, Westminster, on 27 January 1793. But others were less predictable, as when Daniel Turner preached *An Exhortation to Peace, Loyalty and Support of Government* on 9 December 1792 to a congregation of Dissenters at Abingdon. He told them that the trouble-makers were deists and men of no religion, but that Dissenters, although friends to civil and religious liberty, were enemies 'to all licentious violence against the Government', and should have nothing to do with insurrections.[26] But if not yet quite predictable, this was a clear sign of how things were going. After the outbreak of war between Britain and France in February 1793, pro-Revolution sermons almost disappeared; certainly they were virtually never published, even if they were preached. The fast day decreed on 19 April 1793 brought forth a large spate of patriotic and loyal sermons.[27]

In two sermons, *The Man of Sin* and *The Age of Unbelief*, preached at Spring Garden Chapel in January and February 1794, William Jones developed the millenarian theme which he had touched on in his first sermon on the Revolution in October 1789. The personal delusions of 'prophets' like Richard Brothers have given millenarian interpretations of the French Revolution a bad name. In fact, a number of cautious,

[24] *John Bull in Answer to his Brother Thomas.*
[25] See entries for 24, 28 November, 8, 11, 15, 17, 21, 29 December 1792, 11, 12, 19, 26 January 1793; vol. III, pp. 389–400; vol. IV, pp. 2–4.
[26] S. Hayes, *A Sermon Preached in St Margaret's Church, Westminster, January 27 1793* (London, 1793); D. Turner, *An Exhortation to Peace, Loyalty and Support of Government* (Henley [1793]), pp. 8–10.
[27] See, for examples, Richard Beadon, *A Sermon Preached before the Lords* (London, 1793); G. I. Huntingford, *A Sermon Preached before the Honourable House of Commons at the Church of St Margaret, Westminster, on Friday, April 19, 1793* (London, 1793); W. Gilbank, *The Duties of Man* (London, 1793).

studious and sensible men pondered the accounts in the scriptures of the events which would presage the Parousia and considered how these could be related to those events through which they had recently lived, and they did so in language infinitely more restrained and temperate than that employed by Burke in his *Letters on a Regicide Peace*.[28] Historians know now, of course, that the Revolution was not the immediate herald of the Second Coming of Christ, but if they wish to understand both the spiritual mentality and the political perceptions of late eighteenth-century churchmen, they must take the measured, chiliastic scholarship of men like Samuel Horsley and William Jones seriously.[29]

Jones observed that sound lessons could be learned from the Revolution: politicians could consider the dangers of innovation to government, while Christians could think on the last things – though he recognised that such points had been made so often that a sort of moral fatigue was setting in. He concentrated on one of the less frequently invoked of the apocalyptic texts, II Thessalonians 2.3–4. Here St Paul explained that in the last days, before the coming of Christ in judgement, there would be a falling away (Jones supplied the stark word 'apostasy'), a 'Man of Sin' would rise up (Jones explained this could be a whole people not just an individual) against 'all that is called God' (Jones insisted that this meant God's vice-gerents on earth, i.e. Kings and rulers), and usurp the temple of God (converting it, Jones explained, into the temple of man).

For many years, Jones argued, this prophecy had been clouded in mystery, but could now be clearly seen:

in a neighbouring country, a direct apostasy hath taken effect. The Christian religion hath been renounced; not negatively, through corruption of manners, or neglect of truth; but positively, publicly, and in solemn form. The restraining power of government and the obligations of law...[have been] absolutely *taken out of the way* and abolished. The *will* of a wicked nation hath been admitted as the only sovereign *law* now to be obeyed.

Previously, religion and government had restrained man's sinful nature; now, as St Paul predicted, all restraint had been thrown aside by the French, their churches had been shut up or dedicated to the worship of the idol reason, and 'Government murdered in the person of their prince'.[30]

[28] Edmund Burke, *Three Letters Addressed to a Member of Parliament on the Proposals for Peace with the Regicide Directory of France* (London, 1796–7).
[29] R. V. Brothers, *A Revealed Knowledge of the Prophecies and Times*, 2 vols. (London, 1794); Lambeth Palace Library, MS 2809, W. J. Palmer's transcript of Samuel Horsley's Papers, vol. XI, on prophecy, fos. 111–84, notes on the Apocalypse, fos. 199–252, and six letters to the author [G. Goring] of 'Anti-Christ in the French convention' [1797], fos. 255–352. A general survey is provided by Clarke Garrett, *Respectable Folly: Millenarians and the French Revolution in France and England* (Baltimore, Md., 1975).
[30] Jones, *The Man of Sin* in his *Works*, vol. VI, pp. 316–34.

As he had done in earlier sermons, Jones traced this apostasy back to the growth of deism in seventeenth-century England. He claimed that Christianity was 'a scheme of facts', whilst infidelity was 'a scheme of abstract reasoning'. Reason was the wisdom of man, but faith was the wisdom of God. Reason might argue that power came from the people, but faith revealed that government was ordained by God. Deism led to atheism and admitted a worm to the root of the tree of life. The Enlightenment may have appeared innocent, but it was deadly:

A few years ago, it seemed as if the infidel party trusted to scoffing and jesting and pleasantry, and meant no more than to *laugh* the Gospel out of the world if they could. These were the coruscations of wit, which played in the air for a while, and pretended to be gentle and harmless; but they were soon changed into the thunders of persecution, and followed by torrents of Christian blood.

Jones took comfort that what he had experienced had been predicted in the Scriptures, and he felt sure that the horrors he saw around him could end only with the Parousia.[31]

Many other preachers, who did not take the millenarian road, also considered the Enlightenment as the precursor of the Revolution. In his *Reflections*, Burke argued that religion had to be destroyed before political revolution was possible. This theme appeared in a number of sermons, both before and after November 1790, but the allegation of a conspiracy by the *philosophes* to destroy religion and so make political revolution possible, did not become commonplace until 1797 and 1798, following the publication of the English translation of the Abbé Barruel's *Memoirs Illustrating the History of Jacobinism* (1797) and John Robinson's *Proofs of a Conspiracy Against All the Religions and Governments of Europe* (1797). Then, sermon after sermon explained how religion was the support of government and the cement of society, and how the anarchy and revolution in France could not have taken place unless Christianity had first been destroyed by the infidels.

When the Vicar of St Alkmond's, Shrewsbury, preached a sermon before the North Staffordshire Yeomanry on 25 September 1798, he launched into a bitter and passionate attack on the *philosophes*. From Voltaire, he argued, had come

a monster, that now stalks through the earth with gigantic strides, and threatens every throne and every altar; that with the voice of a lamb has the teeth of a lion, and with the insinuating sound of 'liberty and equality' in its mouth, conceals the regicide's dagger, under its blood-stained robe. This monster, a spurious philosophy, makes matter think, denies the immortality of the soul, represents death as an eternal sleep, and, as its highest climax in blasphemy, denies the being

31 Jones, *The Age of Unbelief* in his *Works*, vol. VI, pp. 335–62.

of God. In its political creed it is equally bold and execrable. The boasted 'rights of man' are nothing but a licence to pillage and murder, without any regard to rank, to the dictates of justice or mercy, of friendship or of blood; and to sanction an unprovoked and direct attack upon all property.[32]

Nor were these views limited to Anglican reactionaries, but could be heard from Dissenters who had earlier welcomed the Revolution. One such was Robert Hall, who preached a sermon on *Modern Infidelity Considered with Respect to its Influence on Society* at the Baptist Meeting in Cambridge in November 1799. He argued that a belief in God and in a future life established a moral code and sanctions which restrained men and ordered them in their social relationships. He shuddered at the prospect of relying merely on coercion, 'if nothing but the power of the magistrate stood between us and the daggers of assassins'. He characterised the French Revolution as 'a grand experiment on human nature', and suggested that the main passion it had revealed was vanity. Political power had never before circulated through so many hands; all wanted to possess authority, but none wanted to obey, and the ensuing torrent had overwhelmed law, order and civilisation.[33] By 1799, these were views from which few English preachers, of whatever denomination, would have dissented.

Indisputably, the French Revolution was a frequent topic of *discussion* in English sermons in the 1790s, but can sermons properly be regarded as a medium of *debate*? Debate implies people speaking, listening and replying about issues on which there is a significant divergence of opinion between them. There are, indeed, a number of obvious examples of this happening on a superficial level, but it may appear that more often clerics, usually of a reactionary nature, were using, or abusing, their privileged position in the pulpit, to air their political prejudices, vent their passion and spleen, and indulge in diatribes against the Revolution and all things French. While it is not difficult to illustrate this tendency with individual examples, to characterise the political sermons of the 1790s as a whole in this way would be misleading.

As well as some discussion of events in France, there was also a more significant debate about the values which should inform any judgement of the Revolution. In essence, the reaction to the French Revolution was not the initiation of a new debate in the pulpits, but rather the addition of another layer and a new dimension to an old one. That debate, moreover,

[32] Richard de Courcy, *Self-Defence not Inconsistent with the Precepts of Religion* (Shrewsbury, 1798), p. 19.
[33] R. J. Hall, *Modern Infidelity Considered with Respect to its Influence on Society* in his *Works*, vol. I, pp. 1–80, quotations pp. 24, 38–39.

was not a strictly secular, political one, but a major branch of theological discourse.

There was, in fact, relatively little discussion in secular terms of the superficial events of the Revolution in these sermons. Almost all would have agreed that the pulpit was not the place to discuss matters which were *purely* political. But there was widespread agreement on the propriety of investigating the relationship between government and religion, for this was a well-established branch of political theology. The vast majority of these political sermons discussed the theological issues which lay behind recent events in France and in Britain, and sought to relate these to a Christian understanding of government, society and human nature.

Before the Revolution broke out, there was in Britain a fairly clear idea of the proper relationship between religion and government. It was religion which conferred on governments political legitimacy, and which imposed on subjects a political obligation of obedience. The notion that governments were ordained of God, and that Christians were required to be faithful subjects, was drawn largely from the apostolic epistles. As such, in its broadest sense, it was accepted by all Christians, but the doctrine allowed some scope for interpretation. The form in which it existed in England on the eve of the French Revolution had been forged from the medieval and Renaissance concepts of kingship, through the Reformation of the sixteenth century, the civil war of the 1640s and the Revolution of 1688. In its most extreme form, the doctrine could be used to defend the principle of passive obedience and non-resistance, but by the 1780s everyone agreed that these were 'exploded theories'. The crucial issue was the right of rebellion. If subjects were obliged to accept the government under which they found themselves, as St Peter and St Paul had urged their contemporaries to accept the rule of Caligula and Nero, how could the events of 1688–9 be justified?

The solution, almost universally accepted, was that while government as a general concept was the ordinance of God, the particular form of government in any one country was the ordinance of man and could be changed in extreme circumstances. The crucial question, of course, was what constituted those extreme circumstances, and on this there was little agreement. Views on this varied within the established church, between Christian sects, and over time.[34] Men like George Horne and William Jones never denied the solution, nor repudiated the Revolution of 1688, but they clearly regarded it as an embarrassment best ignored, lest it led men to think that further change was legitimate. Other, like Richard

[34] These are fully discussed in Robert Hole, *Pulpits, Politics and Public Order in England 1760–1832* (Cambridge, 1989).

Watson, considered that the doctrine allowed some degree of constitutional reform without endangering the sacerdotal basis of political obligation.[35]

The political theology of other Christian denominations was even more complex than the range of views within the Anglican Church. Sects outside the established church who had enjoyed only limited toleration, and whose civil and political rights were still curtailed, could be expected to look favourably on the prospect of some degree of change in the constitution of church and state. Moreover, it might be expected that the range of views on church government, which was one of the issues which divided the sects, would be reflected in attitudes to secular government. To some extent this was so; certainly Congregationalists and Independents were unsympathetic to the notion of hierarchy; most nonconformists, along with Mark Wilks, felt little sympathy for the French church when its wealth was attacked; and within the Catholic Church, Cisalpines, like Joseph Berington, looked more favourably on the Revolution in its early days than did the Ultramontanes.[36] But while some Catholics supported the Revolution, most Methodists opposed it, and the secular politics of denominations cannot simply be extrapolated from their ecclesiology. More important was their concern for civil and political rights, but even here one cannot assume that because they opposed the restriction of political rights on the basis of religious affiliation, they were opposed also to a limitation on social and economic grounds. These views of the denominations, in turn, affected those of the Anglican establishment which feared that support for constitutional change could lead to a loss of its privileges. Pulpit discussions of the French Revolution in its early years have to be read in the light of this denominational and ecclesiological situation.

Views on the circumstances in which constitutional change was justifiable had been hardening in the decade or so before the outbreak of the French Revolution. The rebellion and loss of the American colonies, the Gordon Riots, and social change, dislocation and unrest in Britain, led to a general re-emphasis on the obligation of obedience. The homily laid down to be read on the political fasts and feasts was that against disobedience and wilful rebellion of 1570, and therefore predated the seventeenth-century changes in government and political theory. Its strictures on political obligation were still acceptable in the late eighteenth

---

[35] R. Watson, *Christianity Consistent with Every Social Duty*, 9 March 1769, *Sermons on Public Occasions and Tracts on Religious Subjects* (Cambridge, 1788), pp. 5–26.

[36] Joseph Berington, *The Rights of Dissenters from the Established Church* (Birmingham, 1789). See also, E. Duffy, 'Joseph Berington and the English Cisalpine movement 1772–1803', unpublished Ph.D. thesis (University of Cambridge, 1973), and Hole, *Pulpits, Politics and Public Order*, pp. 25–7, 105–6, 117.

century, however, and in 1792 it came into its own. The arguments of the mass of political sermons which followed the publication of Part Two of *Rights of Man*, and almost all of the politico-religious tracts of December 1792 to February 1793, are drawn directly from this homily and that of 1547 on *Obedience to Rulers*.[37] Not only William Jones's John Bull letters and Hannah More's *Village Politics*, but also the stream of pamphlets produced for and published by the Association for Preserving Liberty and Property are, in part, direct translations into popular language of the political theology of these Edwardian and Elizabethan homilies.

Constitutional arguments of legitimacy and obligation were dominant in sermons and tracts up to this critical winter of 1792–3. Thereafter, social arguments concerning the value of religious restraint on individual consciences came to predominate. As men increasingly saw what they regarded as anarchy in France, so they came to reflect on the nature of the social fabric and the crucial importance of the religious warp within that weave. Coercion could deal only with a minority of lawbreakers; a successful society had to be based on a broad acceptance of a moral code. But such was the nature of man that unless that code were enforced by religious sanctions, by the threat of Hell and the promise of Heaven, operating within people's consciences, it could never be effective. Remove religion, and society would begin to disintegrate. Political liberty, which depended upon the moral behaviour of citizens, was impossible, and only a despotic government could delay the slide into total anarchy.

There was little new about these arguments except their frequency and intensity. One branch of this doctrine related to the social hierarchy being divinely appointed, and the requirement of people to accept life in that social rank in which God had chosen to place them. This argument is heard, not only from establishment pulpits, but also from these non-conformist preachers who eschewed any idea of an ecclesiastical hierarchy.[38] The social doctrine depended upon two presuppositions: first, a belief in Christian eschatology; secondly, an acceptance of the Christian view of the nature of man as an essentially flawed creature, the heir of Original Sin. It was this doctrine which led to pulpit debate on the Revolution, especially from 1793 onwards, being increasingly concentrated on the Godless nature of the Revolution and the influence of the *philosophes* upon it.

Just like the constitutional argument, so this social debate needs to be

---

[37] R. Bond (ed.), *Certain Sermons or Homilies (1547) and a Homily against Disobedience and Wilful Rebellion (1570): A Critical Edition* (Toronto, 1987), pp. 161–73, 207–59.

[38] See, for example, E. V. Verson, *A Sermon Preached before the Lords, January 30, 1794* (London, 1794); J. Owen, *Subordination Considered on the Grounds of Reason and Religion* (Cambridge, 1794); S. Bradburn, *Equality, A Sermon on 2 Cor. vii. 14* (Bristol [1794]); J. Crowther, *Christian Order: Liberty without Anarchy* (Bristol, 1796).

read in a wider theological context if we are to understand its discussion of the Revolution aright. As William Jones repeatedly pointed out, deism did not begin in France, but in England with the seventeenth- and early eighteenth-century sceptics, Herbert, Toland and Bolingbroke. This led not only to the deist *philosophes* in France, but also to Arianism and Socinianism in Britain. These English unitarians and 'rational Christians' posed, in the eyes of orthodox Christians, a threefold danger. First, they denied the divinity of Christ and so weakened his authority and took a step towards deism. Secondly, they depended upon reason rather than revelation and would accept only those parts of scripture which were supported by (or, at the very least, were consistent with) human reason, again weakening the authority of Christian moral teaching. Thirdly, they took an optimistic view of the nature of man, radically at odds with the doctrine of Original Sin, so undermining the whole basis of the social doctrine.

A significant number of the protagonists in the pulpit debate had, in the years before the outbreak of the Revolution, preached and published attacks on deism and unitarianism. Samuel Horsley (whose Martyrdom Day sermon, preached before the House of Lords in January 1793, and Episcopal *Charge* to his clergy in 1796 were paradigm statements of the constitutional and the social doctrines respectively) had preached a powerful archidiaconal *Charge* in 1783 passionately attacking Joseph Priestley, the unitarians, and 'rational Christianity', for weakening the moral force of revealed religion. William Jones had published his *Reflexions on the Growth of Heathenism among Modern Christians* in 1776, and reissued it in 1794 observing that this edition was 'more seasonable than the first; now we have been witness to the profane affectation of Heathen manners by the Philosophers of France; with its malignant affects on Religion, Government, and the Peace of the Christian World'.[39]

These two pillars of the establishment said nothing, however, which was not repeated by the Baptist, Robert Hall, in his sermon *Modern Infidelity Considered with Respect to its Influence on Society* in 1799. Hall had welcomed the Revolution in 1791; now he condemned it for its infidel origins. This change of position was a common experience. Most clergy who had not already adopted it were caught up in the passion which followed the conspiracy theory popularised by Barruel and Robinson in 1797, and this led many to denounce French atheism from their pulpits. Here was a doctrine to which all trinitarian Christians, established and dissenting, Catholic and Protestant, could subscribe. In a rare moment of unity, Christians stood together to condemn the infidelity on which the

---

[39] Jones, *Reflexions on the Growth of Heathenism among Modern Christians* in his *Works*, vol. III, p. 425.

Revolution was based, and the moral anomie and social dislocation which would follow the adoption of such a theology.

'Rational' Christians rejected the notion of a moral code revealed to man by God. Joseph Priestley adopted a utilitarian conception of morality, learned from experience, while Richard Price believed that the moral sense was innate, and independent of faith, opinion or will. But both men were agreed in rejecting the doctrine of Original Sin. Price believed that man's natural state was virtuous, and that if a system of minimal government gave him absolute liberty, then he would be good. Priestley too believed that man was capable of achieving perfection and on this belief developed his theory of progress.[40] Price and Priestley's English critics observed that this doctrine of progress and perfectibility was shared in France by Turgot and Condorcet, and at times they appeared to imply that all the *philosophes* subscribed to it, quite ignoring the Voltairean strain of pessimism.

When preachers reflected upon the events in France in the 1790s, they did so in the light of this well-established theological dispute concerning the inherent sinfulness of man and the theory of perfectibility. The essence of the soterial theology which lies at the heart of the Christian faith is contained in the sequence of the Creation, the Fall and the Redemption of humankind by the atonement won by Christ in his sacrifice upon the cross. To deny the Fall and reject the concept of Original Sin was to remove the necessity for the Redemption and to render the Crucifixion irrelevant. A humankind which was capable of self-perfection had no need of a divine sacrifice to atone for its sins. What was in dispute was not just two different views of the nature of man, but an understanding of the relationship between man and God which lay at the very foundation of Christian theology. Although the argument centred around the social and political consequences of these differing views of human nature, the preachers were well aware that infinitely more was at stake in the debate than a system of government.

An acceptance of the essential sinfulness of the human race, led men, it was argued, to a state of humility. The moral code, revealed to mankind by God, enjoined benevolence as a moral duty and a religious obligation, and castigated self-interest and selfishness as a sin. This made men both amenable to government and considerate towards their fellow creatures. It led men to accept laws and respect the social framework. When men considered their interests within the eschatological dimension of eternal

---

[40] J. Priestley's introductory essay in *Hartley's Theory of the Human Mind* (London, 1775), pp. xlii–xliii; *A Sermon Preached at the Gravel Pit Meeting on April 19, 1793*, pp. 31–5; R. Price, *Review of the Principal Questions in Morals* (1757), 3rd edn (London, 1787), pp. 64, 171–96.

life, their conduct on earth was more likely to accord with those standards of social behaviour consistent with government.

The *philosophes* and revolutionaries taught, it was alleged, that enlightened self-interest would lead to universal benevolence. This notion was derided as unrealistic in innumerable sermons. Instead, it was argued, the assertion of human perfectibility would give rise to vanity, and this was the essential quality of the infidel, just as humility was of the Christian. Self-importance, self-interest and selfishness characterised the actions of the Godless man. Since he had no faith in the prospect of eternal reward or punishment in a future life, there was no constraint upon the free exercise of his selfish will.[41]

Christian and infidel attitudes to the concept of human will perhaps best illustrate their differences of outlook. For the Christian, the will was something to be curbed or broken. Man should subject himself instead to the will of God enshrined in the revealed moral code. Infidels, it was alleged, were led by vanity to exercise their individual will in a capricious and selfish way which made society unstable and government impossible. Each man did as he chose, pursuing his own self-interest, without any restraint. This was the problem which Hannah More addressed in her most theologically forceful tract, *The History of Mr Fantom*. Here Fantom, the vain Jacobin, dreams that he would 'alter all the laws, and do away with all the religions, and put an end to all the wars in the world. I would everywhere redress the injustice of fortune, or what the Vulgar call Providence'. By contrast, Trueman, the practical Christian, feels 'more called upon to procure the happiness of a poor neighbour, who has no one else to look to, than to form wild plans for the good of mankind, too extensive to be accomplished, and too chimerical to be put into practice'. Through Trueman, More delivers her verdict on the Jacobins:

The connection of jacobinism with impiety is inseparable. I generally find in gentlemen of your fraternity an equal abhorrence to Christianity and good government. The reason is obvious. There are restraints in both; there is subordination in both. In both cases the hatred arises from aversion to a superior.[42]

The debate on the French Revolution which was conducted in England

---

[41] Edmund Burke, *The Works*, 6 vols. (London, 1877–83), vol. II, p. 536; *Reflections on the Revolution in France and on the Proceedings in Certain Societies in London Relative to that Event* (London, 1790), ed. Conor Cruise O'Brien (Harmondsworth, 1968), p. 256; *The Correspondence*, vol. VI, p. 215, vol. IX, p. 387; G. I. Huntingford, *A Sermon Preached before the Lords on May 25, 1804* (London, 1804); J. Randolph, *A Sermon Preached before the Lords on March 12, 1800* (Oxford, 1800).

[42] Hannah More, *The Works of Hannah More*, 11 vols. (London, 1853), vol. III, pp. 1–42, quotations, pp. 12, 19, 34.

through the media of sermons and tracts was not, in the main, one inappropriate to the pulpit. It was, broadly, developed within a theological discourse. It did not consist merely of secular, political comment on contemporary events in France, but it related these to a complex and well-established political theology. The discussion was largely confined to the theoretical implications of events, and therefore, in a sense, the inaccuracies, limited knowledge and misconceptions about events in France were unimportant. The political theology which emerged did not really depend on evidence from the French experience to prove the impossibility of an atheist state, or the corruption of human nature. To rely upon such evidence would be to argue according to the secular standards of the rationalists and materialists the preachers despised. Human corruption, original sin and a divinely imposed political obligation of obedience to established governments, they believed, were revealed to man by God through the Scriptures and the church. This theology might help to explain, or even to predict, happenings in France, but those events could not prove or disprove doctrines which God had revealed. The debate showed how close these men still considered the relationship between religion and politics, between political theory and political theology to be. But the subject and centre of that debate was the theology, not the events in France. Those events provided a new and stimulating context in which to re-explore and develop a political theology which was long established and still evolving.

2   Interpretations of anti-Jacobinism

John Dinwiddy

During the last dozen years, something which looks rather like a consensus has developed, to the effect that in the political debates of the 1790s the conservatives or anti-Jacobins had the better of the argument. Harry Dickinson, for example, says that it can be argued quite strongly that the radicals were defeated, at least in part, 'by the force of their opponents' arguments'.[1] This remark has been cited by Ian Christie, who has described the intellectual defences of the Hanoverian regime as 'formidable', and by Jonathan Clark; while Philip Schofield has endorsed another remark of Dickinson's about the appeal and intellectual power of late eighteenth-century conservative ideology.[2] Faced with this phalanx, one feels rather as Horne Tooke must have felt in about 1800; and I have no intention of making a frontal assault on it. Nor do I favour a reversion to an earlier consensus, which Harry Dickinson has quite rightly criticised: the consensus among historians operating in the Whig tradition of English radical and labour history, who regarded the intellectual case for extensive political reform in the late eighteenth century as unanswerable, and who treated the case *against* reform with facile neglect.[3] All I want to do is to ask some questions about the new Dickinsonian consensus: to ask, for example, what assumptions and contentions are being made by the various members of the phalanx, and in what senses it can really be said that the arguments of the anti-Jacobins were stronger than those of their opponents.

[1] H. T. Dickinson, *Liberty and Property: Political Ideology in Eighteenth-Century Britain* (London, 1977), p. 272.

[2] Ian R. Christie, *Stress and Stability in Late Eighteenth-Century Britain: Reflections on the British Avoidance of Revolution* (Oxford, 1984), p. 159; J. C. D. Clark, *English Society 1688–1832: Ideology, Social Structure and Political Practice during the Ancien Régime* (Cambridge, 1985), pp. 199–200; T. P. Schofield, 'Conservative political thought in Britain in response to the French Revolution', *Historical Journal*, 29, 3 (1986), p. 604.

[3] P. A. Brown's *The French Revolution in English History* (London, 1918), contains a couple of pages on Burke's thought, but nothing else on the intellectual reaction except a single quotation from Hannah More's *Village Politics*, and a remark that Burke's arguments were 'parodied by the host of anti-Jacobin writers'; G. S. Veitch's *The Genesis of Parliamentary Reform* (London, 1913), paid even less attention to the ideological response to radicalism, though it included several chapters on repression.

In his chapter – or lecture – on 'The intellectual repulse of revolution', Ian Christie gives some attention to the Burke–Paine controversy; and he claims that while Paine's perception of what was happening in France was superficial, Burke's 'penetrated to the heart'.[4] Burke discerned, or claimed to discern, in 1790, elements or tendencies within the Revolution, and especially within its ideology, that were leading ineluctably towards social breakdown and lawless tyranny. In 1792–4, much of what he had predicted did actually occur; and for Christie the events of these years are a vindication of Burke's analysis and of his perception of a 'destructive, murderous' elements at the heart of the Revolution. In support of this kind of interpretation Christie can cite some formidable authorities – especially François Furet, or at least the Furet of *Penser la Révolution Française*,[5] as well as earlier writers such as Talmon; and the ideological determinism that infuses Furet's interpretation still seems to be fashionable in French Revolution scholarship. It has met with some opposition lately, however;[6] and there is another tradition of interpretation which does not see the Terror as the predetermined outcome of developments that had taken place in the opening year or two of the Revolution. This alternative tradition goes back as far as Mallet du Pan, who argued in his *Considérations sur la nature de la Révolution de France* in 1793 that the increasing violence of the Revolution was attributable largely to the counter-revolutionaries, whose desperate attempts at reaction gave strength and opportunity to extremists on the opposite side.[7] Also, of course, the alternative tradition has put much emphasis on the impact of invasion and total war; and one can add that Furet Mark I – the Furet who published *La Révolution* with Denis Richet in 1965 – belonged to a large extent to that tradition, explaining the *dérapage* (the skidding-off course) of the Revolution principally in terms of counter-revolution and war.[8] If this interpretation is regarded as more right than wrong, then the Terror cannot be plausibly construed as the natural fruit of the doctrine of popular sovereignty and as the culmination of trends manifest to Burke in 1790. Much of what Burke predicted may have occurred – but for reasons which lay *outside* his analysis.

Christie goes on to say in his lecture: 'To contemporaries then, and to us now, the clash between Burke and Paine over the French Revolution

---

[4] Christie, *Stress and Stability*, pp. 170–1. See also Roger Scruton, 'Man's second disobedience: a vindication of Burke' in Ceri Crossley and Kay Small (eds.), *The French Revolution and British Culture* (Oxford, 1989), pp. 187–222.

[5] (Paris, 1978); Eng. trans. *Interpreting the French Revolution* (Cambridge, 1981).

[6] See, for example, Norman Hampson, *Prelude to Terror: The Constituent Assembly and the Failure of Consensus, 1789–1791* (Oxford, 1988).

[7] Jacques Mallet du Pan, *Considérations sur la nature de la Révolution de France* (London, 1793), pp. 17–18, 50; cf. Robert R. Palmer, 'Reflections on the French Revolution', *Political Science Quarterly*, 67 (1952), p. 76.

[8] François Furet and Denis Richet, *La Révolution*, 2 vols. (Paris, 1964–5), vol. I, ch. 5.

epitomized the confrontation between conservatism and revolution.'[9] That is certainly one way of seeing the Burke–Paine controversy. But it seems to me that there is another way of seeing it: as a confrontation, not between conservatism and revolution, but between conservatism and redistributive radicalism. The essence of Paine's critique of the late eighteenth-century government machine in England was that it was mainly a device for raising money from the consuming population at large and transferring it into the pockets of place-holding members of the oligarchy; whereas it *could* operate, he believed – if it was turned into a genuinely representative government – to transfer resources in the opposite direction, raising money by progressive taxation and using it to finance such things as old-age pensions and popular education. In 1800, nettles were selling at Oldham for tuppence a pound (according to William Rowbottom's diary), while Parson Woodforde was sitting down one day to 'a boiled rabbit and a goose', the next day to 'boiled pork and a roast pheasant', and the next day to 'cod-fish and oysters and shrimp-sauce and a couple of partridges roasted, etc.'.[10] A few years earlier, Paine had published his *Agrarian Justice*, in which he said that the current state of civilisation presented a horrifying contrast of affluence and wretchedness; and he went on to say, in explaining that the problem could never be solved by private charity: 'It is only by organizing civilization upon such principles as to act like a system of pullies, that the whole weight of misery can be removed.'[11]

Burke, at much the same time, was formulating one of the most extreme arguments for economic *laissez-faire* that has ever been written. During the crisis of 1795 he was deeply alarmed by the arguments being expressed by Samuel Whitbread and others to the effect that the authorities should interfere at least temporarily with the labour market or the market for provisions by fixing minimum wages or maximum prices. It was vitally important, Burke maintained, to resist any idea that it was 'within the competence of government, taken as government, or even of the rich, as rich, to supply to the poor those necessaries which it has pleased Divine Providence for a while to withhold from them'. And he went on to say, in words that Marx not surprisingly picked up later, that the people should be made to realise that their hardships could not be alleviated by any breach of 'the laws of commerce, which are the laws of Nature, and

[9] *Stress and Stability*, p. 170.
[10] MS diary of William Rowbottom, under 20 April 1800, Oldham Public Library; *The Diary of a Country Parson: The Reverend James Woodforde, 1758–1802*, ed. J. Beresford, 5 vols. (London, 1924–31), vol. V, p. 282.
[11] M. D. Conway (ed.), *The Writings of Thomas Paine*, 4 vols. (New York, 1894–6), vol. III, p. 337. See also Gregory Claeys, *Thomas Paine: Social and Political Thought* (London, 1989), pp. 196–208.

consequently the laws of God'.[12] He opposed any measure of a
redistributive tendency – and he included the fixing of minimum wages in
this category, as being tantamount to an 'arbitrary division' of the
employer's property among those he employed – on the grounds that once
the sanctity of property suffered any infringement, the way would be open
to wholesale levelling. He went so far as to argue in the *Reflections* that it
was good for vast accumulations of property to exist and to be rigidly
protected, for they then formed 'a natural rampart about the lesser
properties in all their gradations'. Paine, on the other hand, maintained
that some degree of redistribution would make property *more* secure by
reducing the resentments it aroused. He said in arguing for the
introduction of a death duty to finance old-age pensions: 'To remove the
danger [to property], it is necessary to remove the antipathies, and this can
only be done by making property productive of a national blessing,
extending to every individual.'[13]

It seems to me that there are dimensions of the Burke–Paine
confrontation or comparison which those who side with Burke are
inclined to ignore; and I feel also that those who emphasise the strength
of conservative thought in general in the 1790s are apt to show similar
selectiveness. Philip Schofield, in his very interesting study of conservative
'high theory', shows how quite sophisticated lines or argument were
developed on the basis of different traditions of eighteenth-century British
thought: theological utilitarianism, social contract theory and the natural-
law tradition. What one does not get from his work, it seems to me – aside
from a brief summary of some of Paine's more vulnerable arguments – is
a sense of the range of *dialogue* that was in progress in the 1790s, and a
recognition that although in some areas the conservatives were able to
counter radical arguments quite cogently, there were other areas where
they had to resort either to evasiveness, or to misrepresentation, or to
some fairly transparent special pleading. Before the emphasis on the
strength and superiority of conservative argument in the late eighteenth
century is endorsed, one would do well to compare (for example) William
Paley's arguments against parliamentary reform with Thomas Holt
White's *Letters to William Paley…on his Objections to a Reform in the
Representation of the Commons* (1796), a pamphlet in which much of the
nineteenth-century utilitarian case for representative government was
adumbrated, and which was to be described by John Colman Rashleigh
in 1820 as perhaps the ablest work published on the side of constitutional

---

[12] *Thoughts and Details on Scarcity* in F. W. Rafferty (ed.), *The Works of the Right
Honourable Edmund Burke*, 6 vols. (Oxford, 1907), vol. VI, p. 22; cf. Karl Marx, *Capital*,
trans. E. and C. Paul (London, 1974), p. 843n.

[13] Edmund Burke, *Reflections on the Revolution in France and on the Proceedings in Certain
Societies in London Relative to that Event*, ed. Conor Cruise O'Brien (Harmondsworth,
1968), p. 140; Conway, *Writings of Paine*, vol. III, p. 341.

reform.[14] In combatting Paley's view that no new mode of election to the House of Commons promised 'to collect together more wisdom, or produce firmer integrity' than the existing system, Holt White wrote: 'Something more than large property, external eminence, and shining talents are requisite in an assembly of Legislators,...because these qualities do not necessarily involve an IDENTITY OF INTEREST between the Governed and their Governors.'[15] Similar points were made by Thomas Cooper in 1792 and by John Thelwall in 1795:

I have always thought that it will be found on examination (whether pursued with a view to mere Theory, or the evidence of past facts) that every Government has been and will be conducted for the advantage in the first instance of the *Governors*, whoever they are: and the whole secret lies in making those the *actual* Governors, whether directly or indirectly, whose Interests and Welfare are intended to be the main object of the Government.[16]

The plain and simple fact is, that...the great body of the people are neglected, because the great body of the people are not represented in the legislature; and those who make the laws are not at all dependent upon their favour or approbation.[17]

It was in this line of argument, rather than in the more easily contestable doctrines of natural and historic rights, that the core of the radical case lay.

A work of Paley's which Schofield wisely treats as beneath his attention is *Reasons for Contentment, Addressed to the Labouring Part of the British Public.* Jonathan Clark does mention it, however. He says that because radical historians hold such texts up to derision, we lack scholarly studies of them; and he himself characterises the pamphlet as a 'classic and lasting formulation of the Anglican argument for the rule of law and social subordination in an inegalitarian, Christian society'.[18] But the only evidence he adduces for awarding it this status is the fact that the tract was reprinted in a Manchester newspaper two days before Peterloo; and I personally find it hard to believe that anyone with any critical sense, or indeed, sensibility, could ever have read the work without objections crowding into his mind. A sample of such objections expressed by a contemporary can be found in *A Letter to William Paley...in Answer to*

[14] Cf. J. R. Dinwiddy, 'White, Thomas Holt (1763–1841)' in Joseph O. Baylen and J. Goseman (eds.), *Biographical Dictionary of Modern British Radicals, 1770–1830* (Hassocks, 1979), vol. I, pp. 528–9.
[15] [Thomas Holt White], *Letters to William Paley, M. A., Archdeacon of Carlisle, on his Objections to a Reform in the Representation of the Commons* (London, 1796), p. 30.
[16] Thomas Cooper, *A Reply to Mr Burke's Invective against Mr Cooper and Mr Watt, in the House of Commons, on the 30th of April, 1792* (Manchester, 1792), p. 27.
[17] John Thelwall, *The Tribune*, 3 vols. (London, 1795–6), vol. II, p. 82.
[18] Clark, *English Society*, p. 262.

his Reasons for Contentment (1793). The anonymous author protested not only against the insultingly specious comparisons between the 'cheerfulness and serenity' associated with a life of labour and the satiety and worry associated with a life of wealth. He also protested – much as Bentham did in his devastating critique of Mr Justice Ashhurst's *Charge to the Grand Jury of Middlesex*[19] – against the airy assertions that were made about the English legal system. According to Paley, 'it is rather more the concern of the poor to stand up for the laws than of the rich; for it is the law which defends the weak against the strong, the humble against the powerful, the little against the great'. For Paley's critic, the Combination Laws were a standing refutation of any such pretence.[20]

What I have been suggesting is that to assert that the anti-Jacobins had the better of the argument simply in terms of argument involves value-judgements which are questionable – or at least involves a tendentiously *selective* approach to the debate. It has to be said, however, that there was one level of conservative ideology – exploited by Paley among others – which the radicals had some difficulty in coping with directly. Clark says that in his *Reasons for Contentment* Paley saved his trump card till the end: 'If in comparing the different conditions of social life we bring religion into the account, the argument is still easier. Religion smoothes all inequalities, because it unfolds a prospect which makes all earthly distinctions nothing.'[21] This quotation recalls, of course, Burke's admonition in the *Reflections*: 'The body of the people...must labour to obtain what by labour can be obtained; and when they find, as they commonly do, the success disproportioned to the endeavour, they must be taught their consolation in the final proportions of eternal justice.'[22] (It also recalls Mary Wollstonecraft's response to Burke: 'It is, Sir, *possible* to render the poor happier in this world, without depriving them of the consolation which you gratuitously grant them in the next.'[23]) However, it is argued by Clark that Anglican 'political theology' was a major element in the strength of conservative thought in general in the 1790s and of Burke's thought in particular. 'Burke's achievement in his later works,' he says, 'was to give eloquent but unoriginal expression to a theoretical position largely devised by Anglican churchmen.'[24] Earlier writers, of

---

[19] '*Truth* versus *Ashhurst*' in John Bowring (ed.), *The Works of Jeremy Bentham*, 11 vols. (Edinburgh, 1843), vol. V, pp. 231–7.

[20] *Reasons for Contentment, Addressed to the Labouring Part of the British Public* in *The Works of William Paley, D. D.* (London, 1835), p. 568; Anon., *A Letter to William Paley, M. A., Archdeacon of Carlisle, from a Poor Labourer in Answer to his Reasons for Contentment* (London, 1793), pp. 12–13.

[21] Paley, *Reasons for Contentment*, p. 571.   [22] Burke, *Reflections*, p. 372.

[23] Mary Wollstonecraft, *A Vindication of the Rights of Men* (London, 1790), p. 136.

[24] Clark, *English Society*, pp. 200, 249.

course, such as the New Conservatives of the Cold War period, have argued that the essence of Burke's thought was religious, thereby, in C. B. Macpherson's words, putting the basis of his thought 'beyond the reach of criticism, which is no doubt where Burke intended it to be'.[25] But Clark's interpretation is distinctive in that he sees the Burke of the 1790s not as a defender of all religion, but as a defender of trinitarian religion; he had come to the view, says Clark, that 'Anglican Christianity was established not merely because it was expedient but because it was true'.[26]

This raises some interesting questions, but also doubts. What is beyond doubt is Burke's belief that an established church – indeed a union of church and state which 'consecrated' the latter – was highly desirable for a number of reasons: among others, so that those who contemplated any reform of the state should do so with reverence and caution, approaching (he says) 'to the faults of the state as to the wounds of a father, with pious awe and trembling sollicitude'.[27] Also, to maintain the credibility and value of the state religion, it was necessary that those in positions of political authority should subscribe and be seen to subscribe to its doctrines. 'They would find it difficult,' Burke says, 'to make others to believe in a system to which they manifestly gave no credit themselves.'[28] Yet there is little to suggest that he was interested, for their own sake, in the *doctrinal* differences which separated the Church of England from Dissent. He explicitly disowned, in the *Reflections*, those 'miserable bigots...who hate sects and parties different from their own, more than they love the substance of religion'; and in his speech of 11 May 1792 on the issue of toleration for the Unitarians, he said that he regarded the question *not* as a theological one, but as 'a question of legislative prudence upon a point of policy'.[29] It is also noteworthy that at much the same time as he was defending the Church of England as essential to the English state, he was stressing the value of the old Catholic Church in France and the value of the Hindu religion to the society of India.[30] It is true that Burke had a clear perception that any notion of a 'double truth' in John Burrow's sense of the term, implying a disjunction between the truth of a belief and its social value,[31] should not if possible be allowed to surface. This perception is evident in a fascinating passage in his early notebook:

If you attempt to make the end of religion to be its utility to human society,... you

---

[25] C. B. Macpherson, 'Edmund Burke and the New Conservatism', *Science and Society*, 22 (1958), p. 238.   [26] Clark, *English Society*, pp. 251–2.
[27] Burke, *Reflections*, p. 194.   [28] *Ibid.*, p. 200.
[29] *Ibid.*, p. 257; W. Cobbett (ed.), *Parliamentary History of English from the Norman Conquest in 1066 to the Year 1803* (London, 1817), vol. XXIX, p. 1382.
[30] C. P. Courtney, *Montesquieu and Burke* (Oxford, 1963), pp. 135–6.
[31] J. W. Burrow, *Whigs and Liberals: Continuity and Change in English Political Thought* (Oxford, 1988), p. 57.

then change its principle of operation, which consists on views beyond this life, to a consideration of another kind, and of an inferior kind; and thus, by forcing it against its nature to become a political engine, you make it an engine of no efficacy at all. It never can operate for the benefit of human society but when we think it is directed quite another way.[32]

However, in spite of this perception, and in spite of Burke's grandiloquence on the subject of religion in his later writings, I agree with Victor Kiernan that the importance he attached to the social and political value of religion was clearly discernible through his rhetoric. And Kiernan may be right in suggesting that Wilberforce's 'vital Christianity' was of greater utility from a hegemonic point of view *because* its priorities were more patently spiritual. Wilberforce (in Kiernan's words) 'did not appear to set up religion for the sake of the State: religion made its own infinite demands, and wholesome political consequences followed merely as a by-product'.[33] One can see how Burke's emphasis on the threats to religion and the established church could have added to the cogency of his work in the eyes of those who had an interest in the preservation of the existing order. But his remarks on religion leave an erastian after-taste that probably restricted their appeal, as compared with the headier impact of Evangelicalism.

A similar point can be made more broadly, in regard to the Anglican political theology that Clark so much esteems. He emphasises – as Dickinson and Schofield do in relation to secular political theory – that the writers of the nineties were drawing on a longstanding eighteenth-century tradition. Much the same thing was said nearly forty years ago by Bernard N. Schilling. He quoted an array of passages from both mid-eighteenth-century and late eighteenth-century writers, contending that religious belief was vital to the welfare of society and that an established church was vital to the stability of the state.[34] But he did not see the reiteration of these well-worn themes as indicative of the *strength* of conservative argument in the 1790s. Nor, one may add, does Nancy Murray, author of the most impressive study of the Church of England in that decade. It is true, of course, that the French Revolution unleashed an unprecedented quantity of Anglican tracts and published sermons in which traditional political theology was deployed for anti-Jacobin purposes. But while the scale of this output was very large, Murray attributes this in part to the fact that such publications seemed 'the most

---

[32] M. V. F. Somerset (ed.), *A Notebook of Edmund Burke* (Cambridge, 1957), p. 67.

[33] V. Kiernan, 'Evangelicalism and the French Revolution', *Past and Present*, 7 (1952), pp. 47–9.

[34] Bernard N. Schilling, *Conservative England and the Case against Voltaire* (New York, 1950), especially ch. 9, 'Religion as the support of government'.

likely road to preferment';[35] and she sees the content of this body of work as stale and repetitive, and as limited in its impact on uncommitted opinion by its failure to engage in any but a crudely negative way with the criticisms that were being levelled against the established order. Most orthodox defenders of the alliance or union between church and state were unreceptive to criticisms of either the secular or the ecclesiastical hierarchy, and justified both in terms of their combined roles in promoting a well-ordered and harmonious society. For writers on the evangelical wing of the church, on the other hand, this sort of complacent analysis, even when combined with fierce denunciations of French atheism and barbarity, seemed unlikely to carry widespread and lasting conviction.

Their message was not that everything was as it should be, but that *moral* reform was required among the higher orders as well as among the lower; that too much of the established church was marked by a 'barren formality' (Hannah More's phrase for the religion of the *Anti-Jacobin Review*); that religion should bind all classes together in a common pursuit of salvation; and that, in the words of one of the reports of the Society for Bettering the Condition of the Poor, 'rank, power, wealth, influence, constitute no exemption from activity, or attention to duty; but lay a weight of real, accumulated responsibility on the possessor'.[36] The *Anti-Jacobin Review* may have been shocked by evangelical attacks on the moral and spiritual shortcomings of the opulent and privileged, but it seems likely that Murray and Kiernan are right in suggesting that the brand of religion which did most to counter political radicalism was the evangelical brand:[37] and it did so more by *outflanking* the radical case, or by diverting the discourse from political into spiritual and moralistic channels, than by confronting radical argument directly. It is not, of course, necessary to suppose that this was a deliberate manoeuvre, or that there was anything insincere about the beliefs of the Evangelicals. What Bentham called 'interest-begotten prejudice' works in a variety of oblique and unselfconscious ways; and 'hegemonic' ideas – ideas which help to sustain the position of an elite or superior class, or to deflect threats to it – do not need to be adopted deliberately for 'hegemonic' purposes in order to be so described: indeed it is arguable that the less consciously they are used for such purposes, the more effective they are likely to be.

[35] Nancy U. Murray, 'The influence of the French Revolution on the Church of England and its rivals, 1789–1802', unpublished D.Phil. thesis (Oxford University, 1975), p. 316.
[36] *Ibid.*, pp. 290 and 367, and chs. 7–9 in general; Hannah More to William Wilberforce, 11 September 1800, in R. B. Johnson (ed.), *Letters of Hannah More* (London, 1925), p. 177; *Reports of the Society for Bettering the Condition and Increasing the Comforts of the Poor*, 7 vols. (London, 1798–1817), vol. II, pp. 27–8.
[37] See also Richard A. Soloway, 'Reform or ruin: English moral thought during the first French republic', *Review of Politics*, 25 (1963), pp. 110–28; Robert Hole, 'British counter-revolutionary propaganda in the 1790s' in Colin Jones (ed.), *Britain and Revolutionary France: Conflict, Subversion and Propaganda* (Exeter, 1983), pp. 64–8.

It has to be admitted, of course, that there were important senses in which the conservatives did prevail over the radicals in the debate of the French revolutionary period. For one thing, this was clearly the case in terms of *volume*. As Gayle Pendleton has conclusively shown, the conservatives produced and sold many more publications. It is also plain, however, that many writers on the conservative side were either place-holders or place-hunters. Of the attributable publications classified by Pendleton as having substantial political content of a conservative kind, well over half – nearly three-fifths – were written by people who were identifiably part of the patronage network, either as recipients of government money or as clergymen of the Church or England.[38] As for the volume of sales, it needs to be remembered that many conservative tracts, especially at the popular end of the spectrum, were purchased in bulk for free distribution, and that their extensive circulation said far more about upper-class anxiety to instil anti-Jacobin news than about the lower-class appetite for them. Francis Freeling reported from the General Post Office to the Crown and Anchor Association that 'vast quantities of Judge Ashhurst's Charge' had been sent 'to every Post Town in the King-dom' for circulation.[39] But how many people reacted to the work like Bentham? Or like the author of *Justice to a Judge*, who in response to Ashhurst's claim that the law only laid such restraints on the actions of individuals as were necessary for the safety and good order of the com-munity, asked whether the game laws were necessary for this purpose.[40] Or like the anonymous correspondent of Reeves, who wrote: 'Poor Ash-hurst's Weakness and Folly has damned him and his Understanding for ever, such time-serving pimps are a disgrace to any professional character whatever.'[41]

Even when such points have been taken into account, it doubtless remains true that the great majority of those defined by Burke in *Letters on a Regicide Peace* as 'the people'[42] – a great majority (shall we say) of the pamphlet- and newspaper-reading public – *was* more conservative than radical. But how far the same could be said of the rest of the people – of the labouring classes who made up two-thirds of the population – is another matter. There is much evidence to suggest that in the earlier 1790s the popular mood was predominantly anti-Jacobin, and that radicals

---

[38] Gayle Trusdel Pendleton, 'English conservative propaganda during the French Revolution, 1789–1802', unpublished Ph.D. thesis (Emory University, 1976), pp. 56–7, 185–6. See also Emily Lorraine de Montluzin, *The Anti-Jacobins 1798–1800* (London, 1988).

[39] Francis Freeling to [? John Reeves], 28 December 1792, British Library (BL), Add. MSS 16923, fo. 146.

[40] Anon., *Justice to a Judge: An Answer to the Judge's Appeal to Justice, in Proof of the Blessings Enjoyed by British Subjects*, 2nd edn (London, 1793), p. 7.

[41] 'Equality' to John Reeves, 16 December 1792, BL, Add. MSS 16923, fo. 4.

[42] Rafferty, *Works of Burke*, vol. VI, p. 128.

(outside one or two places such as Sheffield and Norwich) were conscious of being a minority which faced either apathy or hostility from the bulk of the community. However, E. P. Thompson has rightly emphasised the major shift which took place in what he calls the 'sub-political attitudes of the masses' in the course of the French wars; and there are clear indications that the years 1795–1802 were an important phase in this important change.[43] Whether a serious danger of revolution developed is a problem that lies beyond the scope of this chapter. But it seems that there was at least a great deal of *passive* disaffection among the labouring population in these years of economic distress and political and economic repression (even if this was offset to some extent by the patriotic feeling – patriotic in the modern sense – that was periodically excited by the threat of invasion). It is sometimes suggested, for example by Robert R. Dozier, that by 1794 the loyalists had definitely won the battle for the minds of the people. This seems an unfounded assumption, arising perhaps from the blinkered view that 'the people' in Burke's limited sense was *really* the people. And even in regard to the politically articulate classes, one should bear in mind that the petitions sent to Parliament against the Treason and Sedition Bills in late 1795 carried four times as many signatures as the loyalist counter-petitions: a fact which Dozier completely ignores, saying that the Two Acts were passed 'with relative ease'.[44]

In so far as it can be said that the anti-Jacobins were 'victorious' in the debate of the 1790s, this was due less to the superiority of conservative over radical arguments about the merits or demerits of reform, than to *circumstances*: circumstances which enabled conservative polemicists to misrepresent English reformers as French-style Jacobins,[45] to maintain that French models and experience were more relevant than the American ones which most English radicals preferred,[46] and to assert (as Arthur Young did in 1794) that 'what is *reform* in the commencement becomes *massacre* in the conclusion'.[47] It may be objected that the force of an argument cannot be gauged in abstraction from the context in which it is expressed. That may be largely true: and it is in fact part of my point.

---

[43] E. P. Thompson, *The Making of the English Working Class*, 2nd edn (Harmondsworth, 1968), pp. 85, 202–3, 662–3; John Dinwiddy, 'England', in Otto Dan and John Dinwiddy (eds.) *Nationalism in the Age of the French Revolution* (London, 1988), pp. 66–7.

[44] BL, Add. MSS 27808, fo. 52; Robert R. Dozier, *For King, Constitution, and Country: The English Loyalists and the French Revolution* (Lexington, Ky., 1983), pp. 169–70.

[45] For a spirited response to this mode of attack, see Richard Dinmore, *An Exposition of the Principles of the English Jacobins*, 2nd edn (Norwich, 1797).

[46] Cf. Arthur Sheps, 'The American Revolution and the transformation of English Republicanism', *Historical Reflections/Réflexions Historiques*, 2 (1975), pp. 7–10, 17–18, 22–3, 26–8.

[47] Arthur Young, *The Example of France a Warning to Britain*, 4th edn (London, 1794), p. 219.

Some scholars seem to be to have written about the conservative ideology of the 1790s in ways that suggested that this ideology had an intrinsic strength and superiority which was *not* dependent on the particular circumstances which the conservatives were able to exploit. If they were merely saying that conservative publicists helped to raise an alarm, I should not disagree with them (any more than Schilling would have done). There is no doubt that a great many members of the educated and propertied classes were turned against reform. But how far was it the intellectual cogency of the arguments of Richard Hey, or William Cusac Smith, or Paley, or even Burke, that was *responsible* for turning them against it? The evidence suggests that when Burke's *Reflections* appeared it had a very mixed reception,[48] and that its main effect in the first year or two after its publication was to stimulate the articulation in England of the very ideas that he was trying to counteract. It was only after the September Massacres and the outbreak of war and the onset of the Terror that he came to be widely regarded as a sage.

[48] Cf. F. P. Lock, *Burke's Reflections on the Revolution in France* (London, 1985), ch. 5.

3 The fragmented ideology of reform

Mark Philp

Historians have invoked a wide range of factors to explain why reformers in the 1790s failed to obtain their objectives. Government repression, the strength of the popular loyalist movement, the pervasive influence of a sophisticated conservative ideology, the resilience of the institutions of monarchy, aristocracy and the Church of England, or the pluralism of British culture and the responsiveness of its institutions to the needs of the poor, have all been cited as key factors in this failure.[1] So, too, have the

---

[1] Part of this formulation is owed to Harry Dickinson's opening section to his 'Popular loyalism in Britain in the 1790s' in Eckhart Hellmuth (ed.), *The Transformation of Political Culture: England and Germany in the Late Eighteenth Century* (Oxford, 1990), pp. 503–33. Dickinson is referring to J. C. D. Clark's *English Society 1688–1832: Ideology, Social Structure and Political Practice during the Ancien Régime* (Cambridge, 1985) (for the 'resilience thesis'), and to Ian R. Christie's *Stress and Stability in Late Eighteenth-Century Britain: Reflections on the British Avoidance of Revolution* (Oxford, 1984), (for the 'pluralism and responsiveness thesis'; see also his contribution to this volume. Clark also contributes a 'radical extremism thesis' which neatly complements Dickinson's account of popular loyalism. Compare for example, Clark, *English Society*:

Yet if the facts of suffering, poverty and (what radical intellectuals never saw) the horrors of war failed to be widely translated into popular politics directed against the establishment, a major reason must be the activities of those theorists who, even before 1789, had defined their position in terms so extreme (in relation to society's ruling orthodoxy) that radicalism itself could easily be equated with the destruction of civilisation' with Dickinson's 'Popular Loyalism in Britain (p. 346)...historians have often been so captivated by the noble and heroic efforts of reformers that they have exaggerated their strength and unity. They have usually failed to recognize that the reformers agreed on very little except the need for a more equal representation of the people, that they never developed the organisations, strategies, or tactics capable of bringing irresistible pressure to bear on the governing elite, and that they failed to rally the majority of either the middling or the lower orders behind their political demands' (p. 503).

The 'repression' thesis is given short shrift, on the basis that Clive Emsley's work has shown how much the repression has been exaggerated; see 'An aspect of Pitt's "Terror": prosecutions for sedition during the 1790s', *Social History*, 6, 2 (1981), pp. 155–84; and 'Repression, "terror" and the rule of law in England during the decade of the French Revolution', *English Historical Review*, 100 (1985), pp. 801–25. The thesis does, however, have a long pedigree, starting with many of the participants of the decade, as discussed in my *Godwin's Political Justice* (London, 1986), pp. 224–8.

ideological disagreements amongst reformers and the factionalism in the organisations for reform:

> The reform movement was hopelessly divided on what changes ought to be made and none of the competing elements could rally adequate support in or out of Parliament...The evidence...shows how the radicals were divided among themselves, how most of them failed to take their ideas to their logical conclusions and how all of them failed to devise any effective means of implementing their policies.[2]

It is primarily with this last claim that this chapter takes issue. It does not deny that there were substantial disagreements among reformers over both means and ends, but it challenges the view that these contributed significantly to their failure to achieve parliamentary reform. In doing so, it also seeks to cast doubt upon the adequacy of explanations of the failure of reform which do not recognise that the radical agenda was as much the outcome of the political struggles of the 1790s as it was their cause.

I

There is no doubt that despite the apparently widespread favourable response to the French Revolution and the formidable initial critical reaction to Burke's *Reflections*, by the end of 1792 and throughout the rest of the decade there were deep and obvious divisions in the ranks of those sympathetic to reform.[3] Most obviously there is the split in the Whigs between Portland and the Foxites, but equally important are the tensions between Grey's Friends of the People and the extra-parliamentary organisations for reform.[4] While there are brief moments of temporary and uneasy alliance between parliamentary elites and these extra-parliamentary organisations, the general tenor of their association is one of mutual distrust and antagonism.[5] It is not difficult to identify other

---

[2] H. T. Dickinson, *Liberty and Property: Political Ideology in Eighteenth Century Britain* (London, 1977), p. 271. See also his 'Popular loyalism in Britain in the 1790s'.

[3] On the initial response, see Alfred Cobban (ed.), *The Debate on the French Revolution* (London, 1950); P. A. Brown, *The French Revolution in English History* (London, 1918), ch. 2; Albert Goodwin, *The Friends of Liberty: The English Democratic Movement in the Age of the French Revolution* (London, 1979), ch. 4. A slightly more nuanced picture can be gained from Derek Jarrett, *Three Faces of Revolution: Paris, London and New York in 1789* (London, 1989), and Leslie Mitchell's editorial 'Introduction' to *The Writings and Speeches of Edmund Burke: The French Revolution 1790–1794*, vol. VIII (Oxford, 1990).

[4] Cf. Mitchell, 'Introduction', and John Derry, 'The opposition Whigs and the French Revolution 1789–1815' in H. T. Dickinson (ed.), *Britain and the French Revolution 1789–1815* (London, 1989), pp. 39–59.

[5] The three key periods for co-operation between the parliamentary and extra-parliamentary forces are at the very end of the 1780s, when there was considerable agitation to remove the Test and Corporation Acts, and a good deal of support for the move in Parliament, in 1792 after the formation of the Whig-led Association of the Friends of the People, and again around 1795–6 over the campaign to repeal the Gagging

divisions, for example, between 'Painites' and those operating with a less universalist, more home-grown set of assumptions about the appropriate structure for the British polity – Thelwall, for example, is not a Painite – not a democratic republican.[6] This division is reflected within the reform movement between those with strong 'independent' or Whig leanings, and those whose commitment to France pulls them away from their traditional protestations of the sanctity of the Englishman's liberty towards more internationalist aspirations (which are rarely adequately integrated into a consistent ideological position). Similarly, there are divisions within the corresponding societies – over the discussion of religion, between those with a republican bent and those with more moderate leanings, between local divisions and the central committee over the treatment of certain delegates, and, as the decade wears on, between those who favour radical action and those who lacked the stomach for it or felt it served no point.[7]

The reform movement is also marked, as are most movements, by personal and ideological differences between leading reformers – such as Godwin's disagreement with Thelwall over the 'Gagging Acts', Spence's rather riotous relationship with Bewick, or Ritson's summary dismissal of most of the leading intellectuals associated with the reform movement, bar Thelwall:

To confess the truth, the more I see of these modern patriots and philosophers the less I like them... Their constant cant is, the force and energy of mind, to which all opposition is to be ineffectual; but none of them, I say, has ever chosen to rely upon that irresistible force in his own case. I really think that Thelwall is the best of them, and yet I find myself pretty singular in my good opinion of him.[8]

Acts. In the interim period Fox at first spent much energy attempting to hold the increasingly divided party together, and was forced to do so in ways which muted his endorsement of the reform movement. There was also tension between prominent Whigs and reformers when the former presumed the right to direct the latter's activities. See Goodwin, *Friends of Liberty*, ch. 2, pp. 203–15 and ch. 10; John Erhman, *The Younger Pitt: The Reluctant Transition*, vol. II (London, 1983), pp. 108–10, and 172–4; J. Ann Hone, *For the Cause of Truth: Radicalism in London 1796–1821* (Oxford, 1982), ch. 1.

[6] Gregory Claeys, *Thomas Paine: Social and Political Thought* (London, 1989), chs. 3 and 4; Iain Hampsher-Monk, 'Civic humanism and parliamentary reform: the case of the Society of the Friends of the People', *Journal of British Studies*, 18 (1979), pp. 70–89. See also H. T. Dickinson, *Liberty and Property: Political Ideology in Eighteenth-Century Britain* (London, 1977), pp. 237–69.

[7] See Mary Thale (ed.), *Selections from the Papers of the London Corresponding Society 1792–1799* (Cambridge, 1983), but on secession from the society, see especially pp. 241–52. Some of these divisions were felt still more acutely in the Irish reform movements, particularly on the question of religion. See, Marianne Elliot, *Partners in Revolution: The United Irishmen in France* (New Haven, Conn., 1982), and *Wolf Tone* (New Haven, Conn., 1990).

[8] J. Frank (ed.), *Letters of Joseph Ritson*, 2 vols. (London, 1833), vol. II, p. 69. See also vol. II, p. 117. On Godwin and Thelwall, see my *Godwin's Political Justice*, pp. 117–19 and 196–7, and John Thelwall's *Tribune*, 3 vols. (London, 1796), vol. II, p. vii, and vol. III,

Moreover, the presence of numbers of people whose opinions change in the period, adds to the sense of division and incoherence amongst reformers – whether it be those who renege on their earlier radical enthusiasms, those who are radicalised permanently, or those who move from early but essentially moderate enthusiasm for France ultimately to countenance domestic rebellion and revolution.[9]

Two further, related elements add to the impression of diversity, division and incoherence among reformers. The first concerns the extent to which the principles and ideology of reform are subject to ongoing innovation throughout the period. The second concerns the complex relationship which develops between radicals' aspirations, their commitments and their rhetoric.

There is a growing body of writing detailing the way in which reformers (and loyalists) changed and developed their theoretical positions in response to the arguments and events of the decade. Certainly, it seems that without the impetus of Burke's *Reflections*, Paine would have had little cause to formulate a full natural-rights-based account of popular sovereignty and the limits of government legitimacy. Moreover, it is in responding to Burke that Paine turns to issues of welfare and distributional justice, the fruits of which appear first in Part Two of his *Rights of Man* and, subsequently, under the impetus of a rather different set of events in France, in *Agrarian Justice* – where the intellectual justification for a distributive rather than an entitlement conception of justice is expounded.[10] Similarly, for others 'radicalism' is not a standard which they either stand beside or desert; it is a developing political practice whose principles and ideological commitments are as much forged in the struggle as they are fetched from the arsenal and brought to it. Thelwall's account of his endorsement of a rights-based perspective on government should certainly caution us against thinking that the relationship between political practice and principle is a one-way process:

pp. 103–3; while on Bewick and Spence, see Thomas Bewick, *A Memoir*, ed. Iain Bain (Oxford, 1975), p. 53, and Marcus Wood, 'Thomas Spence and modes of subversion', *Enlightenment and Dissent*, 10 (1991).

[9] We should also recognise that at least some of those who might be claimed to have reneged on their earlier enthusiasms remained profoundly influenced by their earlier sympathies, see David Eastwood, 'Robert Southey and the intellectual origins of romantic conservatism', *English Historical Review*, 104, 411 (1989), pp. 308–31. There is also the vexed question of how committed and realistic many of the more literary radicals were. On which, cf. E. P. Thompson, *The Poverty of Theory* (London, 1978), p. 372, and *The Making of the English Working Class*, 2nd edn (Harmondsworth, 1968), p. 193, with Nicholas Roe, *Wordsworth and Coleridge: The Radical Years* (Oxford, 1988), and my *Godwin's Political Justice*, ch. 10.

[10] See my *Paine* (Oxford, 1989), ch. 3, and Claeys, *Thomas Paine*, chs. 4 and 8 (although, in many respects, Claeys over-emphasises the continuities in Paine's thought, and underplays the impact of Paine's immediate context on his writing).

It was only in the solitude of the Tower [awaiting his trial for High Treason], where the mind had leisure for the investigation of abstract and difficult propositions, that every objection was removed, and I became convinced, that the only practicable means of ameliorating the condition of mankind, is to restore them to the full possession of their just and inalienable rights.[11]

What we get from Thelwall, and from many others on both sides, is a sense of the period as transforming or traumatising people so as to produce highly individual personal and intellectual responses, rather than a pattern of simple conformity to a creed.

The sense of diversity in the radicalism of the decade is enhanced by those analysts of the 'debate on France' who see the decade as marking a break from eighteenth-century traditions of thought and argument.[12] There have, however, been recent attempts, by J. G. A. Pocock and Gregory Claeys, to illuminate the decade by recognising in the assumptions and arguments deployed by reformers the continuing influence of the discourses of country party opposition, civic and civil humanism, and Scottish political economy.[13] At base,

British radicalism...continued to be expressed in terms of a sustained attack on the Whig oligarchy, variously known as 'Old Corruption' and 'The Thing.'...We know that the language in which Old Corruption was defined was by this time a century old, and as much Tory as Whig in its origins and transmission; the time has now come to claim that it remained paradigmatic.[14]

Yet this is a rearguard action, and one which risks conflating different levels of abstraction. A language is not a paradigm, and we should not confuse the weaponry of reformers and radicals with the battle which they were fighting. While many clearly did use the language and imagery of Old Corruption, there should be little doubt that new paradigms of political thought and participation were being tabled. It is one thing to recognise the continued force of the language of 'independence', but quite another to think that this necessarily dominates the new universalist and national forms of political language which are an increasing presence in British political life from the 1760s onward, and which had a major impact on

---

[11] *Life of John Thelwall, by his Widow* (London, 1837), p. 115.
[12] For some commentators, it is precisely in Burke's attempt to purify Whiggism and in Paine's attempt to repudiate Burke that the principles of the two wings of modern liberal thought are forged. See, for example, P. Raynaud (ed.), *Reflexions sur la Revolution de France* (Paris, 1989), pp. lxxxvii–lxxxviii.
[13] J. G. A. Pocock, *Virtue, Commerce, and History* (Cambridge, 1985), pp. 279–94; Gregory Claeys, *Thomas Paine*, and 'The French Revolution debate and British political thought', *History of Political Thought*, 11, 1 (1990), pp. 59–80; see also, Iain Hampsher-Monk, 'John Thelwall and the eighteenth century radical response to political economy', *Historical Journal*, 34 (1991).
[14] Pocock, *Virtue, Commerce, and History*, p. 289.

political debate and practice in the 1790s, even if it was subsequently (if temporarily) eclipsed by older concerns.[15]

The further issue which both adds to and complicates this sense of disorder and which is insistently present as the reader pores over the documents and literature of the period, is the question of how far, or in what ways, people can be taken as meaning what they said. This is not straightforward. For example, as D. O. Thomas has recently noted, when the good Dr Price raised his glass at the commemorative dinner held by the London Revolution Society on 4 November 1790, and proposed a toast to 'The Parliament of Britain – may it become a NATIONAL Assembly', he certainly did not mean what he had said.[16] Nor is Price alone in this. Quite where Horne Tooke stood on a number of rather crucial issues, from monarchy to the use of extra-legal force to encourage Parliament to see the wisdom of reform, remains unclear. And Thelwall's activities did much to leave questionable the extent of his radicalism: 'in nothing was he more representative of his generation than in the unrestrained violence of his rhetoric and in the temporising moderation evident in his own conduct and the political advice he gave to his popular audiences.'[17]

Given the range and nature of the divisions which it is possible to identify among reformers in the 1790s, we have good reason to doubt the adequacy of the various explanations offered for the failure of the reform movement. Such explanations implicitly assume that there is a sufficiently discrete entity, 'the reform movement', with objectives of which success or failure can be predicated. Not only is this assumption questionable, so too is the idea that there is agreement about the nature of the movement. Different explanations of the failure of reform are intimately related to divergent accounts of the nature of that movement, and to conflicting counterfactual claims about the kind of movement it ought to have been for it to have succeeded – the accounts of what did not happen in the 1790s, of why it did not happen, and of how close it came to happening, are far from uncontentious.[18] Nor can differences between accounts of the

---

[15] See Frank O'Gorman, *Voters, Patrons, and Parties: The Unreformed Electorate in Hanoverian England 1734–1832* (Oxford, 1989), pp. 300–16, for an account which carefully avoids equating 'independence' with radicalism. The shift towards a national political agenda and more universal forms of political discourse is reflected in the very language in which political debate was conducted in this period; see Olivia Smith, *The Politics of Language 1791–1819* (Oxford, 1984), and Marilyn Butler, *Burke, Paine, Godwin and the Revolution Controversy* (Cambridge, 1984).

[16] D. O. Thomas, *Response to Revolution* (Cardiff, 1989), p. 41.

[17] Goodwin, *Friends of Liberty*, p. 321.

[18] Cf. Christie's *Stress and Stability*, and Roger Wells's *Insurrection: The British Experience, 1795–1803* (Gloucester, 1983), and *Wretched Faces: Famine in Wartime England 1793–1801* (Gloucester, 1988), and their respective contributions to this volume.

nature of radicalism be settled by appealing to the intentions and activities of the reformers since, as we have seen, different groups (and single groups at different points in time) could have different views of their objectives and of the steps required to achieve them.

Reformism or radicalism in the 1790s is protean stuff. It resists a simple definitive classification of its nature and objectives, and it demands a more complex understanding of its ideology and political objectives than is often offered. To treat reformism or radicalism (or indeed loyalism) as a single, consistent, continuous programme throughout the decade is to ignore, at the very least, the extent to which reformist and loyalist movements shaped and conditioned each others' objectives and tactics, the way that government and judicial action against reformers helped focus and narrow the range of strategies open to them, and the manner in which events in France fed into each group's understanding of the dangers of and potential for reform in Britain. The reform associations of the 1790s did not spring fully formed onto the stage of British politics with a clear sight of their historical destiny.[19] Over a ten- to fifteen-year period, the various commitments towards social and political reform which were first elicited by the opening events of the French Revolution underwent great changes, few of which can be ascribed to the immanent logic of radical principles. On the contrary, many of those principles were themselves the outcome of responses to events, or of reactions to others' responses to events. To analyse the reformism of the 1790s in these terms involves pre-empting questions about why there was no revolution in the period, or about why the reform movement failed, by asking instead how the agenda of radicalism, loyalism and government response was set, and how revolution came to be on it – if indeed it did.

II

That there is a good deal of evidence to show that the reform movement was not united should not surprise us; it is difficult to think of a reform movement or revolution, successful or unsuccessful, without significant divisions. What is at issue is how far these divisions were positive or containable, and how far they brought about the collapse of the reform movement from within. To establish this we need to consider not only how serious these divisions were, but also from where they originated. In the analysis of the reform movement, insufficient attention has been paid to the role played by the broader political context in generating some of the deeper and more debilitating divisions in the radicalism of the 1790s.

[19] Jonathan Clark's caution on the latter point ('historical destiny') in *English Society*, p. 347, needs supplementing by the former ('springing fully formed').

A central element of this broader context is the developing conflict between reformism and loyalism, which occurs not just in the theoretically sophisticated and principled tracts of the 'debate on France' conducted in the opening years of the decade, but also, and equally importantly, in the tide of propaganda which, by 1793, was increasingly displacing the intellectual confrontation from the centre of political activity.[20] To grasp the process of confrontation between the loyalist and reformist presses through the decade, we must recognise that three elements come into play at the beginning of the 1790s in a way which broke apart the existing lines of popular and elite political division: the French Revolution, Burke's *Reflections* and Paine's *Rights of Man*.[21]

The precise impact of the French Revolution is difficult to assess. J. G. A. Pocock has said some very complex things about the problems of translating the French example into English terms and about the use of French rhetoric and symbols in a British context, but these risk missing the simple point that the French Revolution was seen immediately as speaking to an English experience (the Glorious Revolution of 1688) and, having made that connection, events in France provided a running and, it was assumed, relevant commentary on British politics.[22] The outbreak of war between the new republic and the Brunswick coalition, the internationalising of the Revolution, the eventual declaration of war between Britain and France, and the ongoing problems of financing and manning the conflict, inserted into British popular politics an insistent pressure to link experience at home with French affairs. This pressure was not intrinsically more favourable to reformers or loyalists, but its existence gave British domestic political confrontation a momentum it would otherwise have lacked. The other two elements – Burke's *Reflections* and Paine's *Rights of Man* – encouraged this connection and helped frame the interpretation and course of that momentum.

[20] Works which have extended our understanding of the principles in play in the 'debate' include, Clark's *English Society*; Claeys, 'The French Revolution debate' and *Thomas Paine*; Pocock, *Virtue, Commerce, and History*; Dickinson, *Liberty and Property*; T. P. Schofield, 'Conservative political thought in Britain in response to the French Revolution', *Historical Journal*, 29, 3 (1986), pp. 601–20; and Robert Hole, *Pulpits, Politics and Public Order in England 1760–1832* (Cambridge, 1989). But all of these tend to place greatest weight on the first three years of the decade and underplay the less principled aspect of the confrontations which followed.

[21] This is not to deny the influence on the 1790s of the American Revolution, the Wilkes affair, the Wyvill reform associations, or the experiences of the Dissenters in their campaign to remove their disabilities in 1787, 1789 and 1790, but these are not in themselves enough to account for the events of the decade. See Goodwin, *Friends of Liberty*, ch. 2; E. C. Black, *The Association: British Extra-Parliamentary Organization 1769–1793* (Cambridge, Mass., 1963); G. M. Ditchfield, 'The parliamentary struggle on the repeal of the Test and Corporation Acts. 1787–1790', *English Historical Review*, 89 (1974), pp. 551–77.   [22] Pocock, *Virtue, Commerce, and History*, pp. 283–4.

Gregory Claeys has suggested that much of the 'debate on the French revolution' was 'waged in terms not immediately given in the two combatants' main texts'.[23] While this is true, it remains the case that Burke and Paine did much to set the parameters within which the ideological confrontation between loyalism and reform was fought. Burke's *Reflections* sketch a conspiracy theory which his later works paint in in ever more gruesome colours. The works of the Abbé Barruel and his translator merely complete and systematise a project which is implicit in Burke's revolution writings from 1790 onward, and while not all loyalists necessarily saw things in these terms, the very existence of this perspective served to condition loyalist response and to shape its strategies.[24] This is particularly so after the outbreak of war with France, when radicalism could be tainted with disloyalty and identified as an enemy within. Moreover, while Burke's opening salvos against the French were treated by many with a mixture of disbelief, scorn and amusement (with the caricaturists depicting him as a befuddled Quixote, Don Dismallo, tilting at imagined horrors), as events progressed he came to be seen as increasingly prescient. Loyalists could find in Burke ample justification for a strenuous defence of their patrimony, and even if they did not necessarily use the same principles or rhetoric in that defence, his work increasingly set the tone for those attacking radicalism. Indeed, one feature of its success was that its complex and cultivated rhetorical style found (or perhaps called into being) an audience who could recognise in it a clarion call to fulfil their responsibilities.[25]

Paine's *Rights of Man* has a similar impact on the decade, even where his democratic republicanism is not embraced. Paine, more than any other pamphleteer in the initial wave of responses to Burke, endorses the French Revolution by appealing to principles of natural rights and popular sovereignty – principles which question the legitimacy of the British state. And, by his open and inclusive rhetorical style, which constituted its readers as citizens not subjects, and through his own and others' efforts to

[23] Claeys, 'The French Revolution Debate', p. 59.
[24] Abbé Barruel, *Memoirs Illustrating the History of Jacobinism*, 4 vols. (London, 1797–8); and *Application of Barruel's Memoirs of Jacobinism, to the Secret Societies of Ireland and Great Britain by the Translator of That Work* (London, 1798). See Seamus Deane, *The French Revolution and Enlightenment in England 1789–1832* (Cambridge, Mass., 1988), pp. 5–20, and Mitchell's 'Introduction' to vol. VIII of *The Writings and Speeches of Edmund Burke*, on Burke and conspiracy.
[25] The tendency to disaggregate the various elements of Burke and Paine's works – their rhetoric, their audiences and supporters, and their ideas (between, roughly speaking, literary theorists, historians and political theorists) – although often unintended, has had the effect of underplaying the extent to which these elements are indissolubly connected, and consequently, the extent to which what is being mapped out in the opening salvos of Burke and Paine is as much a plan of battle in a practical struggle for political ascendency as the intellectual contours of a new debate on the Whig legacy.

arrange the wide circulation of his work, he ensured that these principles and the example of the French would be firmly lodged at the centre of radical politics throughout the decade. It is possible to imagine French affairs playing a relatively slight role in the British reform movement of the 1790s, but in the wake of Burke's conspiratorial linking and Paine's willingness to endorse the conflation of the French example and the principles of British reformers, events in France assume a direct significance for the British movements for reform. This, in part, accounts for the continuing recourse to imagery and rhetoric borrowed from France, alongside vernacular idioms in the confrontation between loyalism and reformism. Loyalists had to deny the force of 'French principles', and did so by attempting to link them directly to the bloodshed of the decade; radicals might seek to deny the practical example of France, but they remained committed to defending, in some form, the principles it proclaimed. Hence, much of the argument and rhetoric of the decade revolves around the presence or absence of a link between principles and practice in France – with conspiracy theories espoused by loyalists and being countered by reformers and radicals arguing that the bloodshed in France is a result of the conspiracy of European states against her – with Burke's *Reflections* being partly responsible.[26]

In this confrontation, prose, poetry, print, caricature, pottery, painting and even coinage are mobilised, and what began as the 'debate on France' quickly degenerates into a propaganda war.[27] Certain motifs – often drawn from France, or incorporating a French reference point – recur in loyalist writings. For instance, the claim that reformers put into jeopardy that most natural and fundamental unit of sentimental relationships, the family, which begins with the depiction of the treatment meted out to the French Royal Family by the French mob, and culminates in the heart-rending scenes of Louis being taken from his family to be executed.[28]

Loyalism also uses the straight Anglo-French contrast as a way of summarising the respective virtues of loyalism and reform. This is

---

[26]   And didst thou hope, by thy infuriate quill
        To rouse mankind the blood of realms to spill?
        Then to restore, on death devoted plains
        Their scourge to tyrants, and to man his chains?
        To swell their souls with thy own bigot rage
        And blot the glories of so bright an age?
    Joel Barlow, *The Conspiracy of Kings* (London, 1792), p. 12.
[27] See David Bindman, *The Shadow of the Guillotine: Britain and the French Revolution* (London, 1989).
[28] See John Brewer's 'This monstrous tragi-comic scene' in *ibid.*, pp. 22–4. The motif is continued subsequently in caricatures of sexual excess and libertinage amongst the 'Jacobins' and extends through to the pillorying of Godwin and his memoirs of Mary Wollstonecraft.

exemplified in the Murray/Rowlandson print, *The Contrast* (1792), which offers two cameos: one of Britannia, beneath an oak, with lion and liberty cap,[29] the other, a French Medusa, with snakes for hair, one foot on a corpse whose head is impaled on her trident, with the 'lantern' and its traditional sacrifice in the background. England offers: 'Religion, Morality, Loyalty, Obedience to the Laws, Independence, Personal Security, Justice, Inheritance, Protection, Property, Industry, National Prosperity, Happiness.' France: 'Atheism, Perjury, Rebellion, Treason, Anarchy, Murder, Equality, Madness, Cruelty, Injustice, Treachery, Ingratitude, Idleness, Famine, National and private Ruin, Misery.' A more culinary orientated version of the opposition is deftly put by Gillray in *French Liberty, English Slavery*.[30]

The Contrast is just one amongst hundreds of prints which poured into the print shops between the summers of 1792 and 1793. There is also a simultaneous outpouring of loyalist songs and broadsides. The objective was to combat the successes of the radical associations and the dominance of radical literature in the arena of popular political debate.[31] Whether or not the insurrectionary plot of 1792 was an invention, the government certainly seems to have believed that extraordinary measures were required to counter the success of the reform associations and to rally public support as it faced the prospect of war with France.[32] It had become increasingly alarmed at the spread of reform principles after the spring of 1792, when Paine's works were being distributed on an unprecedented scale and the Whig Association of the Friends of the People was formed, and when neither the Royal Proclamation against Seditious Writing of May 1792, nor the inauguration of the prosecution of Paine had had much impact. The alarm had grown with the London Corresponding Society's inauguration of correspondence with the French republic, with the transformation in French military fortunes, and with the recognition that British reformers were increasingly coming to see the

---

[29] On the ambiguous nature of the liberty cap, see James Epstein, 'Understanding the cap of liberty: symbolic practice and social conflict in early nineteenth-century England', *Past and Present*, 122 (1989), especially pp. 86–91.

[30] Although the use of the contrast as a style of print is not restricted to the loyalist camp. See Thomas Rowlandson's *A General Fast in Consequence of the War (c.* 1795).

[31] Both Claeys, in his 'The French Revolution debate', and Gayle Trusdel Pendleton, in her 'Towards a bibliography of the *Reflections* and the *Rights of Man* controversy', *Bulletin of Research in the Humanities*, 85 (1982), pp. 65–103, show that there were more loyalist than reformist pamphlets. None the less, given circulation figures and the evidence of the reform associations, it is legitimate to claim that in the field of *popular* political debate the radicals were ascendant, both in 1791–2, and again, although not continuously, after 1795.

[32] Clive Emsley, 'The London "Insurrection" of December 1792: fact, fiction, or fantasy?', *Journal of British Studies*, 17, 2 (1978), pp. 66–86.

French as champions of universal liberty – and as their best defence against growing domestic repression.[33]

It is in this context that the loyalist movement emerges, and it is against this background that we can recognise that the 'debate on France' has metamorphosed into something rather different.[34] There is a strong sense in which we can see Paine as engaging Burke in a debate of principles,[35] but by the middle of 1792 the term 'debate' is a misnomer – except perhaps in certain elite circles relatively immune from popular politics. The pamphlet has become a weapon; the debate a struggle over popular mobilisation and political ascendancy. In the loyalist propaganda at the end of the year, the cause of reform was being cast as levelling, egalitarian and anarchical. For their part, the radicals focused on their new areas of strength, the circulation of pamphlets through the constitutional and corresponding societies in the metropolis and the provinces. Moreover, by their exclusion from the parliamentary arena, and the challenge posed to their very legitimacy by the Royal Proclamation of May 1792 – an exclusion which the war with France and the increasingly violent direction taken by the Revolution considerably accelerated – the radicals were forced to explore new ways of challenging the political status quo and making the government responsive to their interests. And in being forced to countenance new methods, they also had to recognise the extent to which the stakes were being raised.[36]

There is insufficient space here to detail the highways and byways of this increasing polarisation, and the gradual elimination of the distinction between a reformer and a Jacobin revolutionary. It is a complex map, shaped by the judicious use of prosecutions, propaganda and the creation of states of emergency, with the suspension of habeas corpus, the deployment of the militia, and so on. Some areas of activity are more affected than others; Daniel Eaton, for example, spent some time going to court to answer charges of sedition (with great success), but 'higher' areas of literary activity remain relatively untouched – as with the Godwin circle prior to 1798. But only relatively so: Godwin does not face prosecution, but he plays an important part in the Treason Trials of 1794, and a perhaps less creditable one in the campaign against the Two Acts in 1795;

[33] Goodwin, *Friends of Liberty*, pp. 239–67.
[34] See D. E. Ginter, 'The loyalist association movement of 1792–3 and British public opinion', *Historical Journal*, 9, 2 (1966), pp. 179–90; Austin Mitchell, 'The association movement of 1792–3', *Historical Journal*, 4, 1 (1961), pp. 56–77; R. R. Dozier, *For King, Constitution, and Country: The English Loyalists and the French Revolution* (Lexington, Ky., 1983); H. T. Dickinson, 'Popular conservatism and militant loyalism 1789–1815' in H. T. Dickinson (ed.), *Britain and the French Revolution 1789–1815*, and 'Popular loyalism in Britain in the 1790s'.   [35] See my *Paine*, ch. 3.
[36] See, for example, Goodwin, *Friends of Liberty*, pp 280–2, on the failure of Grey's motion for reform in May 1793, and the message taken from this by the democratic societies.

and throughout the period he is conscious of the government's willingness to transgress people's liberty in the name of resisting reform, and it is unlikely that he felt completely secure from prosecution.[37] In contrast, by 1796 Thelwall had no doubts as to the speed with which his public platform was being eroded by a combination of loyalist statutes and loyalist staves. The activities of the reform societies in the last four years of the century become more covert, increasingly linked with the United Irishmen, and more wholeheartedly subversive.[38] By the turn of the century, political reform was a cause canvassed largely in private and, in at least some areas, it was broached in increasingly insurrectionary terms. The suggestion, then, is that the 'debate' becomes a practical struggle between loyalists and radicals over reform, with the loyalists seeking to discredit their opponents among the political and social elite, and to counter the spread of radical principles and sympathies amongst the lower orders who, as the war became more unpopular and as food shortages fuelled popular discontent, offered an attentive audience for radical propaganda. The radicals in turn attempted to extend popular support and agitation for reform to the point that the government would be forced to concede, but they did so against this background of increasing public unrest. Given that from May 1793, the radicals were effectively cut off from established and respectable methods of reform, they were forced to consider alternatives. Hence the development of conventionist demands which led first to the Scottish Treason Trials, and subsequently, and in part motivated by a fear that the government in England was aiming at a similarly draconian repression, to the call for a British Convention and to the English Treason Trials of 1794.[39] Hence also their later alliance with the popular discontent arising from the war and food shortages in 1795–6 and also again in 1800–1, and their more obscure connections with the mutinies of 1797. But hence, also, the reluctance on the part of some reformers to become involved with these developments, and their unwillingness to follow the path to insurrectionary activity or to risk prosecution and prison or transportation. Government prosecutions for the 1790s are hardly credible as a 'Terror' of the same order as that experienced under both 'red' and 'white' on the other side of the Channel, but the prosecutions are sufficiently numerous, and many are sufficiently

---

[37] On Godwin's view that the government's declaration of war with France was motivated almost wholly by a desire to challenge the spread of French principles, see Bodleian Library, Abinger MSS, dep b. 227/1g. One indication of Godwin's sense of his vulnerability is the withdrawal of the preface to the first edition of *Caleb Williams*.

[38] This is territory best commanded by Roger Wells in his *Insurrection* and *Wretched Faces*, and in his contribution to this collection. But see also Marianne Elliot's *Partners in Revolution*, on the Irish dimension.

[39] T. M. Parsinnen, 'Association, convention and anti-parliament in radical politics, 1771–1848', *English Historical Review*, 88 (1973), especially p. 513.

notorious (particularly the Scottish trials, which may have done much to pre-empt more extensive government action in England), that it is impossible to believe that they had no impact either on reformers' interpretation of what was now politically possible or, more critically, on what price might have to be paid to achieve one's ends. Moreover, in the light of foreign war, domestic repression and a government committed willy-nilly to sticking it out, seemingly regardless of the cost in terms of popular support or the suspension of the shibboleths of the Englishman's liberties, some reformers found themselves forced to revise their estimate of the ends they should pursue – agendas change with circumstances. Of course, to find one's cause forced along a path which must rely on foreign invasion, insurrection and revolutionary excess to achieve its ends is not to be forced to take that path. There are other, more quietist, options. Some took these early – the emigrations of Priestley, Eaton and others; the retirements of Hardy[40] and ultimately of Thelwall himself. The corresponding societies found new leaders, who had gained their political education when the stakes were already raised, and who in consequence might well have found the road to insurrection a less alarming prospect, or a more urgent necessity.

This might be put another way. What forces the debate into the realm of practical political struggle is the government's refusal to contemplate reform. The radicals have no strategy against the government's refusal to negotiate or make concessions, except to try forcing it to pay attention, and as they try to do this they find themselves overstepping the bounds of legality. If it is fair to talk of the radicals losing the debate, it is so only if we also recognise that it is difficult to win a contest when the other side will not play.

We should not, however, overemphasise the radical side of the story as simply a reaction to government intransigence and repression and loyalist intimidation. The loyalist and government reading of radicalism might be a caricatured one – and the smear tactics used against both radical writers and their principles might also consciously exaggerate their evil intent and levelling aspirations – but it seems equally caricatural to think of loyalists or Pitt's ministry as engaged in a wilful conspiracy against the liberties of

---

[40] None the less, Hardy remained an acute interpreter of the political scene. In 1801 he wrote to Major Cartwright that the government had become

terrified at the word *reform* least (*sic*) it should tend to a *revolution* and terminate in a republic – they have effected (*sic*) such a *revolution* in the country which the most violent reformer never had the most remote idea of. The word reform may *now* be blotted out of the vocabulary – repeatedly and honestly have the rulers of this country been told within these forty years of the necessity of a reform in the democratic part of the constitution in order to save the Crown but the die is cast!!!

Cited in John Dinwiddy, 'Conceptions of revolution in the English radicalism of the 1790s' in Hellmuth, *Transformation of Political Culture*, p. 559.

Englishmen. It may be the case that Pitt could have conceded moderate political reform and found himself at the head of a more united and loyal people, but there seems to have been no way that he could have been certain of this outcome, and there were grounds in the activities of the radicals for wishing to temporise on reform. Once the war with France began, and given the direction which events in France had taken, reform seemed pregnant with even greater dangers.[41] While loyalism seemed to offer confirmation of the backing of the bulk of 'the people', it is also clear that the movement lost a good deal of its impetus by the middle of the decade.[42] Moreover, although the Volunteers were partly an outgrowth of the loyalist movement, and were a major adjunct to domestic policing, they were not without their dangers.[43] There were, then, times when the government felt the reform movement was a threat to internal stability and the continuation of the war. Perhaps this is not surprising since it did much to ensure that the cause of reform was a lost one, unless reformers could gain substantial extra-parliamentary leverage against the government, but this should not obscure the fact that this was precisely what reformers were increasingly trying to do. The logic of confrontation between the reform movement and government and loyalist forces is such that each provides ample confirmation to the other of their threat.

To see why radicals might have taken positions which might further stimulate government measures against them, we need to look not simply

[41] Consider, for example, the remarks made by Lord Grenville in his letters to his brother the Marquis of Buckingham:

> it is perfect blindness not to see that in the establishment of the French Republic is included the overthrow of all the other Governments of Europe (17.9.1794);...I do verily believe that we must prepare to meet the storm here...It seems too probably that it is decreed by Providence that a stop shall be put (for reasons probably inscrutable to us) to the progress of arts and civilisation among us...Do not think me dispirited by what has happened. I see the extent of our danger, and think that danger much greater than is commonly apprehended; but the effect of that opinion on my mind is no other than that of increasing the conviction with which before I was impressed, of the necessity of perseverance and exertion. France and Spain and the Netherlands, and Geneva, most of all (small as it is) show us that this danger is not to be lessened by giving way to it, but that courage and resolution are in this instance, as in most others, the surest roads to self-preservation (27.9.1794).

Duke of Buckingham and Chandos, *Memoirs of the Court and Cabinets of George the Third* (London, 1853), vol. II, pp. 303, 305 and 306–7.

[42] There is little in the petitions to the House of Commons over the Two Acts to give Pitt confidence that he had the backing of the nation. The number of signatories against the Bills substantially outweighed those in support: ninety-four petitions with 130,000, as against sixty-five with 30,000. See *The History of the Two Acts*...(London, 1796).

[43] See David Eastwood's contribution to this volume; J. R. Western, 'The Volunteer Movement as an anti-revolutionary force', *English Historical Review*, 71 (1956), pp. 603–14; John Bohstedt, *Riots and Community Politics in England and Wales 1790–1810* (Cambridge, Mass., 1983), especially pp. 49–51, and pp. 114–6; and J. E. Cookson, 'The English Volunteer Movement of the French wars, 1793–1815: some contexts', *Historical Journal*, 32, 4 (1989), pp. 867–91.

at the way in which paths to alternative forms of reform activity were successively closed, but also at the radical rhetoric which did much to alarm government and which increasingly seemed to lead towards insurrection.

III

There are two aspects of the relationship between rhetoric, ideology and action which demand careful attention. The first tackles the issue of how far reformers and radicals in the 1790s are operating within the established conventions of an attack on 'Old Corruption', and how far we can find in the decade evidence of a displacement of older frameworks of radical thought and their replacement with newer, more universalistic, democratic and populist ideological commitments. The second, but related issue, returns to the questions raised earlier about the connection between radical rhetoric and radical intent.

One consequence of the preceding analysis of the changing logic of confrontation between reformers and loyalist and governmental forces, is that we should be prepared to forego the prospect of identifying a new paradigm for those demanding parliamentary reform. Because radicalism evolves to a significant extent in the process of confrontation, and because, early in the decade, this confrontation becomes one of practical political struggle and propaganda, it is extremely difficult to read off ideology from rhetoric. It is true that there is extensive use, across the board, of the rhetoric of 'Old Corruption', and that the older tradition plays a predominant role in the formal statements of the reform societies,[44] but there is also a great deal of rhetoric influenced by France and tied to the radicals' defence of the right of the French to their Revolution. We have already seen why this should be so: France is pushed firmly into the limelight by Burke, and its centrality to issues of reform in Britain is confirmed by Paine. But events in both Britain and France do much both to continue and to transform the role of French affairs. One reason for the corresponding societies sending addresses to the French republic in the autumn of 1792 was a growing sense that France now stood as liberty's best ally, while Britain seemed to be sinking towards oppression. Some of the analysis of this development was doubtless indebted to 'independent' ideology; but it should also be recognised that one reason for using such language was the purchase it had within British political culture. Even while flirting with 'French principles', reformers could make pointed use of traditional forms of opposition rhetoric. How are we to tell whether or how it was meant?

[44] See Dinwiddy, 'Conceptions of revolution', especially pp. 537–42.

One way of answering this question which follows up the argument presented thus far is to suggest that reformers in the 1790s were faced with at least four reference points when taking their ideological bearings. First, there was the theoretical and principled defence of reform, not just in the works of Paine, Thelwall and other contemporaries, but also in those classical works of republicanism and radicalism which appeared in extracts in journals such as *Pig's Meat* and *Hog's Wash/Politics for the People*, and which were also reprinted and circulated by the constitutional societies. Second, the developing events in Britain and France acted as an ongoing commentary, capable of diverse interpretation, on the principles and prospects of reform. Third, the outpourings of the loyalist presses provided a constantly moving field of rhetorical contest for reformers, whilst also acting as an alternative commentary on France. Finally, there were the existing traditions of political participation, with their rhetoric, expectations and codes.[45] Clearly, each point could be affected by other points; moreover, this is not offered as a definitive account of all potential influences. None the less, we come closer to the realities of the 1790s if we think of people as responding to events, debating issues and affirming or changing commitments within this frame, rather than as subscribing to a particular set of radical principles or a particular ideology. Moreover, if we recognise that the pressure of events in France and from the war with France feed into a polarising conflict between the cause of reform and loyalism, we can also see that as the decade progresses the paradigm of opposition thought is increasingly displaced and its language put to instrumental use. No new framework emerges to replace the old, although there are innovations.[46] Indeed, by the end of the 1800s we can recognise a revival of this ideology. But for a time, during the 1790s, popular political discourse breaks with its traditions, and is best understood as increasingly tactical and innovative. Two areas symptomatic of this movement are the use of French references and motifs amongst radicals, and the development of a distinctive language of protest.

One surprising feature of reform throughout the decade is the persistent use of French reference points. A whole panoply of symbols, images, styles and rhetoric, continued in use amongst radicals throughout the decade[47] – much to the horror of the Committee of Secrecy:

Subsequent to the Declaration of War, which interrupted this System of direct Correspondence and Concert with France, and down to the present Time, the

---

[45] On which, see O'Gorman, *Voters, Patrons and Parties*, especially ch. 5; also John Brewer, *Party Ideology and Popular Politics at the Accession of George III* (Cambridge, 1976), and J. A. Phillips, *Electoral Behaviour in Unreformed England, 1761–1802* (Princeton, N.J., 1982).

[46] See, for example, Claeys, *Thomas Paine* on Paine, ch. 4; Hampsher-Monk, 'John Thelwall'.   [47] Dinwiddy, 'Conceptions of revolution', pp. 537–8.

Society has continued on various Occasions, to manifest their Attachment to the Cause of the French Revolution, and have affected to follow, in their Proceeding, and in their Language, the Forms and even the Phrases which are adopted in that Country.[48]

Reformers' attachment to French principles was signalled in the way they addressed each other, their dress and their hair. Moreover, as the 'Report' suggests, these practices continued after the outbreak of war – as far as the use of 'citizen' is concerned, the London Corresponding Society used it from early in its history, as did some of the more respectable sympathisers (for example, Ritson). At times the use of French symbolism could take a more complex form. When Gerrald was sentenced in Scotland he appeared before his judges with his neck bared, French style, his unpowdered hair hanging loose and his shirt, with a large collar doubled over in the French fashion of the day.[49] While the contrast with his judges was stark, the intent and effect might have been more subtle than merely establishing his heterodoxy. His judges might have been reminded of other occasions on which French necks were bared. If so, the instance is instructive. To stand before his accusers representing the martyred King was to cast them as revolutionists. The tension between this rhetorical strategy and Gerrald's own ideological commitments is immaterial – the point and force of the act is not to take a stand on principle but to discomfit his judges. It is true that the strategy seems to have paid few dividends, save ensuring an equal martyrdom, but it is instructive of the way that symbolism and rhetoric might be used with serious practical intent but without direct ideological import.

A further feature of the identification with the French is the occasional willingness of some reformers to embrace *sans-culotte* and 'Jacobin' as self-descriptions, and the much more common use of 'citizen' amongst themselves:

I am a *sans-culotte*! one of those who think the happiness of millions of more consequence than the aggrandizement of any party junto! or, in other words, an advocate for the rights and happiness of those who are languishing in *want* and *nakedness*; the thing in reality which the *whigs* pretend to be.[50]

Cases of publicly subscribing to 'Jacobin' are rarer; even Richard Dinmore, in his *An Exposition of the Principles of the English Jacobins*, provides only a third-person account of the beliefs of the English

---

[48] *First Report of the Committee of Secrecy, 17 May 1794* (London, 1794). See also the accusation of systematic French design to overthrow the British constitution and all its works, for which the dissemination of French principles is the instrument, in *House of Commons Sessional Papers of the Eighteenth Century: Reports and Papers 1798–9* (Wilmington, Del., 1975), vol. CXXI, 'Report of the Committee of Secrecy', pp. 317–18.

[49] Thompson, *Making of the English Working Class*, p. 139.

[50] *Life of Thelwall*, p. 128.

Jacobins, and Eaton's *Politics for the People* seems keener to reveal the English Jacobins as creatures of the imagination than to endorse the ascription.[51] None the less, Dinmore does suggest that some radicals were prepared to be counted as Jacobins:

I call them jacobins because their enemies chose so to call them, with a view to confusing the public mind; to render it incapable of distinguishing their merit from the brutal cruelty of the second order of French jacobins. This nickname these persons readily adopted. They cared not by what names they were called, which rendered the malice of their enemies pointless.[52]

But there is no doubt as to the widespread use of 'citizen'. Ritson uses it extensively in correspondence, and it became the standard form of address within the corresponding societies.[53]

The preparedness to use such terminology in self-description has obscure roots. The pejorative use of 'Jacobin' may well originate from the time of the reformers' correspondence with the French societies, but it came to have a much greater significance as events progressed.[54] Loyalists increasingly used the term interchangeably, to all intents and purposes, with 'French', it being used to describe all those implicated in the bloodshed in France from, at the very latest, September 1792. It was also increasingly used in association with the term 'leveller', thereby fusing

[51] Cf. *Politics for the People*, vol. I, part 2, no. 5 (1794), p. 15 (see also, 'The origin of Jacobinism', vol. II, p. 178). But the description of them as non-entities is on the same page as the rhyme, 'Marat's descent to the shades':

> The infernal realms, in wild afright, receive his spotted shade,
> Aristocratic imps and fiends were horribly dismay'd;
> They fear'd his democratic rage might all distinction level,
> Make Hell with loud Ça ira's ring, and *Guillotine the Devil*.

[52] Richard Dinmore, *An Exposition of the Principles of the English Jacobins* (Norwich, 1796), p. 6.

[53] See *ibid.*, pp. 37–8. It is difficult to know quite when 'citizen' came into common usage amongst the radicals. Judging from Thale, *Selections from the Papers of the London Corresponding Society*, it seems to become frequent in 1793 and normal from 1794 on; but its presence in records might be a misleading indication of its actual use.

[54] Again, judging when 'Jacobin' became an epithet is also difficult. It appears in loyalist songs from very early in 1793 – as in 'King, liberty, laws', which also appears in the *Anti-Gallican Songster I* (London, 1793), as 'Song' (first line, 'Ye Britons, so brave, so bold and so free'):

> No religion or laws the vile Jacobins own;
> Their God they deny, and their King they dethrone

That they only dethrone their King suggests it was written prior to the King's trial (December 1792). Prior to the end of 1792 there would have been no cause to associate the Jacobins in particular with revolutionary extremism, although thereafter the left sections of the club did play a leading role in the inauguration of 'terroristic' policies. However, the loyalist linking of British reformers and the French Jacobins might well have been grounded on the apparent similarities in organisation and educational objectives between the provincial Jacobin clubs and the British societies.

French and English idioms in the attempt to discredit the movement for reform. When reformers embraced the terms 'Jacobin' or 'leveller', or used other terms valorised by French events (such as 'Convention'), they could have had a number of purposes: to assert the legitimacy of the French Revolution; as part of a strategy to counter loyalist assertions as to their fiendish nature; or as a symbol to elicit affirmations of commitment from fellow radicals and a gesture of defiance and resistance to their opponents.[55] Again, the rhetorical intent and effect is of greater significance than the principles which might be deduced from such a self-ascription. The 'English Jacobins' is a wildly misleading description of British radicals in the 1790s, even if we think it possible to translate the category from the French experience to the English. What it does do, however, is indicate an implicitly international dimension to the radical cause, reinforced by the earlier exchanges of messages and the sending of delegates, which pushes radicalism beyond the boundaries of the more local and confined language of opposition thought. There is no wholesale conversion to French principles or terminology, but either might be invoked as a way of enriching, by universalising, the language of reform. This might be said of the use of 'citizen', which can be used as an equivalent to 'freeman' (possessing civic rights and privileges) but which, in virtue of its place in the French revolutionary lexicon, brings into play more universalist connotations.

The innovative character of radical writing in the period has been the subject of renewed critical study.[56] We should not underestimate the prior existence of a popular print culture, but the period is distinctive in the development of a popular style of political discourse. Paine is an exemplar of this style, but we can also see in the works of Spence, Eaton and others a process of working out ways of communicating effectively with an audience, many of whom are called into political debate on broader, national issues for the first time by the efforts of the corresponding and constitutional societies. This 'democratical' writing is important for the way it constructs its reader, making accessible to all political issues which were customarily shrouded in a refined language which confined them to an educated elite. O'Gorman has made a convincing case for recognising widespread popular participation in elections in the hundred years before the Reform Act, but he has also stressed the localised character of the political issues.[57] The case for claiming innovation in politicisation in the

---

[55] Not unlike the process of the inversion of terms derogatory of certain groups brought about by their positive affirmation by members of those groups – a common enough strategy in black, homosexual and feminist groups in the last thirty years.

[56] Most prominently Smith, *The Politics of Language*, and Butler's collection *Burke, Paine, Godwin*. For a detailed analysis of Spence's methods, see Wood, 'Thomas Spence'.

[57] O'Gorman, *Voters, Patrons and Parties*, ch. 5, 'Ideological aspects of electoral behaviour'.

1790s and 1800s on the part of radicals rests with their introduction of a more abstract and principled form of political literature to a plebeian audience. But these writings are also significant in their development of ways of demythologising elite political discourse, and in undercutting the rituals, symbols and conventions of political, social and religious authority.[58] Although the role of loyalist counter-propaganda in defusing elements of this radical challenge should be recognised, it should not be exaggerated; it is more likely that the *Cheap Repository Tracts* were taken as entertainment than as gospel.[59] But it may well be that the net effect of all this activity is to increase the reader's scepticism towards print culture, and this doubtless works in favour of the status quo.

These examples confirm the importance of moving the analysis of the debate from the level of contrasting political principles and theories to that of the conflicting rhetorical strategies and devices, the developing polarisation of loyalist and reformist claims with its associated denial by the authorities of the existence of a moderate middle ground, and the tactical extension of the boundaries of debate through to sections of the population with little previous involvement in politics. One consequence of doing this is that we have to develop a more nuanced understanding of the relationship between the practical, tactical struggle for reform and the terms which they used to justify, elaborate and reflect upon their activities and objectives. We also need a better understanding of the place of rhetoric and language within the reform movements. Even while recognising the existence of rhetorical flourishes, we need seriously to reflect upon their meaning and function.

For example, how is Thelwall's story, 'King Chaunticlere', for the publication of which Eaton was charged with sedition, meant to be understood? The anecdote follows the story of a slave who had revolted for freedom and was being brutally tortured, but who instinctively defended himself against a blow intended by a companion to put him out of his misery. Thelwall purports to be exploring the distinction between mental and muscular action (or intentional and reflex), to demonstrate

---

[58] See, for example, Eaton's 'Guilemo Pittachio', *Politics for the People*, vol. II, no. 25, pp. 388–9, and vol. II, no. 26, pp. 406–7; it is probable that the piece is by Spence, and it is discussed as such by Marcus Wood in his 'Thomas Spence and modes of subversion'. Also the use of offensive parody in 'The Pernicious Principles of Tom Paine, Exposed in an Address to Labourers and Mechanics by a Gentleman' – where the force of 'gentleman' suggests a class connotation absent from much reform literature. 'Pernicious principles' was published both as a short pamphlet and in full in *Politics for the People*, vol. II, no. 1, pp. 4–9. See also Bindman, *The Shadow of the Guillotine*, especially ch. 8, and the introductory essay, 'This monstrous tragi-comic scene: British reactions to the French Revolution' by John Brewer.

[59] S. Pedersen, 'Hannah More meets Simple Simon: tracts, chapbooks, and popular culture in late eighteenth-century England', *Journal of British Studies*, 25 (1986), pp. 84–113.

that we cannot conclude that the love of life is stronger than the love of liberty:

> I had a very fine majestic kind of animal, a game cock: a haughty, sanguinary tyrant, nursed in blood and slaughter from his infancy – fond of foreign wars and *domestic rebellions*, into which he would sometimes drive his subjects, by his oppressive obstinacy, in hopes that he might increase his power and glory by their suppression.

This cock would not give the farmyard a moment's peace, and despite certain prejudices predisposing him to reverence, Thelwall also felt a degree of aversion to barefaced despotism which suggested to him 'that the best thing to do for cocks and hens, or men and women, was to rid the world of tyrants':

> So I believe, if guillotines had been in fashion, I should have certainly guillotined him: being desirous to be merciful, even in the stroke of death, and knowing, that the instant the brain is separated from the heart, (which, with this instrument, is done in a moment,) pain and consciousness were at an end.

Instead, Thelwall is forced to use a knife and block, which he does to good effect. Beneath the bird's finery he finds it is no better than 'a common tame scratch-dunghill pullet'. But the point of his story is that after the head was cut off the bird continued to bound around, so that had someone tried to knock it down they would have concluded that the bird was trying to save itself, and that this 'proceeded from the conviction that life was worth preserving even after he had lost his head: which, in my opinion, would be just about as rational as supposing that it can be worth preserving to [the] man who is writhing about in *the frying pan of despotism*'.[60]

The story is brilliantly constructed satire on loyalist dogma and monarchical pretensions – one which works even better as a performance than in the written word. But it is far from clear quite what Thelwall (if indeed it is Thelwall) is recommending. How, in particular, is the quite detailed reference to the virtues of the guillotine to be read?! It is worth asking whether Thelwall was just colossally imprudent – or whether it is evidence of a form of collective impudence. It is notable that the meeting broke up in disorder when a minority tried to prevent Thelwall from speaking as he went on to praise the exertions of France in favour of liberty. How much is it the frisson of danger, the thinking of the unthinkable, which generates the disorder? Perhaps what comes out most

---

[60] *Politics for the People; or Hog's Wash*, no. 8 (1793), pp. 102–7. This is reprinted, omitting a report of the subsequent evening's debate, in Butler's, *Burke, Paine, Godwin*. Thelwall later denied that the story was given in these terms, and claimed that Eaton had dressed it up in much stronger terms, *Life of Thelwall*, pp. 108–9.

clearly from this and similar examples is a clear sense that writers are playing with ideas and principles, and with their audiences' intellectual and emotional reflexes. In a great deal of the material of the 1790s, we are dealing less with a clear-cut ideological division with well worked-out opposing principles and more with experimentation, both in the use of particular media and in the position being advanced. Such rhetorical experimentation often leads people to innovate in their commitments and break new ideological ground. Instead of reading these texts, utterances and symbolic statements for the deeper, principled meaning behind them, we should recognise that it is often in their superficial diversity, idiosyncrasy and imprudence that their force lies – a force which affects both the audience and, in many cases, the writer or speaker. There is a temptation when looking at controversies to see writing and speaking as expressing already existing ideas, but there is much to be said for recognising a more complex relationship. It is frequently in the act of writing and speaking that we form ideas and make them choate. This is not invariably the case, but it is more likely to be so when writing and speech become invested with an immediate practical political significance.

There is a final area of concern in the analysis of reformism in the 1790s which requires our attention before returning to the questions raised in my opening statements about the impact of the fragmentation of radical ideology on the prospects of the reform movement. I have argued that we should understand the 1790s in terms of the development of a logic of confrontation and an associated shift from ideology to rhetoric and propaganda. I have also suggested that in this process some people were persuaded that they required new tactics to attain their ends and that, at each step, the stakes in the struggle were raised – both in the sense of increasing the costs of agitating for reform, and in the sense of making moderate reform less likely and less possible. That is, as the decade progresses there is less chance of securing reform, and there is less chance, were such reform to be attained, that it would remain moderate. To complement this account we need some sense of the way that reformers reacted to these changing parameters of reforming activity. Clearly, there were, in fact, many different individual responses, some moving to a withdrawal from political activity, others being willing to countenance armed insurrection, but it is still possible to make some general comments about the processes involved in people's developing commitments.

The least plausible account of radical motivation is an instrumental one in which reformers see reform as a way of improving their lot, but abandon it as a strategy either when they cease to need it,[61] or when they

---

[61] A cynical account of Hardy would suggest that once he thought he could rely on the financial support of his rich friends, he lost interest in the reform movement (he would

see the probable short-term costs outweighing the increasingly improbable long-term gains. This kind of calculation, particularly the latter, probably played some role in people's willingness to remain active in political associations, but to see this as all is to rely on a very emaciated picture of human motivation and to be satisfied with a very inadequate account of the 1790s. We need to combine a more complex account of motivation and ideological commitment, with a recognition of the changing nature of the options and costs faced by reformers, and with an appreciation of the factors which shaped their perceptions of these options. Ideology plays some part in this, but so too does the complex process of identifying interests and making commitments and interpreting and reinterpreting these in a context which increasingly seeks to classify them and their concerns as subversive.

We should begin by recognising that becoming involved in agitation for reform was not a uniform experience. For someone like Fox his flirtation with the reform movement was not radically discontinuous from his previous activities; for someone like Godwin, identification with it offered the prospect of fame and fortune within a literary culture in which he had already played a minor role or even, perhaps, a more glorious role as one of the intellectual leaders of the new society. But for people like Place and Hardy, reform offered a more practical kind of emancipation or empowerment, together with a degree of social mobility. Hardy's comments that in the first five nights he and his first associates in the London Corresponding Society spent the time discussing whether they, as 'treadesmen (*sic*), shopkeepers and mechanics', had any right to seek parliamentary reform, should alert us to the dramatic impact which democratic politics and the spread of Painite and other literature had on the common man. Thomas Preston recorded the awakening he experienced in the 1790s which subsequently led him to trial for High Treason for his part in the 1816 Spa Fields riot:

The increase in reading had dissipated the delusion, and people now knew the meaning of words, whether spoken in the Senate, written in a lawyer's bill of costs, or printed on an impress warrant. The charm of *ignorance* which had so long pulled my mind into comparative indifference at people's wrongs, was now beginning to disappear. The moral and political sum of TRUTH had now arisen. The arguments, the irresistible arguments, laid down by the 'Corresponding Society' had rivetted my heart to the cause of liberty.[62]

That is, for some the experience was transformative – and this sense of personal enlightenment, indeed empowerment, was very much associated

certainly have been imprudent to do so, given that his friends seemed more willing to give out promises than cash). Cf. Hardy's *Memoir of Thomas Hardy* (London, 1816).

[62] *Life and Opinions of Thomas Preston* (London, 1817), p. 13.

with the development of artisan-based organisations which made their own rules and ordered their own proceedings.[63] But it also suggests that the experience could also be welded together with older and often deeply potent popular traditions of thought and practice – not just 'independent' or opposition traditions, but also millenarian and apocalyptic visions. The diverse language, imageries and ideas available to those who now had a sense of a unique destiny in clearing the shrouds of superstition and imposture from the body politic could be combined and utilised in many ways, but not as creeds to conform to so much as a tool-kit with which to innovate.[64]

There is, then, a recurrent sense in the 1790s of people's commitments being transformed, particularly amongst the artisans and the middling orders. This is one factor which distinguishes the popular participation of the 1790s from that which existed in the arena of electoral struggles and which has been brought sharply into focus by O'Gorman. But a further distinguishing feature is that whereas electoral participation is rooted in local issues and reciprocal relations, reformers could interpret their activity in more universal terms, as a matter of moral truth and political integrity. Similarly, this feature also serves to sanctify personal preferences by representing them as demanded by a higher morality, and this in turn may lead people to ignore instrumental calculation: prudence may speak against demanding reform, but truth has the higher claim. And when the force of law is brought to bear against this morality, it loses its impartial character and becomes seen as progressively more corrupt, both forcing and making legitimate, active measures to challenge its authority. This progressive movement towards greater radicalism – this commitment to a radical 'career' – is made additionally attractive to many in the 1790s by the gradual erosion of legitimated alternative forms of political activity. Having made the initial commitment, people rarely fall at the first obstacle.[65] While events at home and in France – the Royal Proclamation, the September massacres, the rise of loyalism and the Reevite Societies, and so on – serve increasingly to stigmatise and increase the costs of radical activity, there were also gains to radicals from this process, in terms of collective solidarity and, through this and the higher public

[63] As Günther Lottes argues, in part in his chapter in this volume, but also in his *Politische Aufklärung und plebejisches Publikum* (Munich, 1979).
[64] The metaphor of 'bricolage' is helpful here; see C. Levi-Strauss, *The Savage Mind* (London, 1968), ch. 1, and Jon Mee's forthcoming *A Dangerous Enthusiasm* (Oxford), ch. 1.
[65] Although Godwin's experience did not extend across the whole social spectrum, it is worth recalling his suggestion that, 'Down to the spring of 1797, when petitions were being sent up from many parts of England for the removal of the King's ministers, scarcely one of those persons who had declared themselves ardently and affectionately interested for the success of the French, deserted their cause'; *Thoughts Occasioned by the Perusal of Dr Parr's Spital Sermon* (London, 1801), p. 4.

profile attained, an implicit affirmation of a new political identity. It might well be, however, that these gains are greater for the newly politicised, those who rise with events, than they are for the older elite whose role in the political and social order might itself be under threat. Further polarisation makes escape routes more attractive – emigration, quiescence, *volte-face* – but again there are class and status differentials. Who can gain by reneging (Mackintosh, but not Place or Hardy); who can afford emigration? Quiescence is not necessarily a more attractive prospect than continued involvement, especially if there are side benefits, such as participation and status gains, a sense of empowerment, and so on, or where there are innovations in tactics which offer renewed promise of results, as in their association with the anti-government feeling stemming from food shortages and the war in 1795–6, and in the use of mass meetings in 1795. While the escalation of conflict did threaten to impose high costs, many of those agitating for reform would also have been insulated in their perception of these costs by group norms. Furthermore, the reformers' increasing confrontation with the law, and their notable success in using the courts as a platform for their cause, would have both confirmed their sense of the urgency and legitimacy of reform and decreased their sense of the probable costs of continued agitation.

These considerations are an essential background to the analysis of radical rhetoric. It seems plausible to read stories, such as Thelwall's 'King Chaunticlere', as part of a process of self-definition, involving experimentation with commitments, identities or political positions, which may subsequently be endorsed. Similarly, the juggling with Burke's phrase 'a swinish multitude' by Eaton, Spence and many others, offers an opportunity to speak in a number of different characters, against which the reader can form new perceptions of his or her own. The identities experimented with, as in 'King Chaunticlere', are frequently oppositional and confrontational, and the rhetoric has its share of bravado, but that is part of its point. When challenged, reformers might prove slippery, as in the Treason Trials, exploiting the difference between what might have been said or written and what was really meant; but they might also be drawn into a commitment to the implications of their rhetoric. In this way, political rhetoric serves to explore and reinterpret (and thereby determine) the boundaries of the politically possible and the politically desirable. Paulson, in discussing the French Revolution suggests that, 'If the French example made revolution possible – even desirable – it also, from the events of 1788 onward and at each new stage, served to convince many people that *anything* was now possible'.[66] In his contribution to this volume, Günther Lottes has suggested why British reformers might find

[66] R. Paulson, *Representations of Revolution 1789–1820* (New Haven, Conn., 1983), p. 2.

their political imaginations more constrained than their French counterparts, but as the decade progresses, and the polarisation is exacerbated, those who remained committed to reform would have found the constraints less potent.

Political rhetoric, then, is neither the direct expression of conviction, nor just a joke. It is a way of experimenting with commitment and identity, some of which get full personal endorsement when confrontation necessitates it. But as these commitments are elicited, the actor can become successively more embroiled in confrontations which lead him, or her, down paths and into activities which they would not earlier have countenanced. They are not forced to take this road, but confrontations cannot simply be assessed in terms of prudence – what is at stake for the participants is the strength of their commitments to beliefs and values which have come to play a major role in governing their day to day behaviour – beliefs moreover, which have become increasingly central to their sense of who they are. Going against these commitments involves a certain loss of self, sticking with them offers confirmation.

IV

I began by looking at the role which the divisions in the reform movement have been accorded in the explanation of its failure. As will now be clear, there are good reasons for thinking that the ideological divisions among the reformers are of less significance than some writers have suggested. The movement for reform which develops as the decade progresses is not driven by high theory, but by popular agitation and mobilisation against scarcity and war and in favour of reform. At this level, the diversity of reformist thinking can be seen as positively enriching the process of constructing a radical identity. The range of radical and reformist traditions and texts together with the practical examples of America and France provide a context within which reformers can construct interpretations, identities and strategies. And many of the divisions which do exist, such as that between temperate reformers in parliamentary circles and the extra-parliamentary groups which, by the end of the decade were toying with insurrection, flow less from the intrinsic qualities of radical thought and more from the loyalist reaction and the government's continued refusal to engage in dialogue with the extra-parliamentary groups agitating for reform.

In the final analysis, it is not clear that the fragmentation matters very much in the debate over the prospects for Britain experiencing a French Revolution. It is only on the most simplistic and voluntarist of assumptions that a cohesive revolutionary theory can be seen as a necessary condition for revolution. When we put the more sensible question of why reform attempts fail, we can find the answer without difficulty in the processes of polarisation and confrontation which the conservative reaction initiated, and we can see the willingness to countenance more radical aspirations and methods as an outcome of this exclusion. But the question of whether these ambitions could then have succeeded has little to do with the integrity of radical reform programmes, and much more to do with the extent to which social and economic crises associated with the war also provoked political crises and crises of legitimation – crises which matter most, not among the classes which attend the free and easies of Spencian circles, or indulge in politicised millenarian speculation, but amongst members of the social, political and financial elites of the country. Popular discontent and a radical popular politics may be necessary conditions for revolutionary transformation, but they are not by any means sufficient.

4   Radicalism, revolution and political culture: an Anglo-French comparison

Günther Lottes

I

'Radicalism' has become an established term with regard to the late eighteenth-century movement for political reform in England, whereas the term *radicalisme* is not normally used to designate a particular political group during the French Revolution. We are wont to speak of a radicalisation of the Revolution. But the radicals themselves we call Jacobins, *sans-culottes* or some other contemporaneous name. Any attempt to compare English and French radicalism in the period of the French Revolution should therefore make clear to which political currents it refers.[1]

The term 'radicalism' enters the political language(s) of Europe during the opening decades of the nineteenth century. It seems to have been first used in Britain, from where it migrated to France during the 1820s and via France to Germany during the 1830s.[2] Just like the term 'conservative' which appeared at about the same time, it was used to describe a particular way of dealing with the political heritage of the eighteenth-century revolution in government. Whereas the adjective 'radical' came eventually to be used in a politically neutral sense, the noun never lost the original semantic link with the later eighteenth-century demand to enforce the principle of government by consent without any social reservation. Uncompromising conservatives were never called radicals but found themselves, equally tellingly, labelled die-hards or ultras.[3] A radical was

[1] For the use which is made of the term 'radical' in relation to France see, for instance, the index of Colin Jones, *The Longman Companion to the French Revolution* (London, 1989), or Lynn Hunt, *Politics, Culture and Class in the French Revolution* (Berkeley and Los Angeles, Calif., 1984).

[2] See P. Wende, 'Radikalismus' in O. Brunner, W. Conze and R. Koselleck (eds.), *Geschichtliche Grundbegriffe, Historisches Lexikon der politisch-sozialen Sprache in Deutschland* (Stuttgart, 1984), vol. V, pp. 116–33.

[3] Cf. *The Oxford English Dictionary*, vol. IV, s.v. *die-hard* and vol. XVIII, s.v. *ultra*. The term 'die-hard' does not appear before the twentieth century, while the term 'ultra' seems originally to have been used to denote extremism of any kind. But through the French usage and as the term 'radical' gained ground, it became increasingly associated with conservatism.

someone who adhered unflinchingly to the leading principles of what Robert Palmer has named the 'democratic revolution' of the later eighteenth century.[4] He would neither sacrifice those principles to the exigencies of a historical compromise with the political forces of the *ancien régime*, nor acquiesce in a political culture overgrowing and stifling its democratic origins, be they supposed or real.

As radicalism and conservatism built up political traditions for themselves as well as for their respective adversaries, these names came to be applied to the corresponding political currents in the revolutionary period itself. In England the term 'radical' was eventually extended back to include all those who had advocated a significant extension of the suffrage and a thorough reform of Parliament culminating in the demand for universal suffrage, equal representation and annual parliaments in the 1790s.[5] It was even read back into the seventeenth century, although there was no real continuity of discourses behind the apparent similarities between mid-seventeenth-century levellers and late eighteenth-century Jacobins.[6] In France, where the Revolution soon became the point of reference for all political camps, other terms were at first used to express continuity. When the term 'radical' was imported from England, it was used to designate a continuity of content which it was difficult to acknowledge openly. However, there can be no doubt whose political executors the French radicals purported to be. They stood for the republican form of government, for human rights and individual liberty, for universal suffrage and last, but by no means least, for a vigorous anti-clericalism which made them claim the *philosophes* as their ideological ancestors in pre-revolutionary France.[7]

Both in England and in France the roots of radicalism are thus to be found in the closing decades of the eighteenth century when the twin concepts of government by consent and popular sovereignty were taken to their logical conclusion. And English and French radicals also had much

---

[4] Robert R. Palmer, *The Age of the Democratic Revolution: A Political History of Europe and America*, 2 vols. (Princeton, N.J., 1959 and 1964).

[5] See *The Oxford English Dictionary*, vol. XIII, s.v. *radical*; for the historiographical tradition cf. among many other works, C.B.R. Kent, *The English Radicals* (London, 1899); Simon Maccoby, *The English Radical Tradition 1763–1785* (London 1952), as well as his *English Radicalism 1762–1785. The Origins* (London, 1955), and *English Radicalism, From Paine to Cobbett* (London, 1955). More recently H. T. Dickinson, *British Radicalism and the French Revolution 1789–1815* (London, 1985).

[6] See, for example, R. L. Greaves and R. Zaller (eds.), *Biographical Dictionary of British Radicals in the Seventeenth Century*, 3 vols. (Brighton, 1982), or H.-Chr. Schröder, *Politischer Radikalismus im 17. Jahrhundert* (Göttingen, 1984) = *Geschichte und Gesellschaft* (special edn), 4 (1984).

[7] Cf. Jacques Kayser, *Les Grandes Batailles du radicalisme 1820–1901* (Paris, 1962); F. Furet, 'Révolution française et tradition jacobine' in Colin Lucas (ed.), *The French Revolution and the Creation of Modern Political Culture. The Political Culture of the French Revolution*, vol. II (Oxford, 1988), p. 295.

in common. Their intellectual origins, their political ideas and the institutional solutions they believed in were in many ways similar. On the other hand, it is clear even from what we have so far said about the two radicalisms under consideration that they differed in important ways. And if we turned to the radical tradition of other countries, we would find that radicalism was a head with many faces. It was a European phenomenon inasmuch as the 'democratic revolution' had been one. But it was a distinct national phenomenon inasmuch as this revolution had been experienced in different ways. A comparative approach may thus help to evaluate the nature and the potential of radicalism in the various contexts in which it appeared. Within the limits of this chapter I can only presume to do this for England and France.[8]

Very broadly speaking, European radicalism was the political result of the new philosophy of the seventeenth and eighteenth centuries, which had discovered individual man as the irreducible basic unit of the social world. It had applied this principle mercilessly to one field of knowledge after the other: to philosophy and psychology, to religion and ethics, to social philosophy and economics. The defenders of the established order and of the traditional ways of thinking were driven mad by the dynamics of this methodology, which sacrificed accumulated human wisdom and centuries of historical experience with a stroke of the often polemical pen. Within two or three generations the new concept of individualism had exploded such time-honoured notions as the ideology of order, with its insistence on a divinely ordained social hierarchy, and the moral obligation of a Christian to perform the duties of the social station assigned to him. By the middle of the eighteenth-century the once noble edifice of traditional knowledge was so derelict that it had become uninhabitable for all but the most immune to the spirit of the times.

The ground was now well prepared to tear down the last wall supporting the old structure by applying the methodology of individualism to the realm of power and government. The following decades witnessed

---

[8] There have been few attempts at a comparative analysis. Palmer's classic *The Age of the Democratic Revolution*, as well as Gwyn A. Williams's *Artisans and Sans-Culottes: Popular Movements in France and Britain during the French Revolution*, 1st edn (London, 1968), tend to reduce the comparative dimension to the juxtaposition of events and socio-political conditions. Much the same is true for the collection of valuable essays edited by Eckhart Hellmuth, *The Transformation of Political Culture: England and Germany in the Late Eighteenth Century* (Oxford, 1990). In the discussion of this chapter, it was asked why I had not included Scottish and Irish radicalism in my comparative approach. My answer was that the choice of the phenomena to be compared in an analysis of this sort depends on the questions which are asked. My concern in this chapter is not with problems like radicalism and cultural hegemony or religious background and potentials for politicisation, but with the differences between the English and the continental attitudes towards the concept of popular democracy and the appearance of the people on the political stage.

a politicisation of individualism which led naturally to the emergence of political radicalism in England as well as in France. For nobody who took the principle seriously could escape its logic. Political participation could no longer be conceived of as a privilege of the few, whoever these might be. It was the undeniable right of every citizen. The proud *Declaration des droits de l'homme et du citoyen* introduced this reasoning into its very title: manhood and citizenship were one. There was, of course, the practical difficulty of organising such political participation in a great nation state. But did not the idea of representation, that great innovation of modern political theory, provide a perfect solution? As yet unaware of such intrinsic problems of representation as Edmund Burke was broaching in his speech to his Bristol electors, radicals on both sides of the Channel shared the conviction that individualism in politics meant universal, i.e. manhood suffrage and equal representation.[9]

English and French radicalism also articulated these ideas in the same political languages: that of natural-rights philosophy, of civic humanism and of philosophical psychology.[10] But they spoke these languages with distinct accents. This becomes particularly obvious in the case of civic humanism. In England a vigorous participatory political culture had interacted and was interacting with the semantics of this political language since the seventeenth century, whereas the French version of civic humanism was much less empirical and more utopian.[11] English and French radicalism thus drew on quite different dialects of the same political language. And they did so in a context which made this difference even more marked. While English radicals could and had to refer to an existing representative system, French radicals breathed the purer air of theoretical discourse. When the time for political action had eventually come in 1788–9, they faced a much more formidable task. They had to deal with an absolute monarchy which was unable to break out of the golden aristocratic cage in which it had placed itself and to accept an historical compromise. And they had to erect a representative system which satisfied the dictates of reason perfectly.

Let me elaborate this contrast by highlighting three distinctive features.

---

[9] See J. R. Pole, *Political Representation in England and the Origins of the American Republic* (London, 1966), parts 4 and 5.

[10] See Iain Hampsher-Monk, 'The idea of property in eighteenth century British radicalism' in Günther Lottes (ed.), *Eigentum im englischen politischen Denken* (Bochum, forthcoming), and his 'Civic humanism and parliamentary reform: the case of the Society of the Friends of the People', *Journal of British Studies*, 18 (1979), pp. 70–89.

[11] Nothing like J. G. A. Pocock's work (*The Machiavellian Moment. Florentine Political Thought and the Atlantic Republican Tradition* (Princeton, N.J., 1975)) on civic humanism in the Atlantic republican tradition is available for France, although this political language was by no means confined to England. Cf., for instance, E. Lawson, *The Spartan Tradition in European Thought* (Oxford, 1969).

82   *Günther Lottes*

To begin with, I will try to assess the relative weight of the question of sovereignty in English and French radical discourse. I will then consider how the approach to the problem of representation differed in both cases. And, lastly, I will turn to the practice of radicalism and ask how it shaped the radical tradition in both countries.

II

Late eighteenth-century English radicalism had little or no need to debate over the question of sovereignty. This had been answered very effectively, though not openly, in the Glorious Revolution. For more than a century the much vaunted doctrine of the mixed constitution had not only conferred the blessings of classical political theory on the English constitutional trinity of King, Lords and Commons, but served as a rhetorical smoke-screen produced consciously and unconsciously, to obscure the revolutionary transfer of sovereignty.[12] Even so it remained apparent for everyone who had eyes and wanted to see that in 1688–9, Parliament had established itself as the true sovereign of Britain. And within Parliament the House of Commons had undoubtedly achieved preponderance. The Crown and the Lords had for the most part accepted this arrangement and refrained from bringing to bear the institutional weight they were accorded in constitutional theory. Instead, they preferred to build up political influence in the lower house through the extensive use of patronage and by manipulating the representative system. Corruption became, in fact, something like a constitutional technique which spared all sides the grim reality of a theoretical debate.

By the end of the eighteenth century the transfer of sovereignty from the prince to the political nation was so much taken for granted that not even the radicals felt compelled to abandon the constitutional rhetoric surrounding it.[13] John Jebb, who among the mainstream radicals of the late 1770s and early 1780s came closest to the idea of popular sovereignty, found it possible to reconcile this notion with the doctrine of the ancient constitution:

The king, the house of lords, and the commons, fairly and adequately represented in parliament, are to be considered, with respect to each other, as free and independent: while the constitution subsists, they are equally exempt from the

[12] For the debate, see C. C. Weston, *English Constitutional Theory and the House of Lords* (London, 1965), and Pocock, *The Machiavellian Moment*, part 3, especially chs. 12, 13 and 14.
[13] On the constitutional and political situation in the latter part of the eighteenth century, see Ian R. Christie, *Myth and Reality in Late-Eighteenth-Century British Politics and Other Papers* (London, 1970).

most distant idea of mutual coercion and control ... This doctrine, I trust, will not be found in the least to militate against the acknowledged right of the people to new-model the constitution, and to punish, with exemplary rigour every person, with whom they have intrusted power, provided, in their opinion, he shall be found to have betrayed their trust.[14]

In other words, the distribution of power in the British constitution was not a matter of right but one of expediency and, above all, a trust which could be revoked.

Jebb almost got carried away by the logic of his own argument when he added that this applied only to a 'period, when, from the acquiescence of the people, it plainly appears to be their will, that the form of government, already established, should continue in existence', but not to 'that solemn hour, when the delegates of a state, chosen according to forms, which not law and custom, but necessity and expedience shall prescribe ... shall sit in awful judgement upon the traiterous invaders of their rights'.[15] Yet Jebb also demanded that such a constitutional convention should act 'in conjunction with the king, and hereditary nobility', arguing that the people, the 'commonalty at large', in their collective capacity were the third branch of the legislature.[16] Another prominent radical, Major John Cartwright, expressed himself in a similar vein. Like so many others he saw no contradiction in combining his adherence to the ancient constitution with a demand for universal suffrage built on a trenchant criticism of all political privilege.[17]

Such arguments were possible because it was not the share of the King or the Lords in the constitution's balance of sovereignty which mattered to the radicals. The issue for them was that a political elite in control of the electoral system denied the nation at large its sovereign right to assent to the laws which bound it. They did not see that a thorough reform of Parliament would necessarily have brought into open confrontation the question of sovereignty – less because the crown retained so much power, than because a political elite deprived of its means of control might well have sought shelter behind the King. Nor could the radicals admit the constitutional function of corruption, since doing so would have been self-defeating and would have turned the intellectual world of civic humanism upside down. It was unthinkable that there could be virtue in corruption.

That it was possible to express radical ideas in an accepted constitutional

---

[14] John Jebb, *The Works, Theological, Medical, Political and Miscellaneous ... with Memoirs of the Life of the Author*, ed. John Disney (London, 1787), vol. II, pp. 467–69.
[15] *Ibid.*, p. 496.   [16] *Ibid.*, vol. III, p. 288.
[17] Cf. John Cartwright, *The Legislative Rights of the Commonalty Vindicated: Or Take Your Choice* (London, 1776), and for his thinking in the 1790s, *The Commonwealth in Danger* (London, 1795), especially pp. 83ff.

language was to prove crucial in the 1790s when English radicalism first became a political force – one which could not be ignored because of the popular support it was apparently able to muster. The popularity of Tom Paine's *Rights of Man* is misleading. Undoubtedly, Paine had much to say to the radical reader. But he did not become the theoretical mastermind of a new radicalism of the 1790s. A study of the radical pamphlets and magazines of the period indicates that his work had less impact on the ideas and the political language of the reform movement than has often been supposed, and makes one wonder if the immense success and the notoriety of the work were not due more to the shock reaction of the establishment.[18]

In any case, instead of embracing Paine's irreverent description of the mixed constitution as a Government of 'this, that and t'other',[19] the leading radical societies took pains to stress the uncompromising constitutionalism of the movement for parliamentary reform. This was not merely done to evade repression, although it helped the defendants in the Treason Trials of 1794. The radicals of the 1790s simply continued the discourse of the preceding decade when they conceived of universal suffrage, equal representation and annual Parliaments as a restoration of the constitution.[20] It is true that some theorists like John Thelwall, Thomas Spence and William Godwin went far beyond this frame of reference. But with the possible exception of Thelwall,[21] their impact was either negligible or confined to the intelligentsia. And it is also true that we do not know enough about the views of the rank and file of the movement to be sure that a veneer of radical constitutionalism did not

---

[18] Paine's role is still rated high in recent research. See the editor's introduction to this volume which refers to the most important works in the footnotes. Much weight is usually given to the great number of copies of the *Rights of Man* which were sold or distributed. Sales figures are, of course, of great importance. And nobody would deny that Paine was widely known. On the other hand, who would conclude from the sale of the little red book in the late 1960s and early 1970s that Mao had a lasting and penetrating influence on the world-view of the students' movement? For my own argument concerning the influence of Paine, see my *Politische Aufklärung und plebejisches Publikum. Zur Theorie und Praxis des englischen Radikalismus im späten 18. Jahrhundert* (Munich and Vienna, 1979), pp. 267–9.

[19] W. M. van der Weyde (ed.), *The Life and Work of Thomas Paine* (New Rochelle, N.Y., 1925), vol. VI, p. 87.

[20] Cf., for a good example, London Corresponding Society, *Address to the Inhabitants of Great Britain* (London, 1792), or the *Declaration of Constitutional Rights of KING, LORDS, and COMMONS, of Great Britain* of the *Society of the Friends of the People in Southwark* (British Library (BL) 8135 b.b. 8/22); see also Lottes, *Politische Aufklärung und plebejisches Publikum*, pp. 267–70.

[21] Thelwall's importance as a political thinker and as a leading radical intellectual in closer contact with the membership of the movement than most has long been neglected. See, however, my own attempt at an interpretation in *Politische Aufklärung und plebejisches Publikum*, pp. 270–84, 298–9, 327–34 and, more recently, Iain Hampsher-Monk, 'John Thelwall and the eighteenth century radical response to political economy', *Historical Journal*, 34 (1991).

hide much less reassuring political passions. The work of some propagandists like Daniel Isaac Eaton, and the few traces that we have of the mood which prevailed in the divisions of the London Corresponding Society, at least suggest that there was an undercurrent of *sans-culottism* to which the ancient constitution meant little and which would have given short shrift to the interests it protected.[22] Most of the more articulate reformers, however, were unable to break free from the political language of the established system in which their political consciousness had been formed.

Together with the craving for political respectability which burned in men like Thomas Hardy and Francis Place, this attachment to the established constitutional language worked as a means of secondary integration. It gave English radicalism a residual affirmative character which in practice made its far-reaching demand for democratic representation susceptible to being outmanoeuvred by John Bull constitutionalism, or to being bought off by piecemeal political reform.

In France, in contrast, the question of sovereignty was central to radical discourse. It had been debated in various forms in all political camps throughout the eighteenth century. Yet the nation's claims in this respect had been put forward most effectively, not by radical thinkers like Jean-Jacques Rousseau, but by the conservative magistrates of the high courts of justice who formed the *opposition parlementaire*. In their struggle against the absolute monarchy, they had developed a doctrine of the nation's rights which had contributed to the formation of a political consciousness among the *menu peuple* in pre-revolutionary France.[23] At times, the awe-inspiring men of the robe whose world was so far removed from that of the common man had nonetheless been so popular that the people had staged mass demonstrations in their support.[24]

The doctrine of the magistrates was built on the idea that God's creation was a trust to be administered by man in reverence and with responsibility. The absolute monarch was sovereign in an institutional sense only. Just as he could not claim a right to infringe God's commandments and the teachings of the church, so he was bound to

[22] See, for example, Public Record Office (PRO), Treasury Solicitor's Papers 11/956/3501/part 1, Report on the Meeting of the General Committee of the London Corresponding Society on 3 July 1794.

[23] G. Rudé, *The Crowd in History: A Study of Popular Disturbance in France and England 1730–1848* (New York, 1964), p. 51, even refers to the *parlement* of Paris as the political educator of the 'lower orders'. On the *opposition parlementaire* in general, see the account by J. Egret, *Louis XV et l'opposition parlementaire* (Paris, 1970).

[24] Cf. W. Doyle, 'The parlements of France and the breakdown of the old régime, 1771–1788', *French Historical Studies*, 6 (1970), pp. 415–58, and his concise assessment in 'The parlements' in K. M. Baker (ed.), *The French Revolution and the Creation of Modern Political Culture. The Political Culture of the Old Regime*, vol. I (Oxford, 1987), pp. 157–67, especially pp. 160–1.

respect the particular sociology of this creation which the magistrates conceived of in terms of the ideology of order. God had created society as a hierarchically ordered universe, assigning every man a station which gave him duties to perform for the social whole but also rights to claim. The fact that the creation had been and was changing (which posed so great a problem for natural philosophy) was accounted for by the idea that all movement found expression in legal relations. The social world was thus a structure of legal titles unfolding in time which the sovereign was obliged to respect. At any given point in history the sovereignty of the ruler meshed with the sovereignty of God and of the world produced by history. Applied to eighteenth-century France this reasoning resulted in a specifically conservative and defensive concept of the nation's share in the sovereignty which, however, had a wide appeal, because it protected the rights of the small master and the journeyman, to whom it conceded a just price, as much as those of the *rentier* or the *Pair de France*.[25]

This popularity came abruptly to an end on 21 September 1788 when the *parlement* of Paris decreed that the States General should convene according to the forms observed in 1614. The decision came as a shock to a nation full of hope and confidence. When the nation needed it most the *opposition parlementaire* seemed to have changed sides and joined the ranks of privilege. Within weeks the conservative doctrine of sovereignty disintegrated. The nation redefined itself in the light of this experience as an association of useful men living for, not off, society, as an association not of equals but of equally unprivileged men. By January 1789 the Abbé Sieyès's provoking questions concerning the Third Estate gave expression to the new idea of national sovereignty which prepared the ground for the Revolution.[26] From it all thought of privilege was banned. Legal titles turned into civil rights; the appeal to the past was replaced by the appeal to the future; and the insistence on order and moral obligation gave way to the praise of liberty.

The difference from the English experience has to be emphasised. In England the answer to the question of sovereignty integrated the radicals, if only in a secondary sense, into the existing political culture. In France, on the contrary, the nation had to find a different answer to the same question and was forced to sever the bonds which connected it with a legitimising past. The immediate consequence of such a dynamic and even aggressive notion of national sovereignty was that it left no room for the kind of constitutional compromise which the British constitution offered as a solution to the question of sovereignty, regardless alike of all theoretical objections and of the realities of the political process. The idea

---

[25] See my forthcoming book, *Aufklärung und konservatives Denken. Studien zur Frühgeschichte des Konservativismus in Frankreich und England* (Sigmaringen Torbecke).

[26] Abbé Emmanuel-Joseph Sieyès, *Qu'est-ce que le tiers état?*, 3rd edn (Paris, 1789).

that the monarch had a *proprio iure* claim to a share in the sovereignty was inadmissible, for that would have meant admitting just that kind of inherited title from the past which the new-born nation had purged itself of. If the constitution which the nation would now have to give itself provided for a King or, more precisely, for the office of a King this was simply a matter of political convenience. But the debate on the veto soon made it clear to all political groupings that it was hard to escape the logic of the events of 1788–9. There had not been enough time for the nation to forget its triumphant political self-discovery, nor for the monarchy to lose enough political weight to become a negligible constitutional factor. Moreover, the reaction of those few conservatives who were prepared to take a chance in the political arena of revolutionary France left no doubt that they intended to use the veto as a bulwark to control and, if possible, halt the revolutionary process.[27]

Finally, Louis XVI was not the kind of monarch who inspired confidence in the experiment of a constitutional monarchy. He alienated even the moderate representatives of the new political order because he was as unable to give up the notion of his own personal sovereignty as he was unwilling to take the step from *premier gentilhomme* of the aristocratic political nation to the national monarch, which alone could have kept his head on his shoulders. French radicalism was thus inevitably driven towards republicanism. This proved to be of more than national importance. For French historical experience created a political pattern which was to fascinate and to horrify Europe for much of the nineteenth century.

III

Let me now turn to my second point of comparison. The radical answer on both sides of the Channel to the question of representation was, of course, universal suffrage and equal representation. But this identity of political aims hides the fact that the ways in which political representation was envisaged in the two political cultures differed in some important respects. Once again it mattered that the English radicals looked to an established representative system which they wanted to reform, while the founding fathers of French radicalism had to work on practically virgin political soil. The problems on which each side focused were therefore different.

English radicals could and did concentrate on voting rights and electoral districts, but paid surprisingly little attention to such questions as

---

[27] See my 'Die Französische Revolution und der moderne politische Konservativismus' in R. Koselleck and R. Reichardt (eds.), *Die Französische Revolution als Bruch des gesellschaftlichen Bewußtseins* (Munich, 1988), pp. 618–22.

the control of the representatives or the nature of the mandate in the representative democracy they wanted to create. This is hard to explain since there is ample evidence that they were fully aware of the problems involved. The constitution of the London Corresponding Society, for instance, took exemplary care to provide for the most direct kind of democracy. Delegates to the General Committee, which was the legislative body of the society, were to be instructed and had to report back to their divisions before they could decide on matters on which they had not received instructions. The only discretionary power left to the delegate was thus to decide whether he had been instructed or not concerning the matter under discussion. But he could hardly make much of it. For every delegate had a subdelegate at his side who had no vote and was, strictly speaking, not allowed to join in the debates. Officially he was only to replace the delegate if he should be unable to attend a meeting. But his real function was that of a watch-dog who would keep the division informed about the conduct of its delegate. Moreover, the constitution permitted a referendum on all fundamental questions. These regulations were by no means a dead letter.[28] In many disputes within the London Corresponding Society, it was the practice of democracy which was at issue.[29]

Why, then, did so little of this discourse on democracy reappear in the programme for parliamentary reform? Surely, it could not have been presumed that the rules which governed the relationship between Parliament and the republic of gentlemen would also apply in the kind of mass democracy which would result from the introduction of manhood suffrage. And it is hardly imaginable that the radicals really believed annual parliaments to be an adequate solution. Why did these experts on the strangest kind of franchise arrangement in the most rotten of boroughs have so little to say about how elections should be organised in the brave new world of universal suffrage and equal representation? Why were powerful conservative answers to the radical challenge, such as the doctrine of interest representation, so little understood and so unsatisfactorily dealt with? Was it just that, like the constitutional framework as a whole, a great deal of English representative practice was simply taken for granted? It does seem that political representation formed so natural a part of English political culture that the advocates of radical reform had a blunted sensibility to its problems.

A similar effect was produced by the fact that the English radicals were

---

[28] London Corresponding Society, *The Report of the Committee of Constitution* (London, 1794); *The Report of the Committee, Appointed to Revise and Abridge a Former Report on the Constitution* (London, 1794).

[29] See, for example, PRO, Treasury Solicitor's Papers 11/954/3498, Grove's Report of the Proceedings of Division No. 2, and the discussion in my *Politische Aufklärung und plebejisches Publikum*, pp. 184–218, especially pp. 184–207.

in a position to attack the existing representative system for deviating from its own implicit principles. They were eager to discover corrupt practices of all sorts and expose such absurdities as rotten boroughs, because they believed that their revelations would arouse the indignation of all sensible men to a degree which Parliament could not permit itself to ignore. Eventually, they hoped, the pressure of public opinion would become so great that Parliament would yield and reform itself.[30] Edmund Burke, as sharp-eyed as ever before the truth of his own predictions overwhelmed his common sense, was not deceived by the radical rhetoric of restoring the constitution. He was immediately aware that the French Revolution gave a dangerous boost to the democratic reinterpretation of the 1688 settlement which had been going on for some time. It threatened to turn radicalism from a fringe phenomenon into a political force. Burke's reaction reveals once again, this time from the opposite angle, the political soil on which English radicalism had grown. For Burke tried to counteract the radical reinterpretation of British political culture by rethinking Whiggism in a conservative fashion.[31]

In setting all hope on the moral force of public opinion, the English radicals assumed that the seed of the democratic revolution had already been sown in 1688–9 and, at the same time, took account of the sovereignty of the very Parliament they criticized. This was the essence of the strategy of constitutional information to which English radicalism adhered throughout the closing decades of the eighteenth century. It was a strategy deeply rooted in the political culture to which the Revolution of 1688 had given rise. But the radicals' staunch belief in its potential for reform rested on their inability to recognise the socio-political function of the deformations they wished to correct. They never realised, for instance, that the constitution could do without a general social restriction of the vote only because the ruling class was in perfect control of the electoral system through the very absurdities they attacked.[32]

This very shortcoming, however, gave English radicalism a distinctly moral appeal which outweighed its apparent lack of practical political imagination. English radicalism claimed, on the whole quite successfully, to be the conscience of a political culture based on representation. As such, however, it shared the fate of most consciences. For its admonitions

---

[30] For the strategy in general, see E. C. Black, *The Association: British Extra-Parliamentary Organization 1769–1793* (Cambridge, Mass., 1963), and T. M. Parsinnen, 'Association, convention, and anti-Parliament in British radical politics, 1771–1848', *English Historical Review*, 88 (1973), pp. 504–33.

[31] See my forthcoming *Aufklärung und konservatives Denken*.

[32] On the complexities of the system, see the magisterial work by Frank O'Gorman, *Voters, Patrons, and Parties. The Unreformed Electorate in Hanoverian England 1734–1832* (Oxford, 1989).

were only heeded when the pangs could no longer be ignored, and when that happened it was soothed at the lowest possible cost. For over a century the indignation about defects in the representative system which radical propaganda aroused was easily bought off by piecemeal reforms. And the radicals themselves were often deceived about the real political importance of these measures because they underestimated the expertise of the ruling class in manipulating electoral systems.

In France, on the contrary, there was no tradition of representation on which to build. It is true that there was continuity of a sort with the forms of representation which had been used in the elections for the States General.[33] But these arrangements were traditional only in an artificial sense and had to be revised anyway when the regional structure of France was revolutionised. The institution of the new electoral system thus inevitably became a battleground where the various political factions could and had to test their relative strength.

As a matter of course French radicalism raised its head in the debate about the first electoral law after the fall of the *ancien régime* which was eventually passed on 22 December 1789. Robespierre, the arch-radical who was soon to be called the incorruptible, was among the first to attack the distinction between active and passive citizens as utterly incompatible with the Declaration of Rights and the principle of national sovereignty. He did not leave it in doubt that he regarded property as a natural right. But he fought passionately against the idea that the size of a man's property could be made the measure of his right to political participation. Could a nation, only weeks after it had broken the chains of inequality which it had carried in the past, fail to pass the test of the future? Had the Revolution really been nothing more than a change of yokes, putting the aristocracy of money in the place of the aristocracy of birth?[34] Robespierre refused to believe this. And the Abbé Gregoire, Marat, Desmoulins and many others followed suit.[35] They lost the battle over the definition of national sovereignty, just as they were to lose the war. But the constitution of 1793, the first which was written with a radical pen, provided for manhood suffrage, single-member constituencies of nearly

---

[33] E. Schmnitt, *Repräsentation und Revolution. Eine Untersuchung zur Genesis der kontinentalen Theorie und Praxis parlamentarischer Repräsentation aus der Herrschaftspraxis des Ancien Régime in Frankreich (1770–1789)* (Munich, 1969).

[34] Maximilien-François-Marie-Isidor Robespierre, 'Sur la nécessité de révoquer le decret sur le marc d'argent' in J. Poperen (ed.), *Robespierre. Textes choisis*, 3 vols. (Paris, 1974), vol. I, p. 67.

[35] On the early debate about representation, see K. M. Baker, 'Representation' in Baker, *Political Culture of the Old Regime*, pp. 233–57, and P. Guenniffey, 'Les assemblées et la représentation' in Lucas, *Political Culture*, pp. 469–92.

equal size and direct elections.[36] It established a constitutional norm to which French radicalism was to turn throughout the nineteenth century. The consequences of the debate about property qualifications were far-reaching. Whereas the campaign against corruption gave English radicalism a moral appeal, the attack on property qualifications for the right to vote inflicted the stigma of class treason on the French radicals despite the support they could draw on from 1789. As early as that, the Revolution revealed itself as an ambiguous heritage for the propertied classes.

The radical advocates of national sovereignty did not take long to realize that a representative system without social restrictions was no sufficient guarantee for democracy. It remained to ensure that the represented could control their representatives between elections. The revolutionary democrats were keenly aware of the problem even if they did not go so far as Rousseau in his fundamental criticism of representative government.[37] In a speech before the Convention on 10 May 1793, Robespierre made some far-reaching proposals which confirmed his reputation as the guardian of the people's political rights. He blamed the constitution for taking all possible precautions to prevent an insurrection of the people, but none against 'la revolte de ses délègués'.[38] At that stage the incorruptible seems still to have been confident that it was not only possible, but easy to find a way to organise democratic control which would be 'equally distant from the storms of absolute democracy and the perfidious tranquility of a representative despotism'.[39]

Drawing on the tradition of civic humanism, Robespierre called for constitutional safeguards against the concentration and the misuse of power.[40] He demanded that the people be given the right to revoke the mandates of their representatives, and suggested that all those who had been entrusted with power should be formally exonerated at the end of their term of office by their constituents. There was to be no need to convict them of any misconduct. A simple vote of no-confidence was to suffice to make them ineligible for office in the future.[41] Moreover, Robespierre set great hopes on the total publicity of all political proceedings. He declared:

---

[36] For the text, see Jacques Godechot, *Les Constitution de la France depuis 1789* (Paris, 1970), pp. 79–92, and especially pp. 83–6, for the articles referring to the electoral systems and representation.

[37] See I. Fetscher, *Rousseaus politische Philosophie. Zur Geschichte des demokratischen Freiheitsbegriffs* (Frankfurt, 1975), pp. 276–306, especially pp. 276–91, on the Jacobin attitude towards Rousseau.

[38] Robespierre, 'Sur le gouvernement représentatif' in Poperen, *Robespierre. Textes choisis*, vol. II, p. 143.   [39] *Ibid.*, p. 147.   [40] *Ibid.*, p. 148.

[41] *Ibid.*, p. 153.

The whole nation has the right to know the conduct of his mandataries. If it was possible the assembly of the delegates of the people should deliberate in the presence of the whole people. A vast and majestic building with room for 12,000 spectators should be the place where the legislature holds its sessions.[42]

Less than a year later the champion of the people's rights had turned into a defender of revolutionary government which suspended popular participation in politics and presumed to act as popular sovereignty's virtuous and disinterested guardian.[43] He was in all probability sincere when he said that the revolutionary government would only be a temporary measure which it had been necessary to take because the republic was beleaguered by enemies on all sides and threatened by treason from within. But his speeches suggest that his change of mind also had more fundamental reasons. Even he was beginning to revise his ideas on democracy and national sovereignty in a way which was to give the word 'temporary' a quite contrary meaning, for it seems that the people whom he had once hailed as the fountain of virtue and the pillar of the republic had lost the confidence of its most fervent spokesman.

The story of the first French republic need not occupy us here at any length. It has often been told and from many angles. The class constellations and the telling ambiguities of the economic and social policies of the Convention have rightly received great attention. In this chapter I want to emphasise another aspect which has become of singular importance for the history of democracy in general and for the history of radicalism in particular. The first years of the republic saw a confrontation between two concepts of democracy equally radical in their interpretation of the principle of popular sovereignty, but radically different in their understanding of what popular government really meant. The climax of this confrontation came after the destruction of the Girondins when no common enemy remained against whom the popular movement could be used as a weapon. The Jacobin radical democrats and the *sans-culotte* radical democrats now faced each other unprotected by the masks of rhetoric and idealisation. It was a great moment in the history of democracy. Suddenly and quite unexpectedly the democrats met the *demos* which they had idealised but never really looked in the face. To their surprise and horror they found themselves confronted with a quite different idea of democracy.[44]

---

[42] *Ibid.*, p. 150.
[43] On this point, cf. G. Rudé, *Robespierre. Portrait of a Revolutionary Democrat* (New York, 1975), part 3, ch. 1.
[44] See my 'Demokraten und Sansculotten. Zur Gründungsgeschichte kleinbürgerlicher Protestbewegungen' in E. Wangermann, B. Wagner and M. Weinzierl (eds.), *Ça ira. 200 Jahre Französische Revolution* (Vienna, 1991). With J. L. Talmon, *The Origins of Totalitarian Democracy* (London, 1952), in mind, we might also invoke the idea of a totalitarian democracy.

Sans-culotte democrats deeply mistrusted the representative democracy which the Jacobin radicals clung to. They knew instinctively that representation could not but lead to the formation of a new political class, 'an aristocracy of representatives' as they called it tellingly,[45] which would forever stand between them and their sovereign will. The *sans-culottes* had instead an almost physical understanding of national sovereignty and popular government. To them they meant the bodily presence of the sovereign and direct democracy of a kind which would not be satisfied with such constitutional tricks as instructions for delegates or the possibility of revoking a mandate. Moreover, the *sans-culotte* democrat mistrusted the democracy of the word which the Jacobin radicals practised in their clubs as well as in the National Convention.[46] Words tended to obscure things; they placed themselves in some incomprehensible manner between the people and political power. The aristocracy of representatives was also an aristocracy of the word, whereas *sans-culotte* political culture was essentially non-discursive. There, words served other purposes. They were integrated into group rituals and had to evoke solidarity and courage. Finally, *sans-culotte* democracy showed shockingly little regard for the civil liberties of the individual which the Jacobins would not deny, even if they were ready to suspend them in a state of emergency to save the Revolution and the republic. For the *sans-culotte* democrat democracy meant popular justice which could be and was used to punish all sorts of nonconformity. The suspect was guilty for the simple reason that he could be suspected, and any deviation from a common norm of behaviour was grounds for suspicion.[47]

Despite these differences it was difficult for the radical democrats to suppress the popular movement which they had so often used and which had, after all, established an independent claim to the Revolution in the dramatic summer and autumn of 1789, and many times since. But Robespierre argued ingeniously that the people's idea of democracy endangered the people's revolution. In his speech on 5 February 1794 he defined democracy, clearly distinguishing it from spontaneous and unorganised popular interventions into politics:

Democracy is not a state in which the people, split into a hundred thousand fragments, decides the fate of society at large by taking isolated, hasty and contradictory measures. In fact, such a government has never existed; and if it

---

45 Quoted by Albert Soboul, *Les Sans-culottes parisiens en l'an II. Mouvement populaire et gouvernement révolutionnaire (1793–1794)* (Paris, 1968), p. 104.

46 Cf. E. Kennedy, *The Jacobin Clubs in the French Revolution: The First Years* (Princeton, N.J., 1982), and still C. Brinton, *The Jacobins* (New York, 1930).

47 See Soboul, *Sans-culottes*. This very readable abridged edition of Soboul's *thèse* gives a vivid description of political life in the sections of Paris. More theoretical in his approach to the problem of democracy is K. Tonnesson, 'La démocratie directe sous la Révolution française – le cas des districts et sections de Paris' in Lucas, *Political Culture*, pp. 295–307.

were ever to exist it would lead the people to despotism. Democracy is a state in which the sovereign people, guided by laws of its own creation, directly discharges such functions as are within its powers to discharge: those that are not, it delegates to others.[48]

Robespierre still admitted that democratic control remained a problem in a system based on representation, but he now offered a solution which civic humanism had always turned to in order to overcome contradictions: the appeal to virtue. It was the virtue of the representatives which would ensure that revolutionary government would not itself degenerate into representative despotism.[49]

IV

The clash of Jacobin and *sans-culotte* democracy highlights a problem which was to accompany radicalism throughout the nineteenth and early twentieth centuries not only in England and France but everywhere, and which leads me to my third and last point of comparison: how did the radical avant-garde conceive of their relationship to the mass basis which they tried to create for themselves and for whose political rights they fought?

In England this problem posed itself at first as one of mobilisation. As early as the 1770s the radical advocates of a thorough reform of Parliament had realised that they would not get very far if they relied on the educated public alone. The sort of mass pressure which was needed to overcome the resistance of Parliament could only be generated if the radical propaganda reached people farther down the social scale. This, however, meant that propaganda techniques had to be developed which the uneducated mass would be able to comprehend. In August 1782, for instance, a circular of the Society for Constitutional Information called for 'essays...in the Country papers, addressed to the collective body of the people, descriptive of their primary rights as commoners of this country, and calling upon them to reflect how deeply every individual is interested in the proposed reform'. These addresses were to be written 'in a language adapted to the comprehension of the unlearned, and yet demonstrative to the most enlightened'.[50]

In the 1790s, when English radicalism for the first time came into actual contact with the man in the street, mobilisation remained, of course, an

---

[48] Robespierre, 'Sur les principes de moral politique' in Poperen, *Robespierre. Textes choisis*, vol. III, p. 113. The translation follows Rudé, *Robespierre*, p. 120.

[49] *Ibid.*, p. 117.

[50] Society for Constitutional Information, *Constitutional Tracts*, 2 vols. (London, 1783), vol. I, p. 57.

important concern. But the dissemination of constitutional information, even on a level 'adapted to the unlearned', no longer seemed sufficient. The corruptibility and political apathy of the common people began to be seen as the lesser problems. Rethinking and extending the paradigm of civic virtue, the radical avant-garde became much more worried by the incapacity for political participation which they observed in the mass of the people. Was it really desirable to give the vote to 'tradesmen, shopkeepers, and mechanics'[51] who lacked the knowledge and the judgement to use it responsibly? Was it not 'madness to reform before we instruct?'[52] As in France, the realisation that the empirical *demos* had little in common with the *demos* of the radical imagination demanded a major revision of radical strategy and thought. The English radicals concluded that mobilisation would have to go hand in hand with the political education of the recruits to the cause, and, in a wider sense, of the population at large. In the event, the reform movement concentrated on the political socialisation of its following to an extent which endangered its capacity for mass mobilisation. The London Corresponding Society, for instance, adopted rules to regulate the conduct of its members which it required fervent believers in the cause and ascetic natures to accept.[53] The divisions were turned into political classrooms from which all plebeian sociability was banned. Drinking, eating and smoking were forbidden,[54] and doorkeepers were used to make sure that only sober and decent persons were admitted into the room. No wonder that attendance was often poor even if the rules were not rigidly enforced.[55]

The educational programme of the reformers clearly went beyond the dissemination of political knowledge. It goes without saying that the lecture courses and reading lessons which the reforming societies organised were used to criticise the prevailing political conditions and to propagate radical ideas. But they claimed to do more than this because their ultimate aim was to enable the political apprentice to acquire political knowledge on his own without intellectual guidance. This may not have been the case; but the claim in itself is important. Moreover, the mass membership was to be trained in the democracy of the word. The members of the society were to be made familiar with the rules of rational debate and to learn 'the great moral lesson to "hear and forbear"' as Francis Place put it.[56] The foremost duty of a member of the London Corresponding

[51] BL, Add. MS 27, 814, fo. 26.
[52] PRO, Treasury Solicitor's Papers 11/954/3498 fol. 9; see also London Corresponding Society, *Report on the Constitution*, p. 5.
[53] See my *Politische Aufklärung und plebejisches Publikum*, pp. 207.
[54] BL, Add. MS 27, 808, fo. 10.
[55] See E. P. Thompson, *The Making of the English Working Class*, 2nd edn (Harmondsworth, 1968), pp. 167–9.   [56] BL, Add. MS 27, 808, fo. 60.

Society was thus 'to habituate himself both in and out of this Society, to an orderly and amicable manner of reasoning'. He was 'specially to observe the following Rules of ORDER' which were detailed instructions about how to behave in a debate.[57]

Looking back not in anger but with complacency, Francis Place showed little interest in what had happened to the cause of parliamentary reform. He underlined instead that even if the London Corresponding Society had not gained its political ends,

the moral effects of the society were very great indeed, it induced men to read books, instead of spending their time at public houses, it induced them to love their own homes, it taught them to think, to respect themselves, and to desire to educate their children...In fact it gave a new stimulus to a large mass of men who had hitherto been but too justly considered as incapable of any but the grossest pursuits, and sensual enjoyments.[58]

No doubt Place saw things through rose-coloured spectacles.[59] But it should not be overlooked that the radical reformers kept the mass movement active for four years, despite the war with France, and lost ground only through unprecedented governmental pressure. This would not have been possible if political education had only been imposed from above but not sought from below. Men like Thomas Hardy and Francis Place were not typical of the radical reformers of the 1790s, but they certainly represented the type of citizens which the movement wanted to produce: hard working, sober, disinterested and enlightened men who proved that democracy was possible after all, and silenced the argument that only property guaranteed a level of education without which political participation would be hazardous.

In France such a strategy of political education would have been abortive. The radical intelligentsia may have seen the need for it. Robespierre, for example, spoke of the necessity 'to create a new people' when he presented to the Convention the plan for national education produced by his Montagnard colleague Lepelletier.[60] But even if the political situation had permitted the people's gradual preparation for democracy, it is unlikely that the popular movement would have been docile enough. The *menu peuple* never forgot that it had an independent claim to the Revolution. After the flight of the King had sealed the fate of the moderate revolution, their hour had come again. And this time they

---

[57] London Corresponding Society, *Report on the Constitution*, p. 6.
[58] BL, Add. MS 27, 808, fo. 60.
[59] PRO, Treasury Solicitor's Papers 11/965/3510, A/ part 5; 'Voluntary examination of Gosling' gives a quite different description of the division meetings.
[60] Robespierre, 'Plan d'éducation nationale de Michel Lepelletier' in Poperen, *Robespierre. Textes choisis*, vol. II, p. 159.

were determined not to pave the way for others. The invasion of the sections of Paris gave the popular movement a permanent organisational structure of its own, where the club rules of the revolutionary intelligentsia did not apply and where it could acquire that distinct political identity which has been sketched above.[61]

Under these circumstances the revolutionary democrats in the Legislative Assembly and later in the Convention regarded a strategy of repressive alliance as their only choice, even if this meant walking a political tightrope. The idea was to use the *sans-culottes* as a weapon against the enemies of the Revolution, while keeping them at a good distance from all positions of real power. The Robespierrist wing of the radical revolutionaries was the last to fall off the rope. They used the popular movement quite successfully against their rivals in the power struggles among the revolutionary elite, but also managed to keep it under control. Whenever the political pressure from below became too great, they used the safety valve of concessions in economic and social policy without yielding to the *sans-culotte* idea of a moral economy.

The climax in this drama of ambiguity came when the Convention eventually decided to establish a revolutionary government to overcome the manifold difficulties with which it was faced. In the years 1793 and 1795 the idea of a democracy by substitution was born in which a disinterested, austere and virtuous revolutionary democratic elite took the place of a people as yet unfit to fill its proper place. Naturally, the substitute *demos* could ill afford to tolerate the real *demos*. And it had less and less need to do so, for the Terror deprived the popular movement of its political utility while fostering the people's illusion that revolutionary justice was finally done. The functions which the 'people in action' had fulfilled in the revolutionary process were all effectively taken over by the revolutionary government itself. There was now no more need for a *Journée* to break a political deadlock, to keep alive the idea that the Revolution revenged the wrongs done to the people or to inspire fear in the hearts of all enemies of the Revolution. The bureaucrats of the Terror performed these tasks much more efficiently and, so it appeared to the self-appointed guardians of the popular sovereign, much more virtuously. The radical democrats were finally in a position to get rid of popular government. The independent organisational base of the *sans-culottes* came under attack early on when the sections of Paris were forbidden to sit *en permanence*. In the following months one after the other of the popular societies founded to counteract this measure fell silent as the pressure from above mounted. The elimination of the popular leadership

[61] Cf. M. Genty, *Paris 1789–1795. L'Apprentissage de la citoyenneté* (Paris, 1987).

came next. By the time the Thermidorians dealt the last blow to the popular movement it had lost most of its former striking force.

Nineteenth-century French radicalism came back to the specific historical constellations and options of the years 1792–5. The strategy of repressive alliance can be detected, if only faintly, in the July Revolution of 1830 and reappeared in the policies of the provisional government during the Revolution of 1848. The twin concepts of revolutionary government and democracy by substitution were rethought in paradigmatic manner and absorbed into the revolutionary socialist tradition in the course of the nineteenth century. At first, Buonarotti combined them with a conspiracy theory which reduced the concept of revolution to the idea of a *coup d'état* engineered by professional revolutionaries. Then Blanqui added the notion of an educational dictatorship which was to make use of the totalitarian potential of state power revealed during the Jacobin democracy by substitution to create a people worthy of democracy.[62]

[62] Cf. Furet, 'Révolution française et tradition jacobine', pp. 335–9.

5 Revolution, war and the nation state: the British and French experiences 1789–1801

Clive Emsley

Britain and France were the principal opponents in the French revolutionary and Napoleonic wars. From the French Revolution emerged an ideology which, during the first half of the nineteenth century at least, was to fire political debate and action in Europe. Britain, in turn, was the home of the pamphleteer who was to produce the most potent counter-revolutionary ideology, Edmund Burke. Yet while they were opponents, in broad areas, the Revolution and the war produced similar experiences and developments in the two countries: the Revolution both excited political debate and prompted checks on this debate – the new intensity and style of war reinforced these developments; revolution and war required, and fostered, mass participation and as ruling groups and their opponents struggled for the hearts and minds of the respective populations so intolerance towards heterodoxy worsened; revolution and war engendered a new style of militaristic nationalism in both countries. Moreover, action by one state necessitated a reaction by the other; in the processes of ideological, organisational and nationalist development the two warring states fed off each other. The British state[1] emerged essentially unscathed from the experience of war and the fear and threat of revolution; but while the Revolution brought dramatic changes to the French state, it will be argued here that the pressures and strains of war during the 1790s fostered the recreation of a centralised system which differed from its predecessor largely inasmuch as it was far more competent.

I

Debate about the origins and nature of civil government had been central to the Enlightenment. In many respects Britain and France had provided models for different kinds of government in this debate: Britain (or rather

---

[1] Throughout this chapter I will use the term 'the British state' with reference to the apparatus of government of England, Ireland, Scotland and Wales. However, the constitutional ideology which I contrast with that of France is essentially English.

more specifically England) with a boasted balanced constitution of King, Lords and Commons; France with an absolutist monarchy and professional bureaucracy. While there were those who professed to abhor everything about the other country, there were others who sought to learn from, and to advocate change along the lines of, the other.[2] Political ideas and principles were important to the way in which governments acted in both countries during the eighteenth century; they spurred government apologists to explain and to justify the existing systems and practices, as much as did the need to respond to critics and reformers. Events in France in 1787–9 naturally intensified political debate within that country; the financial crisis, the summoning of the Estates General, the call for the *cahiers des doléances*, all suggested that some kind of change was not only necessary, but was also likely. In Britain the coincidence of revolution in France with the centenary of her own Glorious Revolution initially fostered a self-satisfaction among conservatives that France was at long last following the lead taken in Britain 100 years before. But this coincidence also excited and encouraged different kinds of reformers: those campaigning for the abolition of slavery, those who wanted a repeal of the Test and Corporation Acts, and those who, relatively quiescent for the past five years, sought a measure of parliamentary reform. For some parliamentary reformers the French Revolution suggested that the French would now overtake British claims to being in the forefront of constitutional monarchism and individual liberty. Some reformers fell away from the cause as the French Revolution lurched into republicanism, regicide and terror; others positively gloried in the use of French terms such as 'citizen' and *sans-culotte* even when such terms became more subversive with the outbreak of war. As the 1790s wore on, punctuated by acute provision crises and with the demands for more and more men and more and more money to fight the war against France, some British radicals, stiffened by Irish rebels, entered the twilight world of conspiracy hoping for some kind of insurrectionary upheaval along the lines of events in France.

The early 1790s saw the first significant appearance of ordinary working men participating in political action and debate on their own account. Gwyn A. Williams has insisted that, '[N]o matter how radical the differences between the two countries, in both Britain and France, it was in 1792 that "the people" entered politics'.[3] The class element here has skewed perspectives on the period and the recent fascination with 'history from below' has led, perhaps, to an overconcentration on radical ideology

---

[2] Derek Jarrett, *The Begetters of Revolution: England's Involvement with France 1759–1789* (London, 1973).

[3] Gwyn A. Williams, *Artisans and Sans-Culottes: Popular Movements in France and Britain during the French Revolution*, 2nd edn (London, 1989), p. 4.

and on the development of popular movements, both French *sans-culottes* and British 'popular' Jacobins. Intellectual debate about the nature of civil society was conducted at a high level in both countries, at least in the early years of the Revolution. In France the deputies of the National Assembly wrestled with questions of man's political rights and the relationship between the constitutional monarch and the representatives of the nation. A mass of legislation was passed, not the least of which was that concerning local government and seeking to restore the natural areas and boundaries of local life, and that which established a central and uniform system of justice. Faith in 'the people' and their use of their new 'liberty' was naive and contributed, in the long run, to many of the Revolution's problems; but here were political actors, inspired by political principles and theories, seeking to regenerate their country. The revolutionaries of all factions were conscious of living '[d]ans ce siècle de lumières, où la sain philosophie a repris son empire'.[4] It was precisely the appeal to philosophy and the inspiration of abstract concepts and theory which were the focus of Edmund Burke's conservative counterblast of November 1790, *The Reflections on the Revolution in France*. But while he was the first, and undoubtedly the most influential and long-lasting, Burke was not the only conservative commentator who reacted to the Revolution and raised the temperature of political debate; there were, for example, over sixty British-born contributors to the first six volumes of that scourge of radicalism, *The Anti-Jacobin Review*.[5] Burke's diatribe also brought forth a flood of responses of which Tom Paine's *The Rights of Man* is unquestionably the raciest and best-known, but, in comparison with, for example, James Mackintosh's *Vindiciae Gallicae*, it is by no means the most intellectually coherent and cogent.[6] Furthermore, while much history from below has concentrated on Paine and popular radical literature, criticism of Pitt's government and of his war policy, as well as demands for reform continued to be made at a more intellectual level throughout the 1790s, especially among Dissenters in the Midlands and the north.[7]

The intellectual debates were popularised and simplified into propaganda and slogans in both Britain and France. In France this was integral

---

[4] This from the speech of the Vicomte de Noailles during the celebrated debate on the abolition of feudalism, 4 August 1789, *Archives Parlementaires*, série I, vol. VIII, p. 344.

[5] Emily Loraine de Montluzin, *The Anti-Jacobins 1798–1800: The Early Contributors to the 'Anti-Jacobin Review'* (London, 1988).

[6] James Mackintosh, *Vindiciae Gallicae. Defence of the French Revolution and its English Admirers against the Accusations of the Right Hon. Edmund Burke* (London, 1791).

[7] J. E. Cookson, *The Friends of Peace: Anti-War Liberalism in England 1793–1815* (Cambridge, 1982). For the intellectual debate in general, see H. T. Dickinson, *Liberty and Property: Political Ideology in Eighteenth-Century Britain* (London, 1977), chs. 7 and 8; T. P. Schofield, 'Conservative political thought in Britain in response to the French Revolution', *Historical Journal*, 29, 3 (1986), pp. 601–22.

to the Revolution from the beginning; the Third Estate was drawn into participation in politics by the calling of the Estates General, and was barraged with polemic of which the Abbé Sieyès's questions are the most well-known and were, for contemporaries, the most pertinent: ' 1. Qu'est-ce que le Tiers état? TOUT. 2. Qu'a-t-il été jusqu'à present dans l'ordre politique? RIEN. 3. Que demande-t-il? A ETRE QUELQUE CHOSE.'⁸ The Revolution gloried in the sovereignty of the people, therefore the people had to be educated as well as wooed and won. While such propaganda was initially directed at the more well-to-do, the 'active citizen', and while it is clear that such citizens were keen to be rid of their lower-class street allies, numbers of the latter did play an active role in political life until they were disqualified by new legislation in 1790. Some then continued to involve themselves in political debates through the popular societies, and radicals maintained their appeals to, and propaganda for, the 'passive citizens.'⁹ However, from the very beginning toleration and the liberty of the press were undermined by the excitement and single-mindedness of men convinced that their assessment of the remedies for society's ills were the only ones acceptable. Even in the early months of the Revolution, journalists and propagandists who dared to criticise the idols of the day were subjected to threats and intimidation.¹⁰ The reformers in the National Assembly themselves received great quantities of unsolicited advice and censure from more progressive thinkers and publicists. The first regular number of Jean-Paul Marat's *L'Ami du Peuple* appeared on 12 September 1789 and it was intended, its editor explained, to be written in the 'severe but honest tone of a man who wishes to tell the truth without breaking the conventions of society';¹¹ but Marat's tone could often be intolerant. As the Revolution lurched from crisis to crisis so such intolerance grew, and when war put the very existence of the Revolution at stake, the opportunity for political debate and opposition was effectively silenced.

The police of eighteenth-century Paris were always concerned about subversive talk, though they found little evidence of it at least before the middle of the century. Mid-eighteenth-century Paris had about one drinking place for every 200 inhabitants,¹² yet it does not appear that any were noted for the kind of political discussions to be found in a few London, and even English provincial, taverns, where artisans, well versed

---

⁸ Abbé Emmanuel-Joseph Sieyès, *Qu'est-ce que le tiers état?*, 3rd edn (Paris, 1789).
⁹ R. B. Rose, *The Making of the Sans-Culottes* (Manchester, 1983).
¹⁰ W. J. Murray, *The Right-Wing Press in the French Revolution 1789–92* (London, 1987), pp. 15 and 100–2.
¹¹ Louis R. Gottschalk, *Jean-Paul Marat: A Study in Radicalism* (Chicago Press, Ill., 1967), p. 53.
¹² Thomas Brennan, *Public Drinking and Popular Culture in Eighteenth-Century Paris* (Princeton, N.J., 1988), pp. 76, 272–3.

in the political ideology of the seventeenth century, debated among themselves and with their social superiors.[13] The 'freeborn Englishmen' had no plebeian equivalent in France, and while the Frenchmen had taken to the streets to defend their *parlements*, there had been nothing in France to match the sustained lower-class participation in the Wilkes disorders. Propaganda about the French Revolution was not circulated for the great mass of the British population until 1792. That year saw both the growth of the popular radical societies, like the London Corresponding Society and the Sheffield Society for Constitutional Information, and as, towards the end of the year the victories of the French armies and the publications of the radical societies appeared to be winning more and more adherents, so loyalists counter-attacked with the creation of the Associations for the Preservation of Liberty and Property against Republicans and Levellers and with publications of their own. In the indirect, decentralised fashion, typical of the eighteenth-century British state, the courts were enlisted to silence the radical propaganda; and as, from 1 February 1793, Britain found herself enmeshed in the new kind of war, so popular radicalism was more readily equated with succouring an atheistical, levelling creed. The propertied classes had no intention of letting the lower orders be drawn into the political nation as actors, but they recognised that they had to counter the heady appeals to the rights of man and the sovereignty of the people. The mass of the population had to be convinced of why it was in their interest, and indeed in the order of things, that society and the political structure should not be changed radically. British propaganda stressed that this was a new kind of war against 'An Enemy of a new kind...who fights not merely to subdue States, but to dissolve Society – not to extend Empire, but to subvert Government – not to introduce a particular Religion, but to extirpate all Religion.'[14] Paid Treasury writers like John Bowles pitched their argument at the more educated level of society; other conservative propagandists, most notably Hannah More, directed their attention to those lower down the social scale. Besides the perceived need, simply because of the Revolution, to address people who were generally outside the political nation, in both Britain and France the new kind of war unleashed by the Revolution, itself required a new kind of mass support. This, in turn, contributed to the propaganda directed towards those previously outside the political nation.

---

13 Nicholas Hans, *New Trends in Education in the Eighteenth Century* (London, 1951), pp. 169–70; John Money, 'Taverns, coffee houses and clubs: local politics and popular articulacy in the Birmingham area in the age of the American Revolution', *Historical Journal*, 14 (1971), pp. 15–47.
14 Anon, *Objections to the War Examined and Refuted by a Friend of Peace* (London, 1793), p. 3.

II

While the Enlightenment prided itself on its reason and its humanity, it was not noted for its pacific nature. The 100 years before the outbreak of the French Revolution had been punctuated by war. Yet as far as the conflict between the major powers of Europe were concerned, these were relatively restrained affairs. The small professional armies of monarchs sought to outmanoeuvre their enemies, only coming to battle when they perceived a distinct advantage, or when battle was unavoidable. There had been considerable debate over the use of skirmishers, and artillery, and over the composition of armies during the century. In 1772 the Comte de Guibert published his *Essai général de la tactique*; the reasoning and significance of the book was initially overshadowed by the victories and reputation of Frederick the Great, yet it provoked increasing interest and discussion.[15] Guibert argued for armies to be much more adaptable in the ways that they deployed on the battlefield; and he believed that the ideal kind of army was one composed of citizen soldiers motivated by patriotism. The Revolution enabled the creation of such armies and ushered in a new style of warfare qualitatively and quantitatively different from its eighteenth-century predecessors. The wars of the French Revolution and Napoleon were no longer elaborate games of manoeuvre by small armies; battles became far more frequent and mass armies set out ruthlessly to annihilate their opponents.

The changes in the French army in the years following 1789 were gradual, and not immediately the product of war.[16] Initially the politicians of the new order sought to repudiate war and had no thought of creating a national, citizen army; Dubois de Crancé, himself a former soldier, proposed that the National Assembly set about organising a new kind of citizen army in December 1789: 'C'est maintenant un droit de tous les Français de servir la patrie; c'est un honneur d'être soldat, quand ce titre est celui de défenseur de la constitution de son pays.'[17] But while Dubois can be said to have been following through the logic of the Declaration of the Rights of Man and Citizen, his fellow deputies did not share his enthusiasm. During the first years of the Revolution the Assembly gradually established control over the army, leaving the King as little more than titular head. As this happened the royal army suffered seriously from collapsing discipline, desertion and the emigration of the bulk of its officer corps. Yet at the same time a new force took shape which was, in

---

[15] Jacques Antoine M., Comte de Guibert, *Essai général de la tactique*, 2 vols. (London, 1772).

[16] The following discussion draws heavily on Samuel F. Scott, *The Response of the Royal Army to the French Revolution* (Oxford, 1978).

[17] 16 December 1789, *Archives Parlementaires*, série I, vol. X, p. 520.

some respects, a citizen army – the National Guard. The National Guards were formed in municipalities in 1789 essentially to restore order. In origin the National Guard was similar to the *milice bourgeois*, the part-time militias of respectable townsmen who patrolled town streets during emergencies under the old regime. The *milice bourgeois* had been at their strongest and most effective in the early seventeenth century; but they were never organised on the scale that was to develop with the National Guard. Legislation introduced in December 1790 proposed to restrict membership of the Guard to the property-owning 'active' citizens. Robespierre objected in terms which reflected Dubois de Crancé's idea of the citizens in arms:

Les gardes nationales ne peuvent être que la nation entière armée pour défendre, au besoin, ses droits; il faut que tous les citoyens en âge de porter les armes y soient admis sans aucune distinction. Sans cela, loin d'être les appuis de la liberté, elles en seront les fléaux nécessaires! Il faudra leur appliquer le principe que nous avons rappellé au commencement de cette discussion, en parlent des troupes de ligne; dans tout état où une partie de la nation est armée et l'autre ne l'est pas, la première est maîtresse des destinées de la seconde.

Robespierre's objections were ignored by the assembly; one member allegedly making the comment 'ce seroit le moyen d'armer des troupes de vagabonds'.[18] In the summer of 1791 the Assembly called for volunteers from the Guard to bolster the line army. The volunteers were to continue to receive their higher rates of pay, to elect their officers, and to serve for the term of one campaign only. The number of these 'National Volunteers' was eventually set at 101,000 men, about two-thirds the size of the remnants of the royal army. The royal army itself gradually shook off the problems of the early months of the Revolution; its *emigré* officers were replaced by experienced NCOs who had close ties with their men and who recognised that they owed their recent personal advancement to the Revolution. Improved conditions and recruitment bounties attracted many young men to enlist in 1791. The war brought further changes. In July 1792 50,000 men were called for, and each department was given a quota of men which it had to find. The same procedure was followed in February 1793 with the departmental quotas on this occasion amounting to a total of 300,000 men, to be drawn from bachelors aged between eighteen and forty. The demand for men later in the year, under the celebrated *levée en masse*, provided for a new influx of young men, so that, for the campaigns of 1794, the French army mustered a strength approaching a million.

The army of the Jacobin republic was new in many different respects. It was younger than its old-regime predecessor. While a majority of its

18 Maximilian-François-Marie-Isidor Robespierre, *Oeuvres complètes*, 10 vols. (Paris, 1950–67), vol. VI, pp. 622 and 611.

recruits still came from traditional recruiting areas in the north and east, there were far more men now drawn from the west and the south, and far more peasants than before. From the beginning many of the revolutionaries had sought a unification of France and the destruction of provincialism – as they saw it, this was part and parcel of the advance of enlightenment and civilisation. The army provided a solid manifestation of this new unified France. Of course there were problems: many peasants remained uninterested in 'France' and did not even speak French. In the Vendée it was the requisition of February 1793 which sparked off the uprising. Many recruits appear to have regarded the war as an inconvenient interruption to their lives, and in their letters home they asked about friends at home, and made the usual soldiers' complaints about food and conditions. But the army also had a stiffening of men who were notable for their intense loyalty to their nation and, after the fall of the monarchy, to their republic. The officers, promoted from the ranks of NCOs, were one such group; the patriotic volunteers of 1791 were another. Besides those letters home which listed complaints, there were also those reflecting pride in, and a dedication to, the army, the nation and the Revolution, in ways that were inconceivable before 1789. 'Je vous dirai', wrote trooper Jacques Tuzot,

que les armées de la République vont bien et bientôt les tyrans seront confondus. Les ennemis de la République étant vaincus, j'aurai encore le bonheur de vous aller embrasser et rester, s'il plâit au ciel, au sein de ma famille. C'est là que je goutterai [*sic*] le torrent de délices que donnent l'égalité et la liberté aux hommes libres. C'est là que le cultivateur travaillera paisiblement dans ses champs et en sentira les doux fruits et jouira tout ensemble de la liberté et de l'égalité.[19]

In addition to its new spirit, the Jacobin army also developed some of the tactical adaptabilities advocated by Guibert. By 1794 the *armée du Nord* was deploying large numbers of light infantry as skirmishers, and was attacking in the shallow columns which were to become a characteristic of the revolutionary and Napoleonic infantry.[20]

While it was by no means as successful as the army, the revolutionary navy underwent similar strains in the period of the constitutional monarchy, and similar subsequent changes.[21] The eighteenth-century battleship was, by the standards of the times, the most technically sophisticated of all the weapons of war; it required capable seamen and capable commanders. Seamen might be recruited from coastal areas, and

---

[19] Quoted in Jean-Paul Bertaud, *La Revolution armée: les soldats-citoyens et la Révolution Française* (Paris, 1979), p. 220.

[20] Hew Strachan, *European Armies and the Conduct of War* (London, 1983), p. 42.

[21] Norman Hampson, *Le Marin de l'An II. Mobilisation de la flotte de l'océan, 1793–1794* (Paris, 1959).

some capable men were promoted to fill the gaps left by *emigré* officers; but the new French commanders were not as experienced nor as skilled as their British opponents, and the Jacobin fleet suffered a serious setback when the loss of Toulon handed a significant percentage of its ships over to their enemies. Even so, massive efforts were made in the naval arsenals to put fleets to sea and to maintain them, and many French seamen fought with the same kind of new, patriotic fervour as the soldiers. Like the soldiers too, the French seamen provided myths and martyrs for the republic, notably with *Le Vengeur du peuple* sunk on the Glorious First of June; and as prisoners of war they maintained this fervour to an extent which frightened many of their British captors.

The French military was not maintained at the levels reached in 1794. There was no new national levy called for until the crisis of 1798 prompted the *loi Jourdan*, the legislation which was to provide Napoleon with his annual intake of conscripts. Many soldiers simply set off for home during the Thermidorian and Directorial regimes. By 1797 the army strength was a little under 400,000 men; however, those that remained with the colours became battle-hardened professionals, loyal to their young generals who led them to victory, glory and booty. They were also loyal to the nation/republic/Revolution as they perceived it, and were ready verbally to chastise those politicians whose behaviour and policies seemed weak or erroneous, and to demand the ferocious punishments of the terror for any supposed or actual conspirators.[22]

The structure of the British army and navy did not change; essentially the stratification of society was present in the armed forces before the war and it was maintained throughout the conflict. What was new, however, were the enormous numbers of men who were now recruited. In 1795 and 1796, in its search for men, the government had recourse to a quota system imposed on different units of local government not unlike the requisitions demanded in France in July 1792 and February 1793. This enormous increase in men may well have had a deleterious effect on the navy where man managements and skilful seamanship were important among the officers. It is arguable that the need for men led to the navy scraping the barrel to officer its warships; such inferior officers, often frightened by the example of events in France, were more likely to provoke discontent among the men on the lower deck, and less likely to respond sympathetically to protests and petitions from the crew, both of which could have contributed to the great mutinies of 1797.

The militia regiments recruited for local defence were embodied on to a regular footing like the line army in the run-up to the war in December

---

[22] Bertaud, *La Revolution armée*, pp. 332–3.

1792; their numbers were augmented in 1797. Men were recruited from the county militia regiments into the line army as the search for men became desperate; it was believed that men accustomed to army life in the militia would be more ready to enlist into the line, and militiamen could be pressurised by officers and NCOs to 'volunteer'. But essentially the ranks of the line army and the navy were filled by traditional methods – recruiting parties, bounties, gentleman officers drawing on their local links, and, of course, the occasional example of chicanery.[23] In addition to the line army, the navy and to the militia regiments balloted within the counties, vast numbers of volunteers also came forward to form part-time auxiliary corps to defend their localities against the threat of invasion and the threat of internal disorder. The Volunteer Movement was not entirely new; some corps had been organised during the American war when, in 1779, there was the likelihood of an invasion by the colonists' French and Spanish allies. During the 1790s however the Volunteer units were not all organised first and foremost to fight the French in case of invasion; as early as December 1792, a correspondent of the Reeves Society suggested organising cavalry corps among men of property to maintain internal order.[24] At the same time many of the urban Volunteer corps were a reflection of the growing self-awareness and civic pride of the developing middle class.[25] The fighting quality of some of the Volunteer units was probably dubious, but they provided a focus for much of the loyalism which manifested itself during the years of the Revolution, and they turned Britain into a militarised society in a way that had been previously unknown, and that was to be unknown for at least another century.[26] By the second half of the 1790s every county had its Volunteer cavalry regiment, and every town had its own infantry Volunteers, proudly parading in their colourful, local design of uniform.

Organising men to fight meant also organising the ideas for which they were to fight. Both Britain and France witnessed significant development of their national imagery during these wars. In France, for a variety of reasons and drawing on a variety of traditions, the abstract, chaste, impersonal Marianne became a national symbol. For the Jacobins of 1793 and 1794, however, the ideal national symbol appears more to have been that of Hercules who went through a series of guises from classical hero,

---

[23] Clive Emsley, *North Riding Naval Recruits: The Quota Acts and the Quota Men,* (Northallerton, 1978); J. R. Western, 'The recruitment of the land forces in Great Britain 1793–99', unpublished Ph.D. thesis (Edinburgh, 1953).

[24] British Library, Add. MSS 16922, fos. 133–4, Sir Thomas Gooch to Reeves, 16 December 1792.

[25] J. E. Cookson, 'The English Volunteer Movement of the French wars, 1793–1815: some contexts', *Historical Journal,* 32, 4 (1989), pp. 867–91.

[26] The fear of France under Napoleon III led to a revival of the idea of Volunteer regiments in 1859, though scarcely on the scale of the period 1794–1805.

to a *sans-culotte* scourge of kings, and back.[27] In Britain, Britannia, not always as demure as Marianne, was enlisted in the struggle against France. So too was John Bull, a much ruder figure than his nineteenth-century manifestations, yet developing many of his later characteristics, notably his paunch, which could reflect both the joys of feasting on the roast beef and ale of 'Old England', in contrast to the miserable food of the French, but also in one of Gillray's most famous cartoons, it had developed from the rich diet of French delicacies provided by Nelson and other sea captains.[28] In many respects John Bull, especially as portrayed in some of Gillray's cartoons, took on many of the physical attributes of George III; one step towards what Linda Colley has described as that monarch's apotheosis during the revolutionary and Napoleonic wars.[29]

National fervour may not have been as apparent in Britain as it was in revolutionary France, and the government may have been reluctant to encourage large-scale national mobilisation because of a general concern about what might develop from massive popular participation,[30] nevertheless, national fervour was not lacking in Britain, and the forms which it took were not dissimilar from those in France. French municipalities and Jacobin clubs sent their volunteers and conscripts to war with patriotic speeches and elaborate theatrical performances. 'Braves citoyens', exclaimed the Mayor of Paris to volunteers leaving for the front in July 1792,

vous vous enrôlez sous les drapeaux de la Liberté; c'est pour la défendre, c'est pour combattre la tyrannie. Votre famille est maintenant au milieu des camps, votre famille est la Patrie; nous devons tout sacrifier à cette mère commune... Perissons plutôt que de souffrir que notre sol soit souillé par l'esclavage. Mais non, les despots seront vaincus; volez à la victoire...

Revolutionary 'hymns' were sung, flags were waved, young men swore loyalty to the republic to defend her to the last drop of their blood.[31] So in Britain men were encouraged off to war with patriotic parades and

---

[27] Lynn Hunt, *Politics, Culture, and Class in the French Revolution* (Berkeley and Los Angeles, Calif., 1984), pp. 93–117.

[28] *John Bull taking a Luncheon – or – British Cooks cramming Old Grumble-Gizzard with Bonne Chere*, 24 October 1798. Thomas Rowlandson's *High Fun for John Bull, or the Republicans put to their last Shift*, 12 November 1798, has a rather similar image as John Bull watches his enemies bake new fleets in an oven for his sailors to carry off.

[29] Linda Colley, 'The apotheosis of George III: loyalty, royalty and the British nation, 1760–1820', *Past and Present*, 102 (1984), pp. 94–129.

[30] Linda Colley, 'Whose nation? Class and national consciousness in Britain 1750–1830', *Past and Present*, 113 (1986), pp. 97–117; see also the comments of John Dinwiddy, 'England' in Otto Dann and John Dinwiddy (eds.), *Nationalism in the Age of the French Revolution* (London, 1988), pp. 53–70, especially p. 69 and n. 59.

[31] Clive Emsley, 'Nationalist rhetoric and nationalist sentiment in revolutionary France' in Dann and Dinwiddy, *Nationalism*, p. 44. The quotation is from C. L. Chassin and L. Hennet, *Les Volontaires nationaux pendant la Révolution*, 3 vols. (Paris, 1899), vol. I, pp. 328–9.

rousing speeches emphasising that they were fighting for their country. In April 1795 Alderman Osbourne of Hull made a rousing speech urging men to enlist under the Quota Act:

A true British sailor bids defiance to the vauntings of the mean sans culottes, and is only desirous to give him the meeting, to show the effect of British beef and grog; both of which, my brave fellows, you know there is great plenty in the *wooden walls of old England!*...The unanimity which you this day see pervade all ranks and degrees of men, evinces an emulation, as it were, who shall do the most to repay those whose services are now called forth to defend their King, their country, their wives, their children, their sweethearts, and, what is still more dear, the glorious Constitution of Old England, from the ravages of the French.[32]

When there was disquiet and disorder over the Supplementary Militia Act at the end of 1796, the *Northampton Mercury* for one urged, 'surely no man, who has any regard or himself, his family, or his country can object to take his chance of being called upon if [an invasion] should arise'.[33] Volunteer companies had their colours blessed in the local church; parsons preached loyalist sermons; 'God save the King' became a rallying cry to be demanded time after time at the theatre; and new verses were written for important occasions. Public events, like the meeting of quarter sessions could provide the opportunity for an eulogy on the blessings of the constitution. Military victories provided opportunities for public theatre and for spontaneous demonstrations, for loyal sentiments, and old fashioned xenophobia, and such sentiments were to be found among groups as disparate as turbulent navvies in Lincolnshire and the correspondents of mutinous seaman at the Nore.[34] Even radicals could warmly praise the courage and the victories of British seamen while, at the same time, castigating the British government.[35]

While British soldiers and sailors may not have written to their families with the same kind of patriotic fervour as some of their French opponents, and while there was no brave new world which they could feel party to creating, yet there was patriotism to be found in the ranks. Seditious papers circulated in barracks at the time of the naval mutinies of 1797 brought loyalist condemnations and offers of rewards for information about the authors and distributors from the soldiers. The written responses, probably, were rarely the work of ordinary rankers, and some

[32] *York Chronicle*, 16 April 1795.   [33] *Northampton Mercury*, 12 November 1796.

[34] For the latter incidents see *The Times*, 24 January 1794, and Clive Emsley, *British Society and the French Wars 1793–1815* (London, 1979), pp. 62–3; for the general incidence of loyalty and patriotism, see the essays of Colley and Dinwiddy.

[35] Gerald Jordan and Nicholas Rogers, 'Admirals as heroes: patriotism and liberals in Hanoverian England', *Journal of British Studies*, 28 (1989), pp. 201–24.

pressure may have been exerted for contributions towards the rewards, but it is rather too cynical to suggest that the loyalist outrage of the troops can be explained solely in these terms. Richard Huddleston, a Catholic gentleman serving as a captain in the Cambridgeshire militia, was reluctant to go to Ireland during the rebellion of 1798; his men, however, were eager and Huddleston, seeing himself as a man of honour, felt compelled to join them.[36] Perhaps the greatest contrast between French and British patriotic rhetoric was to be found in the largely abstract nature of the former and the often materialistic nature of the latter. The French addressed their soldiers and sailors with appeals to natural rights, to liberty and the ideal of the nation, and some of the men responded in kind. In Britain there were appeals to Old England and traditional English liberties, as well as to the need to protect wives and families; but in a way unknown in France appeals to English liberty were also linked quite literally to roast beef and ale.

There were dissident voices of course and the extent and significance of the dissent in Britain has prompted a lively historical debate.[37] British Jacobins would not illuminate their windows for victories, and their houses were attacked by loyalists. The celebrations for Nelson's victory at the Nile in 1798, however, saw attacks of a different nature as some London crowds occasionally turned on military officers.[38] Recruiting, in spite of appeals to Old England, the constitution and to wives and families, could still provoke hostility and rioting. As the 1790s wore on more men appeared in court for damning the King and the war, and for hoping that the French would come, than for publishing seditious libels.[39] Calls for 'God Save the King' in the theatre could be answered with counter-calls. Clearly not every Briton was prepared to lay down his life for 'Old England' or for 'the happiness of living under the British Government'.[40] But then neither was every Frenchman prepared to lay down his life for his new republic; even in 1793 and 1794 peasant recruits walked back home, sometimes even before they had joined their allotted units. Nicolas Drouhet and Jean Leviteau, aged twenty-one and twenty-two respectively, were arrested in *prairial*, Year IV, nearly two years after the decree of the *levée en masse*. According to the local *juge de paix* in their

[36] Clive Emsley, 'The military and popular disorder in England 1790–1801', *Journal of the Society for Army Historical Research*, 61 (1983), pp. 96–102; Cambs. R.O. Huddleston of Sawston, MSS 488/C2/H.D. 204.

[37] See, for example, the contrasting views of Ian Christie and Roger Wells in this volume.

[38] *London Chronicle*, 4 and 6 October 1798.

[39] Clive Emsley, 'An aspect of Pitt's "Terror": prosecutions for sedition during the 1790s', *Social History*, 6, 2 (1981), pp. 155–84.

[40] *The Happiness of Living under the British Government* was a sermon preached by the Revd Thomas Lewis and published in Tunbridge Wells in 1793.

native district of Charente-Inférieure: 'Ces deux individus ont été arrêtés faute de passeports, leur âge et leur interrogatoire fait decouvrir qu'ils étaient de la réquisition, qu'ils avaient reçu une route pour joindre l'armée, et qu'ils retournaient chez eux'.[41] Dissident voices were raised against the authorities in both countries when provisions were scarce, or, as in the case of the arsenal workers at Toulon in 1794 and the ordinary seamen of the British fleet in 1797, when the respective governments appeared insensible to their protests over poor pay or even the lack of pay. But revolutionary and counter-revolutionary slogans shouted by crowds need to be approached with caution. It is not necessarily the case that the use of such terms by rioters protesting over food shortages or recruiting practices in either Britain or France during the revolutionary period reflect a deep commitment to a political cause. It seems more likely that when, for example, in Year III rioters around Rouen shouted, 'Vive le Roi', and took an axe to a tree of liberty, and when, five years later, a notice posted by English food rioters threatened to overturn the constitution and 'Arect a rebublick',[42] they were more intent in getting action over the immediate and pressing need for food (and peace) than, respectively, counter-revolution or revolution. Violent anti-Jacobinism in the Midi may have employed counter-revolutionary rhetoric, but it was also rooted in traditional youth activities, as well as in long-standing intercommunal and personal rivalries.[43] When large-scale insurrection occurred, as in the Vendée in 1793 and as in Ireland in 1798, a multiplicity of factors can be found among the causes – religious, economic, social, a tradition of urban/rural suspicion – as well as commitment to political principles.

III

The first section of this chapter noted the contrasts between the differing constitutional structures of eighteenth-century Britain and France: the balanced constitution of the former; the absolutist nature of the latter. In eighteenth-century France, decisions were made by the King's government

---

[41] Archives nationales F⁷3031, Marchant to Minister of Police(?) 1 messidor, An IV. For French attitudes to recruitment in general, see Alan Forrest, *Conscripts and Deserters: The Army and French Society during the Revolution and Empire* (Oxford, 1989).

[42] For these specific instances see R. C. Cobb, 'Une emeute de la faim dans la banlieue rouennais' in R. C. Cobb (ed.), *Terreur et Subsistences 1793–1795* (Paris, 1965), pp. 301–2; and Public Record Office, Home Office, 42.50, Revd Mr Meyrick to Portland, 12 June 1800. For a general discussion of the use of royalist slogans by draft dodgers from the Revolutionary and Napoleonic armies, see Forrest, *Conscripts and Deserters*, ch 7.

[43] Colin Lucas, 'Themes in southern violence after 9 thermidor' in Gwynne Lewis and Colin Lucas (eds.), *Beyond the Terror: Essays in French Regional and Social History, 1794–1815* (Cambridge, 1983).

and implemented by the state bureaucracy. In eighteenth-century Britain, decisions could be made by the King's government, but they had to go through a much more public form of consultation among representatives in Parliament, and when they concerned internal affairs they invariably had to be implemented by part-time, unpaid officials. At first glance the French system may appear more direct and consequently more efficient, and thus the state – or the apparatus of government – of old-regime France appears the stronger. The Parliament at Westminster did not pass legislation at the whim of the King and his ministers; a current investigation into the ways that laws were passed in the eighteenth-century suggests that MPs took their administrative roles seriously, that there could be serious debate and that men could take stands on matters of principle as well as practicality. Lobbying by interest groups could also be significant in bringing matters before Parliament, as well as in blocking legislation.[44] Pitt's defeat over the fortifying of the dockyards of Plymouth and Portsmouth in 1785 demonstrates that, even when the King's minister invoked ideas of national security after an unsuccessful war, the Commons could not be depended upon for support especially when vast sums of their money, as taxpayers, were at issue. The ways in which eighteenth-century government and Parliament actually worked clearly merits deeper analysis; a serious contrast between the British reliance on part-time officials to administer local government and the French reliance on state bureaucrats would also be of great value. A recent study of the repression of vagrancy in eighteenth-century France suggests that the English system of poor relief, organised and conducted by part-time officials, was more efficient than that of France with its state directives, state financing and professional police.[45] Moreover, with a population just over one-third of that of France, the British state was remarkably successful in organising itself for war during the eighteenth century. Not least among the reasons for this was the British taxation system. Britons were taxed more heavily than the French, but the taxation system was more uniform and, more importantly still, it seemed fair and equitable. Tax collection was an exceptional aspect of the eighteenth-century British state in that it was in the hands of officials appointed by the central government; this also made the British system stand out from the practice of most continental powers, including France. Yet even though it was centralised, the system remained under the supervision of Parliament which received, and debated, regular

---

[44] Joanna Innes and John Styles, 'The "Bloody Code" in context: eighteenth-century criminal legislation reconsidered', unpublished research paper (December, 1984).
[45] Robert M. Schwartz, *Policing the Poor in Eighteenth-Century France* (Chapel Hill, N.C., 1988), pp. 166–71.

accounts and reports.[46] The American War of Independence was the only conflict which Britain lost during the century, yet it was France, on the winning side, which was bankrupted as a result of that war.

Defeat in the American war had alarmed the rulers of Britain; not only was the loss of the thirteen colonies a blow to national pride, but the war had witnessed a resurgence of French naval power apparently putting Britain and the remainder of her empire in greater danger than anyone had perceived for a century. The defeat prompted a major naval-building programme; the darkest hours of the war had witnessed calls for political reform, and had led to 'economical' reform. Yet, when Britain appeared threatened by Painite propaganda in 1792 and then came into open conflict with revolutionary France in 1793, it was essentially the same apparatus of government which had served successfully for most of the conflicts of the eighteenth century which lumbered into action. Though from 1794 Pitt had an overwhelming majority in Parliament, military estimates and new taxes for the war still had to be debated and could be vigorously opposed. It was possible to circumvent some of the procedures in some instances, and the building of barracks was the obvious example, yet such circumventions were rare. Pitt may have contemplated some kind of action against Fox for his political principles and activities, especially when Fox and his followers seceded from parliament in 1798, but the fact remains that Pitt took no action, and it is probably true to say that he and his fellow ministers were as much prisoners of the rhetoric of English rights and liberties as everyone else. The government itself organised a few of the more dramatic prosecutions of British Jacobins; but the overwhelming majority of the 200 or so trials for treason, seditious words or seditious libel were the result of local prosecutions organised either by individual magistrates or by loyalist groups. The government could pass legislation and exhort its supporters to suppress Jacobinism; but if the men in the locality were disinclined, from whatever motives, to take action, then no action was taken. This is not to deny that violence, intimidation, as well as dubious jury verdicts were all inflicted on British Jacobins, but simply to emphasise the fact that the British government relied on well-to-do individuals, in their part-time official capacities, to administer, to protect and to preserve the localities; there was no army of government appointed bureaucrats. Moreover, if the gentlemen of one district decided not to act, then the central government had little sanction. Militia regiments and quota men were recruited and administered by the same part-time, unpaid county officers. Of course the system was open to corruption; local men with part-time official tasks were well aware that

---

[46] John Brewer, *The Sinews of Power: War, Money and the English State 1688–1783* (London, 1989).

they had to live in their community long after any emergency was over, and links with friends and neighbours were stronger than obligations to a distant government. In consequence men might leave their own sons, or friends, or sons of friends, off the militia lists, or take bribes to leave off other names. Yet the system was pliable in the way that the French bureaucracy was not and, perhaps because it was so sensitive to the attitudes of local communities as well as influential local notables, it worked. During the 1790s the men of property continued to have faith in the system, but they also had a vested interest in making it work to preserve themselves from republicans and levellers at home and abroad.

In France the old royal bureaucracy was swept away by the Revolution. Elected assemblies were established in the new departments and some radicals even toyed with the idea of a federalist structure for the country. New state structures cannot be created overnight and then be expected to work with precision and efficiency whatever the circumstances; war highlighted a variety of problems in the new and shaky French state structure. Not the least of these problems were the lack of experience, and the lack of tradition in local administration; these were compounded by the difficulties and dangers of participation in government at both central and local level during a revolution. Serious debate was inhibited by the political climate in the National Convention except among the bravest; bombast, histrionics and appeals to unity may have a part to play in building morale in wartime, and many speeches, notably those of Georges Danton, were significant in this respect; yet heroic speeches do not necessarily make for workable policies. The radicalisation of the Revolution, prison massacres, blows against Girondins, Dantonist moderates and Hébertist extremists, frightened many in provincial France, and many local authorities ceased to meet, concerned about the effects of backing the 'wrong side'. Others rose in revolt; and of course some revelled in radical political action, though not always able to carry their localities with them. The Vendée offers the most extreme example here, with radicals in the town unable to carry the countryside along with their commitment to the new, revolutionary regime; the resulting tragedy, according to one recent historian, witnessed the first example of genocide in modern war.[47] Revolutionary crisis and the needs of war compelled the Jacobins to centralise and to dispatch supervisory political agents into the provinces and to the armies. These *commissaires* and *représentants en mission* were to oversee or to enforce the policies decided in Paris, and they brought the threat of the guillotine with them. This emergency centralisation disappeared with Thermidor, but a viable apparatus of

---

[47] Reynald Secher, *Le Génocide Franco-Français: la Vendée-vengé* (Paris, 1986).

government at national and local level did not emerge under either the Thermidorians or the Directory. Pressure of war and the fear of internal disintegration probably facilitated the acceptance of Bonaparte's coup in 1799, and also facilitated the recreation of a centralised system with state bureaucrats administering the localities. Under the Consulate and subsequent Napoleonic regime the last vestiges of local departmental government all but disappeared and those of municipalities were brought under close state supervision, yet central government was never able to win the acceptance of all local notables to its military policies when the annual demand for conscripts was made.

IV

The Peace of Amiens in 1801 brought an end to the Anglo-French war which had begun in 1793; war was to break out again in 1803 and to continue with a few months respite (April 1814 to March 1815) until 1815. The year 1801 might, therefore, seem a curious place to end this survey. Yet the war against Napoleon was rather different. While some British radicals shifted their admiration for the Revolution to admiration for its most successful son, Britain appeared much more united, particularly while General Bonaparte's Army of England was encamped around Boulogne during 1803 to 1805 awaiting the opportunity to invade. In France, while conscription ensured that people were aware of the continuing military conflicts, the country itself was not menaced by defeat and invasion until the very end, and the vast expanse of Napoleon's empire ensured that the French population need not go hungry as long as there were subject peoples able to provide.

Revolution and the war of 1793 to 1801 left a legacy in both Britain and France. Survival in the war undermined the radicals' concerns about the weakness of the British economy[48] and, in consequence, probably contributed to the nation's growing self-confidence. The very fact that there was no revolution or serious armed insurrection outside of Ireland, together with the ultimate success in the war against Napoleon, confirmed the loyalists belief in the excellence of the constitution, government and administration. There were concerns during the 1830s and the 'hungry forties', but increasingly revolution became unthinkable in Victorian Britain as gentlemen smugly surveyed the disorders elsewhere in Europe and concluded that the limited trouble at home was the result of a good working system. Benthamite reformers may have begun winning arguments during the 1820s and may have been winning ministerial support,

---

[48]   J. E. Cookson, 'Political arithmetic and war in Britain 1793–1815', *War and Society*, 1, 2 (1983), pp. 37–60.

but their dreams of state bureaucrats and a centralised state were only partly achieved, always being tempered and restrained by negotiations with entrenched local government and administration. Officials were less and less part-time, but many remained local rather than national.

If the experience of revolution and war contributed to the stability of nineteenth-century Britain, it also contributed to the instability of nineteenth-century France. The revolutionary decade produced a variety of blueprints for government which were taken up and developed during the nineteenth century; there were several varieties of both monarchy and republicanism, each with its own claim to be the legitimate government. As different groups squabbled, and periodically seized power from each other during the century, so the bureaucracy – the largest in Europe in the mid-nineteenth century – administered the country. This bureaucracy, like the legal system through which and by which it operated, was the product of the Revolution and Napoleon. Many French political activists saw, in their interpretations of the war and the Revolution, models both for others and for France as a leader of 'free' peoples, or peoples, like the Italians and the Poles, struggling to be free. They also saw models for their own action: 1792, for example, provided the heroic demonstration of how to respond to invasion as Auguste Blanqui explained to the Parisians when German troops surrounded their city in 1870;[49] and the professed anti-patriot Hervé could write in *La Guerre Sociale* on 30 July 1914: 'Aujourd'hui comme en 1792, aujourd'hui comme au temps des 'guerres à outrance' qui firent la Commune, notre patriotisme revolutionnaire serait, le cas échéant, le grand ressort et la suprême sauvegarde de la patrie en danger'.[50] Yet if war and revolution left legacies contributing to stability in nineteenth-century Britain and instability in nineteenth-century France, it is also worth emphasising that both countries emerged from the upheavals as rather similar constitutional, liberal states. The revolutionary and Napoleonic wars were the last of a series of conflicts between the two states going back over many centuries. They remained suspicious and at times fearful of each other, yet they were very different in government and legislative structure from the autocratic states to the centre and east of Europe.

[49] R. W. Postgate (ed.), *Revolution from 1789 to 1906* (New York, 1962), pp. 288–9.
[50] Quoted in Catherine Slater, *Defeatists and their Enemies: Political Invective in France* (Oxford, 1981), p. 9.

6 War, revolution and the crisis of the British empire

Michael Duffy

When Britain went to war with revolutionary France in February 1793 it was with expectations of imperial success rather than imperial catastrophe. The evident disorganisation of France and its empire seemed to present a golden opportunity to terminate decisively a century of imperial rivalry. For over two years before the war, Pitt's government had been bombarded with appeals for aid from disaffected French West Indian planters, and with suggestions from eager British officials that now was the time to take revenge for France's part in the loss of Britain's American colonies by seizing its rich Caribbean empire. Ministers resisted, putting their faith in a peace policy to see them through domestic and international dangers, but when that policy no longer seemed viable at the turn of 1792–3 and war seemed inevitable to defend Britain's interests in Holland and the Austrian Netherlands, Pitt privately admitted that the acquisition of the French islands would be an advantage of the coming conflict.[1]

What Pitt said privately was so loudly broadcast by pro-war supporters that opposition pamphleteers specifically condemned 'those who recommend war for speculation' and tried to belittle 'the golden harvest' being held out 'chiefly in the West Indies'.[2] These arguments failed to convince against the case that France could easily be driven from its small trading-stations in India and that Britain could snap up the dynamic core of the French empire of the Caribbean, where an immense capital investment was tied up in a rapidly expanding economy of sugar, cotton and coffee plantations worked by over 600,000 slaves and generating some two-fifths of France's foreign trade and two-thirds of its ocean-going shipping. Such a conquest, urged *The Times* on 8 February 1793, would raise the British empire to a degree of commercial prosperity beyond all

---

[1] Third Earl of Malmesbury (ed.), *Diaries and Correspondence of James Harris, First Earl of Malmesbury* (London, 1844), vol. II, pp. 501–2. See also M. Duffy, 'The impact of the French Revolution on British attitudes to the West Indian colonies' in D. B. Gaspar and D. P. Geggus (eds.), *The French Revolution and the Greater Caribbean* (Bloomington, Ind., forthcoming).

[2] Anon, *Comments on the Proposed War with France...by a Lover of Peace* (London, 15 January 1793), pp. 23, 36–41; Revd C. Wyvill, *A Letter to the Rt. Hon. William Pitt* (London, 9 February 1793).

calculation, while 'It would not be the work of a few years only, but it would require ages for France to recover to the political balance of Europe that preponderancy, which she enjoyed previous to the Revolution'. Despite the appeals of ideologists such as Burke, the war was fought less to destroy the French Revolution than to destroy French power. George III rejoiced that the first Caribbean capture, Tobago, presaged many more, and that 'now is the hour to humble France, for nothing but her being disabled from disturbing other Countries, whatever Government may be established there, will keep her quiet'. This attitude was repeatedly echoed in the press during the early years of the war.[3]

By mid-1794 such an eventuality seemed on the point of fulfilment. The French Mediterranean fleet was partially burnt at Toulon, their Brest fleet defeated at the 'Glorious First of June', and a Caribbean expedition composed of the cream of the Irish army under General Sir Charles Grey and Admiral Sir John Jervis captured Martinique (March 1794), St Lucia and Guadeloupe (April) and Port-au-Prince, the capital of France's richest Caribbean colony, Saint-Domingue (June). Within months however the situation changed dramatically. The government's war strategy looked to secure Britain and its empire by destroying the French navy and its vital imperial mercantile underpinning. In desperation the French regime struck back at Britain's empire with all the revolutionary means at its disposal. Its first agent to investigate the possibilities of assisting Irish revolt, the American Colonel Oswald, reached Dublin in May 1793 and another, the Irish former Anglican curate, the Revd William Jackson, arrived in April 1794. In the Caribbean the Revolution raised a more insidious threat by decreeing the full equality of free coloured peoples in the French islands in 1792. By autumn 1793 agents were being despatched to spread disaffection among the free coloureds in Britain's colonies. In February 1794 the National Convention went further by emancipating the slaves. By that autumn these methods had been exploited to help recover Guadeloupe from British occupation and the victorious Republican Commissioner, Victor Hugues, was looking to resume infiltration into the British islands.[4]

[3] A. Aspinall (ed.), *The Later Correspondence of George III* (Cambridge, 1968), vol. II, p. 46; Sir G. Dallas, *Thoughts upon Our Present Situation with Remarks upon the Policy of a War with France* (1793), pp. 35, 51, 58; J. Durnford, *The Motives and Consequences of the Present War Impartially Considered* (1793), pp. 59, 66–7; W. Playfair, *Thoughts on the Present State of French Politics and the Necessity and Policy of Diminishing France* (1793), pp. 67–77; *War with France the Only Security of Britain* (London, 20 January 1794), pp. 24, 32ff; *A short Exposition of the Important Advantages to be Derived by Great Britain from the War* (1794), pp. 9–10, 13.

[4] Marianne Elliot, *Partners in Revolution: The United Irishmen and France* (New Haven, Conn., 1982), pp. 60–5; British Library (BL), Add. MSS 59, 239, fo. 71, Memorandum 30 December, 1793; E. L. Cox, *The Free Coloreds in the Slave Societies of St Kitts and Grenada 1763–1833* (Knoxville, 1984), pp. 144–5.

By 1795 there was a much greater readiness to respond to the opportunity of proffered French assistance, and Britain was faced with the threatened destruction of its own empire. In May, James Workman in *An Argument Against Continuing the War*, could stress the danger of revolt in Ireland, where, unless the grievances of the Catholics were speedily redressed, the empire might receive its death-blow. Ireland, he pointed out, supplied abundant provisions and manpower for the army and navy which would be lost, while if the Irish ports fell into French hands Britain's oceanic trade would be in dire jeopardy. He also asserted that alarm had spread throughout the British West Indian colonies at the French decree abolishing slavery, and if the French showed their usual energy and good fortune then Britain's rich Caribbean empire would be lost. Between writing and publication, news reached London that large parts of the populations of Grenada and St Vincent had risen in revolt.[5]

II

Britain controlled its empire through a blend of military strength, mutual economic benefit and an opportunist game of divide and rule. The disruption of most or all of these elements in the 1790s released inbuilt tensions within the empire that blew the lid off of a fragile imperial stability. The major local restraint was the divisions within the society of each dominion. Here, in particular, key changes took place which overthrew delicate internal balances and accepted relationships, and the role of the French Revolution was influential amongst factors promoting this.

The United Irishmen's view of the Revolution's effect on the Irish balance was outlined by their emissary, Theobold Wolfe Tone, in his 22 February 1796 memorial to the French Directory.[6] In an Irish population of about 4.5 million, 450,000 constituted the Protestant Episcopalian Anglo-Irish 'Ascendancy', who had acquired five-sixths of the land and had tied themselves subserviently to England on whom they depended for protection and support, and which rewarded them by bestowing on them a monopoly of patronage and preferment. Pitt might have questioned the extent of such Ascendancy subservience: the British government's hold on no colonial ruling elite was automatic. The Ascendancy valued their

---

[5] James Workman, *An Argument Against Continuing the War* (London, 25 May 1795), pp. 11–12, 42. For Ireland's contribution to the British war effort, see R. B. McDowell, 'Ireland in the eighteenth-century British empire', *Historical Studies*, 9 (1974), pp. 57–63; D. A. Chart, 'The Irish levies during the Great French War', *English Historical Review*, 32 (1917), pp. 497–516.

[6] R. B. O'Brien (ed.), *The Autobiography of Theobald Wolfe Tone 1763–1798* (London, 1893), vol. II, appendix 371–83.

Irishness as well as their Englishness and were sensitive to the legislative independence the Irish Parliament had won in 1782.[7] Nevertheless, even the 'Patriot' opposition in that Parliament largely acquiesced in the foreign and domestic policies of successive Lord Lieutenants in the crisis of the 1790s – a factor which helped lead the disillusioned reformist United Irishmen away from parliamentary towards revolutionary remedies.

At the other extreme were the Catholic population estimated by Tone at 3,150,000 which he portrayed as an oppressed and impoverished peasantry resentful at paying heavy rents to Anglo-Irish landlords and tithes to Protestant Church of Ireland clergy. Economic opportunity, however, had raised a respectable Catholic merchant class which, together with a few of the surviving Catholic landed gentry, had organised a General Committee to campaign for full participation in political life from which Catholics were excluded. In between the Ascendancy and the Catholics were 900,000 Presbyterian Dissenters,[8] who Tone identified as mostly engaged in trade and manufactures (though there were many tenant farmers too), and who had hitherto helped sustain Ascendancy rule and thus British control by the animosity between them and the Catholics. With partial political rights themselves they had supported the exclusion of the Catholics.

It was indeed the Presbyterians whom the British government regarded as the potential revolutionaries in Ireland. Belfast began the armed Volunteer Movement which extorted greater economic and political self-government for Ireland between 1778 and 1782, assembling conventions as extra-parliamentary pressure groups. Dissenter resentment remained at paying tithes to the established church and at the continued tight grip on power of the Ascendancy establishment. Amongst them a vociferous Presbyterian radical core continued to demand reform of the Irish Parliament, and this was re-energized by the French revolutionary example. In November 1792 the Foreign Secretary (and former Irish Secretary), Lord Grenville, described them as 'the Republicans of the North' and expressed his 'very great anxiety' that they and the Catholics were drawing together.[9]

This momentous development was described in Tone's 1796 memorial

---

[7] N. Canny, 'Identity formation in Ireland: the emergence of the Anglo-Irish' in N. Canny and A. Pagden (eds.), *Colonial Identity in the Atlantic World 1500–1800* (Princeton, N.J., 1987), pp. 159–212.

[8] F. MacDermott considers this an overestimate of numbers closer to 500,000: *Theobold Wolfe Tone*, 2nd, revised edn (Tralee, 1968), p. 122, n. 1.

[9] Historical Manuscripts Commission Fourteenth Report, appendix part 5: *The Manuscripts of J. B. Fortescue Esq., Preserved at Dropmore*, vol. II, pp. 214, 221–2; Huntingdon Library, California, Stowe MSS, Grenville to Buckingham [15 November 1792].

as 'Among the innumerable blessings procured to mankind by the French Revolution'. The example of French reforming success, the revolution's ecumenicalism and its apparent ability to subordinate clerical power, encouraged a group of radical Presbyterians and Church of Ireland outsiders to look to Catholic help to force reform of the Irish Parliament against the Ascendancy establishment. In October 1791 the Society of United Irishmen was founded in Belfast to establish a union of all Irishmen as a counterbalance to English influence. This would be effected by a complete and radical reform of representation in the Irish Parliament which, to be just, should include participation by all religious persuasions. Within a month a Dublin society was formed on similar principles.

The Society of United Irishmen essentially attracted the radical urban intelligentsia: it was a mixture of predominantly young Church of Ireland, Presbyterian and Catholic members of the professions, frustrated at the barriers to advancement resulting from the tight grip of the Ascendancy establishment, and of members of the mercantile middle class looking for political influence commensurate with their rising wealth. The twelve founder-members of the Belfast society included ten Presbyterian merchants, an army officer and the young Dublin Protestant middle-class lawyer, Wolfe Tone. The Dublin society attracted fifty-six, chiefly Protestant, lawyers (who soon took the lead), 104 merchants, thirty-one textile manufacturers, twenty-four of the medical profession and, among others, thirty landowners. Their proffered support for the campaign for Catholic political rights was welcomed and a significant link established through the appointment as agent for the Catholic Committee in July 1792 of Wolfe Tone, whose '*An Argument on Behalf of the Catholics of Ireland*' (September 1791) focused much of the rationale for the United Irishmen.[10]

The years 1791–2 saw the development of a massive campaign for equal rights for Catholics in Ireland which had the potential for a wider revolutionary movement. The Catholic Committee was taken over by middle-class activists who used their organisational skills to produce an elected convention in December 1792, by-passing the Irish Parliament and petitioning the King directly for redress. At one side stood the United Irishmen, looking to curtail English predominance and secure radical parliamentary reform. On the other was the militant Catholic secret society, the Defenders, product of the violent economic confrontation with Protestants in Armagh and County Down, which stepped up its

---

[10] Elliott, *Partners in Revolution*, pp. 20–34; R. B. McDowell, 'The personnel of the Dublin Society of United Irishmen, 1791–4', *Irish Historical Studies*, 2 (1940–1), pp. 12–53. McDowell's *Ireland in the Age of Imperialism and Revolution 1760–1801* (Oxford, 1979), pp. 351–461, provides a solid account of events summarised in this section.

activities in 1792 to the extent of contemplating an armed uprising and approaching French agents in London for support.[11]

However, although the Ascendancy obstinately opposed all but the most modest concessions, a united revolutionary front had not yet formed. The Defenders were still looking for arms and allies, while the United Irishmen remained but a pressure group. They tried to build a power-base as the essential link between the two great popular organs of anti-Ascendancy opinion – the Volunteers and the Catholic Committee – but never gained dominance in either. Many Protestant Volunteers were alarmed at increasing Defender activity and concerned that the United strategy might produce Catholic supremacy with all its feared dangers to Protestant liberties and property. Equally, while individual Catholics, including Committee members, joined the United Irishmen, no formal engagement was made between the two bodies. Catholic leaders were cautious of Presbyterian motives and preferred to keep them as a weapon in reserve while they used established contacts to deal directly with Pitt's British government.[12]

The opportunity was thus still available to play divide and rule, and Pitt sought to take it by buying off the Catholics through 'affording a prospect of reasonable and honourable concessions'.[13] Pressure was brought on the Ascendancy to pass Catholic Relief Acts in 1792, restoring remaining lost civil rights, and in 1793 granting the vote to those otherwise qualified.

Over an extended period these Acts failed to conciliate Catholics and, instead, contributed to the build-up of tensions leading to the 1798 Irish rebellion. While Catholics obtained the vote, the Ascendancy successfully prevented them from gaining the right of election to Parliament; while prejudice was substituted for legal barriers to hinder their professional advancement. Hence resentment would re-emerge and, now that the Catholics had glimpsed their power, was likely to take an increasingly militant form. At the same time the Ascendancy was demoralised by the way the British government had failed to support them against Catholic pressure, and resorted to increasingly violent measures to repress protest or reform movements, which eventually became counterproductive. A foretaste of future events occurred in the summer of 1793 when poorer

---

[11] Elliott, *Partners in Revolution*, pp. 39–43, and 'The origins and transformation of early Irish republicanism', *International Review of Social History*, 23 (1978), pp. 407, 416, 418–20; J. Smyth, 'Popular politicization, Defenderism and the Catholic question' in H. Gough and D. Dickson (eds.), *Ireland and the French Revolution* (Dublin, 1990), pp. 109–16.

[12] M. Wall, 'The United Irish movement', *Historical Studies*, 5 (1965), pp. 125–33.

[13] Ann Arbor, Michigan, Pitt Papers: Pitt to Dundas, 8 November 1792. See also Dundas to Westmorland, 7 June 1793 quoted in T. Bartlett, 'An end to moral economy: the Irish militia disturbances of 1793', *Past and Present*, 109 (1933), p. 47.

Catholics, fearing they had been sacrificed to serve in a new militia as the price of gaining the vote for their wealthier co-religionists, rioted with greater violence than in all the preceding thirty years of agrarian agitation and were equally ferociously suppressed.[14]

Nevertheless the 1792–3 Relief Acts were significant and, indeed, from the viewpoint of the wider context of the imperial crisis, they were vital. They slowed the potential revolutionary momentum of the Irish confrontation so that rebellion in Ireland broke out three years after it did in the Caribbean, rather than simultaneously. The Catholic Committee dissolved itself in April 1793 and the Catholic leadership largely stood back while the Irish government cracked down on the Defenders, on the old Ulster radicals (banning the Volunteers in 1793), and on the United Irishmen whose demands for parliamentary reform and opposition to the war with France made them particular targets of state persecution. Several United leaders were arrested, their property and printing presses attacked, and the Dublin Society banned in May 1794.

The Relief Acts halted the developing radical Presbyterian/propertied-Catholic alliance and enabled a revival of divide and rule. For a while longer they left the hope that further reform might be attainable by peaceful parliamentary means if a similar campaign to that of 1792–3 could only be relaunched. Thus most of the Catholic and United Irish leadership were still unprepared to commit themselves to armed support for a French landing when the French agents appeared in 1793–4. Only a few would consider it a possibility at some future date, hedged with conditions, and they certainly had no means organised to implement it.[15]

To the initial delay imposed by the Relief Acts in turning reformers into revolutionaries was then added the hope of a change in the Irish government after the Portland Whigs joined Pitt's British government in the summer of 1794. This materialised in the arrival in early 1795 of a new Lord Lieutenant, Earl Fitzwilliam, sympathetic to Catholic emancipation. The Catholics were encouraged to renew their campaign and invited Tone back as their agent in December 1794, but Fitzwilliam went too fast and too far for the British government and was recalled in February 1795. Without his backing the Catholic Emancipation Bill was lost in May. It was these events that finally convinced significant numbers of Catholics and United Irish alike that peaceful methods would not work and turned them into revolutionaries.

But it would take a long time to create an organisation capable of effecting armed revolution. When Fitzwilliam left on 25 March 1795, Dublin could only demonstrate its disapproval by closing the shops and

[14] Bartlett, 'An end to moral economy', pp. 41–64; Elliott, *Partners in Revolution*, pp. 38–9.
[15] Elliott, *Partners in Revolution*, pp. 58, 60–5.

wearing mourning. On the arrival of his successor on 31 March, Dublin rioted. However, that was all: whereas at the beginning of the same month armed rebellion broke out in the British West Indies.

III

One of the most unnerving aspects of the French Revolution for the governments of Europe was the uncertainty of its popular impact. It was difficult to predict what aspirations of which groups or individuals would be fired or where that fire would lead. The British government, controlling an empire whose colonies and provinces had such varying social and historical experiences, became as perplexed as any. In Ireland in the early 1790s ministers expected trouble from the Presbyterian 'Republicans of the North' and ended in 1798 with a rebellion predominantly of the southern Catholic peasantry. In the West Indies they feared general slave revolt only to find rebellion precipitated by underprivileged whites and free coloureds in specific islands.

If divide and rule in Ireland was played among the Ascendancy, Presbyterians and Catholics, in the British Caribbean colonies, it was played out among a population of 50,000 whites, 10,500 free coloureds and 456,000 slaves (estimated c. 1788). On some islands other groups existed who were also brought into the balance against slaves. On the richest, Jamaica, a nativised Maroon population of former runaway slaves successfully resisted attempts to crush them (1730–9) and were bought off by land grants and freedom on condition of returning future runaways and acting as irregulars against slave insurgents or invaders. A similar (as events proved, timely) arrangement was reached with the Maroons of Dominica in 1794, while on St Vincent the counter came from the Black Caribs, over 5,000 strong, natives interbred with escaped slaves, whose successful resistance (1769–73) led to confirmation of their possession of over one-third of the island provided, amongst other conditions, that they would return fugitive slaves.[16]

Frequent slave revolts throughout the eighteenth century, as well as the fact that liberty, equality and fraternity had a far more direct meaning in the Caribbean than in Europe, made the West Indies the initial focus of government fears of revolt as a result of the French Revolution.[17] In the French colonies the principles of the Revolution split apart the white inhabitants, leading to demands for equal rights from the free coloured population, followed by a vast slave revolt in August 1791 that devastated

[16] M. Craton, *Testing the Chains. Resistance to Slavery in the British West Indies* (Ithaca, N.Y., 1982), pp. 81–96, 142–53, 226–7.
[17] Public Record Office (PRO), Colonial Office (CO) 137–89, Grenville to Effingham, 21 April 1791, CO 5/267, Government circular, 11 November 1791.

the Northern Province of Saint-Domingue. There was some dispute between British officials and colonial planters and merchants as to whether a conspiracy on a Tortola plantation in 1790 and a revolt in Dominica in early 1791 were inspired by events on the French islands or by the campaign to abolish the slave trade in Britain. The insurgent leader in Dominica however was a mulatto, Jean Louis Paulinaire, formerly from French Martinique, and by late 1791 colonial governors were starting to restrict or prevent entry from the French islands for fear of importing revolution.[18]

Despite occasional panic-alarms, however, reports to London were generally reassuring as to the basic loyalty of slaves and the unlikelihood of revolt. In view of what happened subsequently, there is an interesting examination in November 1791 of the state of Grenada as part of a wider report on the prospect of slave revolt in the Windward and Leeward islands. The writer, Captain Berkeley, noted that half the planters were French and perhaps not very well affected to the English, but they had a common interest in preventing insurrection and at that moment they felt the mildness and efficacy of British government so much as to be very good subjects. The fear was therefore of the negroes and people of colour, but he asserted that there were not the same odious distinctions against the latter as on the French islands so that he felt them loyal. He remarked that most of Grenada's slaves were newly imported from Africa (and hence believed more likely to revolt than Creoles habituated to slavery), and that the impassable woods of the interior furnished a refuge which made revolt practicable. However, insurgents would need arms from outside since those on the island were held in forts occupied by two British regiments guarding the capital, St George's, and neighbouring settlements. On these grounds Berkeley doubted slave revolt on Grenada.[19]

Within four years, however, almost all of these restraining factors had been disrupted as Grenada became the first part of the British empire in which rebellion broke out. But Berkeley was partially right. Revolt did not begin among the slaves who, where they rose, followed the lead of white and free coloured inhabitants. It was the latter who, when faced by a conjunction of local factors, earlier than Ireland turned to the French Revolution for support.

The white planter elite of the British Caribbean colonies were traditionally more spirited and independent in support of their institutions

[18] Craton, *Testing the Chains*, pp. 180, 224–6; E. Goveia, *Slave Society in the British Leeward Islands at the End of the Eighteenth Century* (New Haven, Conn., 1965), p. 95; L. Honychurch, *The Dominica Story* (Dominica, 1975), p. 78; PRO, CO 137/90, Proclamation, 10 December 1791.

[19] BL, Add. MSS, Grenville (Dropmore) Papers, 'From Captain Berkeley', 18 November 1791. Formerly in BL, Add. MSS 59, 239, this report has been redisposed within the collection beyond the present trace of the author or the British Library staff.

than either the Anglo-Irish Ascendancy or the North American colonists, and they continued jurisdictional clashes with British governors and government throughout the crisis of the American and French Revolutions.[20] Generally however they did not develop separatist tendencies. Fear of French imperial acquisitiveness and of revolt by their massive slave population made them cling to British military support, while a greater social unity than in the former North American colonies prevented major dissatisfactions developing which could be focused into hostility to British rule.[21] Such unity was not however universal and problems existed with the French-settled colonies of Grenada, St Vincent and Dominica acquired in 1763.

Of these Grenada was the most populous, prosperous and most notorious respecting its political and social situation. With the most fertile area open to development, it quickly received considerable British (largely Scottish) settlement and investment. Between 1763–77 its slave population grew from 12,000 to 35,000 and made it the most productive British island after Jamaica. In 1787 it stood second in total exports to Britain and third (after Jamaica and Barbados) in British imports.[22]

The imperial problem remained as in Ireland, however, of how to control an alien, conquered, Catholic population. The solution attempted by British governments in Grenada had been more generous than in Ireland. French planters retained lands granted by the French Crown, and, after initially imposing the traditional colonial administration including the religious Test Acts, a compromise was attempted by order of the Secretary of State over the heads of the colonial legislature by which Catholics were allowed to vote, up to two were permitted to sit in the twelve-member Council and three in the twenty-six-strong Assembly. In addition one Catholic in each parish could be appointed a magistrate and barriers were removed from holding militia commissions. These concessions were strongly resisted by many British colonists both for their effect and because, they argued, only the colonial legislature could establish such internal regulations.

Sufficient ill-will was created for the French colonists to co-operate heartily in the harsh French occupation of the colony after its conquest during the American war in 1779. When Britain regained possession in

[20] E. Braithwaite, *The Development of Creole Society in Jamaica 1770–1820* (Oxford, 1971), pp. 97–107; J. P. Greene, 'Changing identity in the British Caribbean: Barbados as a case study' in Canny and Pagden, *Colonial Identity*, pp. 213–66; Goveia, *Slave Society*, pp. 68–79; J. Millette, *The Genesis of Crown Colony Government. Trinidad 1763–1810* (Trinidad, 1970), pp. 89–101.

[21] T. R. Clayton, 'Sophistry, security, and socio-political structures in the American Revolution; or, why Jamaica did not rebel', *The Historical Journal*, 29 (1986), pp. 319–44.

[22] E. Williams, *From Columbus to Castro: The History of the Caribbean 1492–1969* (London, 1970), p. 105; S. Lambert (ed.), *House of Commons Sessional Papers of the Eighteenth Century* (Wilmington, Del., 1975), vol. LXIX, p. 248, vol. LXX, p. 220.

1784 the British colonists united to prevent the restoration of the earlier religious concessions, successfully obstructing French Catholic admission to the Assembly and initiating measures to appropriate to the Church of England the lands, incomes and churches of the Catholic Church.

In February 1786 nearly fifty French colonists petitioned the British government against this treatment, but it took six years for the Crown's law officers to adjudicate that the earlier concessions were illegal because they had not been enacted by the colonial legislature. In February 1792, Secretary of State Henry Dundas transmitted their opinion that the Catholic claims could not be admitted, and instructions followed in October to enforce the Test Acts and appropriate Catholic churches and church property to the Crown. As if to add insult to injury the new Lieutenant Governor, appointed in August 1792, was the Grenadan planter, Ninian Home, a prominent enemy to concessions to the Catholics from the start.[23]

Consequently, in an extraordinary conjunction of timing, restrictions were reimposed on the Catholics of Grenada at the very moment they were largely removed from Ireland. Such restrictions were the more galling through being administered by an old enemy as Governor, and by a Council socially inferior to the now debarred French Catholic planters. Since many British planters were non-resident, the seven councillors present in early 1795 included only one Grenada planter with two barristers, two merchants, a surgeon and an Anglican minister.[24] It is not surprising therefore that rebellion broke out in Grenada before Ireland, that among the rebels were prominent signatories of the 1786 Catholic petition, and that among the early victims of the rebellion was the Governor described by the rebels as 'le tyran Ninian Home'.[25]

Grenadan Catholic grievances were sufficiently recognised by British ministers on the eve of the rebellion to be specified as a problem to avoid repeating when settling the administration of the 1794 Caribbean conquests of the Grey-Jervis expedition. 'A Grenada Planter' in 1796 considered them 'the principal, if not the sole cause of the present insurrection', and they have been predominantly stressed by the Catholic Grenadan historian, Father Raymond Devas.[26] Important as they were, however, they were not the sole cause of the rebellion, nor were the signatories of the 1786 petition its leaders. Instead they followed the lead of Grenada's Francophone mulattos.

[23] H. T. Manning, *British Colonial Government after the American Revolution* (New Haven, Conn., 1937), pp. 64–5; R. P. Devas, *Conception Island or the Troubled Story of the Catholic Church in Grenada* (London, 1932), pp. 38–96.

[24] PRO, CO 101/34, fo. 12; a Grenada Planter, *A Brief Enquiry into the Causes of ... the Insurrection in Grenada* (London, 1796), pp. 9–10, 13–14.

[25] *British Sessional Papers, House of Commons 1801*, vol. III, p. 247, Fédon's declaration, 4 March 1795.   [26] A Grenada Planter, *Brief Enquiry*, p. 4; Devas, above n. 23.

How far the mulattos who organised and led the 1795 revolt were predominantly influenced by religious grievances is much more uncertain. The Anglican Revd Francis MacMahon, who ministered in an appropriated Catholic church, subsequently declared that he lived on good terms with the insurgent leader Julien Fédon right up to the outbreak. While one Catholic parish priest joined the rebels at once, dressed as an artilleryman, among their first victims was another French priest who acted as steward for an absentee planter – killed by Fédon's subaltern, Jean-Pierre la Valette, as 'an aristocrat'.[27]

For the mulattos, political rights were important irrespective of religious issues. Grenada's rising wealth drew thither a greater free coloured population than to any other British island except Jamaica.[28] They filled the craft and artificer trades of the colony and began working upwards. Of the mulatto leaders of the revolt, la Valette was a tailor; Stanislaus Besson (the second-in-command) was a silversmith who owned a slave; Etienne Ventour owned urban property valued at £50 and eleven slaves; Charles Nogues had begun the transition to the planting elite: formerly a tailor in St George's, acquiring property worth £20 in Gouyave which he sold to Fédon in 1790 and moving on to rent cotton land at Levera; Joachim Philip came from a wealthy family with substantial holdings at St George's and was a cotton planter in Carriacou (a small cotton estate was the cheapest way to get established as a planter).

The Fédons had advanced beyond cotton to coffee. Julien's brother Jean held a 141-acre estate with eight slaves producing coffee and cocoa, while Julien himself held a £20 property in Gouyave and a 360-acre estate with ninety-six slaves, likewise producing coffee and cocoa. Julien was ostensibly the most successful of the mulatto rebels, which may have helped make him leader. There are indications however that in enhancing his position he may have overextended himself financially. Commissioners for forfeited estates reported after the rising that Fédon's Belvidere estate was in possession of the mortgagee who sold it to Fédon but had never received any part of the purchase money.[29]

The picture emerges of a mulatto community starting to prosper economically, developing social and political expectations, which then ran up against restrictions not only on Catholics, but also on men of colour. The Jamaican Bryan Edwards thought them better treated than on other

[27] F. MacMahon, *A Narrative of the Insurrection in the Island of Grenada* (St George's, 1823), pp. 11–13; An Eye-Witness [G. Turnbull], *A Narrative of the Revolt and Insurrection of the French inhabitants in the Island of Grenada* (Edinburgh, 1795), p. 22.

[28] The influx occurred during the French occupation since numbers of free coloureds rose from 210 in 1777 to 1,125 in 1783 when 185 were of British and 940 of French origin. Cox, *Free Coloreds in Grenada, 1763–1833*, pp. 8, 14.

[29] PRO, CO 106/12, Return of forfeited estates, slaves, etc.; a Grenada Planter, *A Brief Enquiry*, p. 61; [T. T. Wise], *A Review of the Events which Happened in Grenada* (Grenada, 1795), pp. 8, 11.

British islands. They could buy land and tenements without restriction and their evidence was accepted in law courts on proof of freedom. But free coloured civil liberties were restricted by Acts in 1786 requiring them to state their residence and prove their freedom, and in 1789 banning them from gaming houses and regulating their dances and nocturnal movements. In 1790 Fédon, Nogues and Besson, with thirty-two others, sought to demonstrate their loyalty by petitioning for protection against the machinations of base and designing Frenchmen from Martinique, but the signal was ignored and an Act of 1792 specifically confined the vote to whites. Another loyalty address in January 1792 attracted only six mulatto signatures. Fédon and his colleagues were absent from it and it might be implied that they were starting to look for other ways to gain full equality.[30] New ways had appeared through the French Revolution. French colonial mulattos took up arms to demand equal rights, and after several false starts the Legislative Assembly finally granted them in April 1792. These events helped produce a petition for equality from Jamaican free coloureds to their Governor in June 1792;[31] on Grenada they germinated far more.

The outbreak of war between Britain and revolutionary France thus saw two considerably dissatisfied groups in Grenada: the French Catholic planters and the largely Francophone mulattos. Their animosity to British rule was reflected in Fédon's words to his captives in 1795 that, 'The island was theirs by right; and you are only intruders; you came from England, that is your country, where you ought to have remained'.[32] Wolfe Tone and his United Irish colleagues were perhaps more eloquent, but the message was the same.

To desire the overthrow of British rule, however, was different from effecting it. Since they were of French origin and France had sent troops to occupy Grenada only fourteen years before, they were probably more ready than the Irish to seek French aid from the start, but France at that stage was in no position to provide it. Only after Grey's expedition faltered through exhaustion and disease in the summer of 1794 did the situation become more favourable to revolt. The Grenada garrison had been drawn away in Grey's offensive and in early March 1795 only 293 soldiers remained. The colony's defence largely depended on the militia whose 771 effectives mustered in August 1794 were composed of 49 per

[30] B. Edwards, *The History, Civil and Commercial, of the British Colonies in the West Indies* (London, 1807), vol. I, p. 387; Devas, *Conception Island*, pp. 97–8; Cox, *Free Coloreds*, pp. 92, 94–5, 170, n. 26.

[31] G. T. Heuman, *Between Black and White: Race, Politics, and the Free Coloreds in Jamaica, 1792–1865* (Westport, Conn., 1981), pp. 23–4; D. Geggus, 'The enigma of Jamaica in the 1790s: new light on the causes of slave rebellions', *William and Mary Quarterly*, 44 (1987), pp. 278–9.

[32] J. Hay, *A Narrative of the Insurrection on the Island of Grenada* (London, 1823), pp. 46–7.

cent British colonists, 11 per cent naturalised (mostly former French) subjects and 40 per cent (largely Francophone) free coloureds. Over half were thus potentially disaffected. By then the French republic had regained a footing in the eastern Caribbean where 1,100 men landed in June 1794 to recover Guadeloupe and 1,500 more followed in December. The latter's arrival, exaggerated by rumour to 6,000, may have been the deciding factor in leading the mulatto dissidents to send la Valette and Nogues to Guadeloupe in February 1795 to seek French aid.[33]

To do so was more fraught with revolutionary implications than the United Irish approach to the French a year later, for in February 1794 the National Convention emancipated all French slaves and its commissioner, Victor Hugues, who carried the news to Guadeloupe in June, built up an army of former slaves to expel the British. To invite French assistance was thus to invite social revolution, yet it was something from which the mulatto slave-owners of Grenada did not shrink or indeed even await the French arrival – perhaps because they felt their colour and education would enable them to retain an influence over the former slaves. When the rebellion broke out, one prisoner watched Fédon offering freedom to five captured slave sailors: 'he took them by the shoulders, turned them out of doors, observing at the same time, they were as free as he was'.[34]

Rebellion took place in the night of 1–2 March 1795 as the deliberately planned action of determined rather than desperate men. They had begun holding nocturnal meetings towards the end of 1794. A belated order by Governor Home to arm the white militia may have precipitated the uprising before they were fully ready,[35] but their emissaries had already returned from Guadeloupe with French commissions, supplies and a proclamation from Victor Hugues ordering the French inhabitants to support them on pain of death. The British colonists were caught by surprise and Governor Home captured. The rising was a bloody affair with eleven of the fifteen British inhabitants of Gouyave and Grenville murdered at the outset, and forty-eight out of fifty-one prisoners executed (including Governor Home) during a British counterattack a month later.

The free coloured rebels were joined within a week by most of the French inhabitants of four of the colony's six parishes (alleging to their prisoners necessity imposed by Hugues' punitive proclamation). The free population, including females, had numbered 2,117 in 1783. The acting-Governor estimated that 600 were rebels in arms by the end of March 1795, though only 366 were specifically named by Act of Attainder on 10 August. The property these owned (and omitting what they rented) was

[33] *British Sessional Papers, House of Commons 1801*, vol. III, p. 200; Cox, *Free Coloreds*, p. 86; PRO, WO1/83, Vaughan to Dundas, 11 January 1795; [Wise], *Review of Events*, p. 11.   [34] Hay, *Narrative*, p. 29.
[35] A Grenada Planter, *Brief Enquiry*, p. 15.

listed in 1797: thirty-eight possessed plantations and 1,770 slaves; 128 other individuals owned another 516 slaves, and seven more owned urban tenements. The free rebels were therefore a mixture of property owners and propertyless, and while all were reported as donning the French national cockade, they were not all Francophone. At least four British-born colonists (including two overseers) joined them.[36]

The rebellion got its mass following, however, from the many slaves who joined it. Grenada's slave population had totalled 26,775 in 1788. Of these a third were French-speaking and many followed their Francophone masters. They had some inkling of the political situation: a prisoner later recalled their sentinels shouting the challenge, 'Prenez Guadeloupe', instead of 'Prenez garde à vous'. An 'Eye-Witness' reported that favourite domestics, drivers, tradesmen and other principal slaves on the estates – those most trusted and best treated – were the first to go over because they were in closest contact with the free coloureds. There was also some reckoning of the chances of success. In late March acting-Governor McKenzie estimated 4,000 negroes with the rebels, and an escapee soon after declared that he had served rations for 7,200 people in mid-March. However, a fortnight after the failure of the British attack on the rebel camp on 8 April, McKenzie admitted that the defection among the plantation negroes had now become general.[37]

From Grenada revolt spread to neighbouring St Vincent where two more dissatisfied groups came together. The Black Caribs were hostile to the creeping expansion of British sugar plantations into land they regarded as theirs. In 1778 they had assisted the French to conquer the colony and were receptive to fresh overtures. Reportedly these were made via the French inhabitants.[38] Most of the Francophone population joined the insurrection, but far less is known about the St Vincent insurgents than those of Grenada. They had, along with the French on Dominica, a separate grievance against British rule in that their original land purchases on these two islands had not been confirmed by the French Crown before they were acquired by Britain in 1763. They therefore had to repurchase their property from their new British rulers – on St Vincent on forty-year leases maximum – with quit rents attached. Although there was con-siderable evasion of rent payments, Governor Orde began to enforce

---

[36] MacMahon, *Narrative*, pp. 12, 24; Cox, *Free Coloreds*, p. 14; PRO, CO 101/34, McKenzie to Portland, 28 March 1795; CO 103/9, Act of Attainder, 10 August 1795; CO 106/12, Return of forfeited estates; An Eye-Witness, *Narrative*, p. 161.

[37] Lambert, *House of Commons Sessional Papers*, vol. LXIX, p. 377; Hay, *Narrative*, p. 42; An Eye-Witness, *Narrative*, pp. 11–12; PRO, CO 101/34, McKenzie to Portland, 28 March, 24 April 1795; D. G. Garraway, *A Short Account of the Insurrection of 1795–96* (St George's, 1877), p. 29.

[38] Craton, *Testing the Chains*, pp. 190–1; C. Shephard, *An Historical Account of the Island of St Vincent* (1831, repr. London, 1971), pp. 38–57.

collection in Dominica about 1790 and the land tenure issue may have encouraged the former French to take the lead.[39] The St Vincent historian, Shephard, describes the secretary of the conspiracy as 'Mons. Dumont' (the honorific prefix surely denoting a white) without further detail, but Governor Seton later picked out Jean Pradie, an old inhabitant possessed of considerable property, as very instrumental in stirring up the French and Caribs at the outset.[40] In contrast to Grenada no mulatto leadership emerged, perhaps because the free coloured community was far smaller.[41] If the first eight executions of insurgents in March/April indicate a cross-section of the rebels, they included three whites (at least two of these smallholders), a Carib, a mulatto and three negroes.[42]

In May 1795 Victor Hugues tried to infiltrate some free coloureds into St Kitts, but until June most of the republican effort went into evicting the British from the French colony of St Lucia. When that was achieved, substantial French assistance was sent across the channel to neighbouring St Vincent. In early June, Hugues also tried to precipitate another rising by landing some 500 men on the north-east coast of Dominica. This produced a revolt by 150 Francophone militiamen on the west coast, but because of the mountainous terrain the two failed to link up. Neither the slaves nor Maroons (bought off in 1794) rose in support, so that quick action by Governor Hamilton surrounded each in turn and forced their surrender.[43]

Two months later insurrection also broke out in Jamaica in a way that shows the effect of the fears now being rapidly built up. It was not the product of French machinations, nor deliberate conspiracy by the insurgents, the Trelawney Town Maroons, largest of the four Maroon communities in the colony. The Jamaican planters were on edge at the revolts in the Windward colonies and at the continuing mulatto and slave insurrections in alliance with revolutionary France that were thwarting British efforts to conquer neighbouring French Saint-Domingue. In consequence, when the Trelawney Maroons showed signs of insubordination, the new Governor, Lord Balcarres, responded with a massive display of force intended to intimidate them into submission. The Maroons, in fact, seem to have been signalling a wish for more land for an expanding population and for the reinstatement of a former popular

[39] Manning, *British Colonial Government*, pp. 181–3; J. Spinelli, 'Land use and population in St Vincent 1763–1960', unpublished Ph.D. thesis (University of Florida, 1973), p. 52.
[40] Shephard, *Historical Account*, p. 75; PRO, CO 260/14, Seton to Portland, 12 January 1797. This may have been the 'Pradie Senior' who Shephard lists as leasing 164 acres in the 1760s (appendix 20, pp. lxvi–lxvii) – the third largest French holding.
[41] In 1787, 300 (*ibid.*, appendix 4, p. iv).
[42] PRO, CO 260/14 Meetings of His Majesty's (HM) Council, 1, 26 April 1795.
[43] Cox, *Free Coloreds*, p. 144; Shephard, *Historical Account*, pp. 107, 113, 120; Honychurch, *Dominica Story*, pp. 80–4.

British superintendent, but the display of force panicked them into insurrection on 12 August 1795 out of fear that they were about to be enslaved. The 600-strong community took refuge in the mountains, ambushing search columns and raiding adjacent plantations which they burnt – six in one week in September – and from which they attracted 150–200 slaves.[44] By late summer 1795 actual or feared insurrection had spread along the length of Britain's West Indian empire.

IV

The British government's response to events in the Caribbean was to organise the biggest single expedition ever yet attempted from Britain. Between August 1795 and May 1796, 35,000 soldiers departed for the West Indies – a marked contrast to the 10,000 belatedly and grudgingly sent to Ireland in 1798, which shows the comparative importance attached to these rebellions at the time.[45]

In the military situation of 1795 the fate of the West Indies was deemed crucial either to the continuance of war or the making of peace. Revolutionary France had pushed the Austrians back over the Rhine, induced Prussia and Spain to make peace and forced Holland to change sides. Short of some sudden internal political or economic collapse, France would not be defeated quickly. If peace had to be negotiated, Britain needed all the Caribbean conquests it could get to try to bargain against French success in Europe: the West Indian revolts not only deflected resources from this fail-safe objective, they threatened to make Britain suppliant to France overseas as well as in Europe. If on the other hand the war continued, Britain faced the destruction of the most valuable part of its overseas empire by subversion. The War Secretary, Henry Dundas, was 'very much alarmed indeed' at the effect of the success of the revolts in Grenada and St Vincent 'upon the disaffected whites, and ill-disposed insurgent Negroes in other islands'. France showed every indication of continuing its counteroffensive, acquiring Santo Domingo in the Spanish peace, occupying the Dutch islands, and with Victor Hugues continuing his insurrectionary designs from Guadeloupe. Dundas dreaded that if the French reinforced the Caribbean first or intercepted the British expedition at sea, it 'would put a decisive end to the war in their favour'.[46]

---

[44] Geggus, 'Enigma of Jamaica', pp. 279–83; R. C. Dallas, *The History of the Maroons* (London, 1803), vol. I, pp. 131–85.
[45] M. Duffy, *Soldiers, Sugar and Seapower. The British Expeditions to the Caribbean and the War against Revolutionary France* (Oxford, 1987), pp. 159–98, 253; T. Pakenham, *The Year of Liberty* (London, 1972), pp. 247–8.
[46] BL, Add. MSS 40, 102, Dundas to York, 28 July 1795; John Rylands Library (JRL), Manchester, English MS 907, Dundas to Pitt, 29 June, 5 July 1795; J. S. Corbett and H. W. Richmond (eds.), *The Private Papers of George, 2nd Earl Spencer 1794–1801* (London, 1913), vol. I, pp. 148–9.

In 1796 Dundas admitted that he would rather hear of 15,000 French landed in Ireland or even Britain than in Jamaica. The former threat might be quickly isolated by Britain's superior navy, but a superior French force in the Caribbean could take a long time to counter and in the meantime devastating economic damage might have been done. The West Indian colonies were easily Britain's largest and most vulnerable overseas financial investment: estimates varied from £37 million to £70 million compared with £18 million invested in the East Indies. Their loss, it was widely believed, would cut up financial credit by its roots. During the previous war George III had warned that they had to be defended even at the risk of invasion of Britain since, 'if we lose our Sugar Islands it will be impossible to raise money to continue the war', and Dundas, who in 1794 considered that 'all modern wars are a contention of purse', feared in 1796 that 'the loss of Jamaica in the present moment and state of the country would be complete ruin to our credit and put you at once at the feet of the enemy'.[47] The losses on Grenada were subsequently reckoned at £2.5–£4.5 million and on St Vincent at £815,532. Such losses could not be allowed to spread, and Pitt's government felt that the only way this could be prevented was by crushing the rebellions quickly, and eliminating the French revolutionaries from the Caribbean so as to prevent revolt being rekindled or extended. Hence the vast (for Britain) force despatched to the Caribbean in 1795–6.[48]

The war begun with such high hopes in 1793 had run out of control by 1795. Dundas wrote on 5 July that 'our West Indian war is just beginning and on very disadvantageous terms'. The assembly of the expeditionary force was troublesome in the extreme. The country's logistical resources were stretched to the utmost. Reports of the immense mortality of Grey's previous expedition led to George III refusing to allow the Guards to be sent, for fear of the effect of high casualties among their socially elite officer corps, and to mutiny amongst some other regiments who lacked royal protection. In Dublin (22–24 August) and Cork (3–5 September), the troops were encouraged into major outbursts of disobedience, which brought all commercial business to a halt, by a disaffected Irish populace still simmering from the Fitzwilliam episode.[49]

Inauspicious beginnings were followed by an equally inauspicious departure, the expedition being repeatedly driven back by storms. Nevertheless, by Spring 1796 a sufficient force had been gathered for Sir

[47] Corbett and Richmond, *Private Papers*, p. 318; Duffy, *Soldiers, Sugar and Seapower*, pp. 16–17; J. W. Fortescue (ed.), *The Correspondence of King George the Third* (London, 1927–8), vol. IV, p. 483; PRO, CO 30/8/157, fo. 176.
[48] MacMahon, *Narrative*, 128; a Grenada Planter, *Brief Enquiry*, p. 123; PRO, CO 261/9, fo. 118; JRL, English MS 907, 5 July 1795.
[49] JRL, English MS 907, 5 July 1795; Aspinall, *Later Correspondence of George III*, vol. II, p. 381; Duffy, *Soldiers, Sugar and Seapower*, pp. 173–4.

Ralph Abercromby to restore the situation. By then the Maroon revolt on Jamaica had collapsed as the Trelawney Maroons became demoralised by their failure to attract wider support, and by the methodical destruction of their provision grounds by the authorities. When bloodhounds were brought in from Cuba to track them down, their morale disintegrated and they surrendered in January. To windward, Abercromby firstly eliminated St Lucia, the nearest French supply base to St Vincent and Grenada, and then suppressed the insurgents in the latter. In June 1796 their main strongholds were stormed and the insurgents overwhelmed. On Grenada Fédon disappeared (and thus gained immortality), but thirty-eight others (predominantly mulattos) were hanged and other white or free coloured participants exiled. Countless rebel slaves caught in arms were executed. The rest were allowed to return to their plantations, although 486 (21.3 per cent) of those belonging to attainted rebels were missing in 1797, and altogether a quarter of Grenada's slaves (*c.* 7,000) were reckoned killed in the revolt. On St Vincent the same happened, with most of the French population being evicted from the colony, as was the entire 5,000 Black Carib community to Honduras. The 586 surviving Trelawney Maroons of Jamaica were sent further afield, first to Nova Scotia and eventually to Sierra Leone.[50]

V

The Irish dissidents not only failed to revolt at the same time as those in the West Indies, but also failed to take immediate advantage of the opportunity subsequently created by the despatch of almost all of Britain's remaining military reserves to suppress the Caribbean revolution.

This slow response was primarily due to the late conversion of the United Irishmen into armed-force revolutionaries and to hesitations as to how to achieve the type of revolution they envisaged. Only in late 1794 did some Belfast members start developing a secret-society organisation, and only in May 1795 did the more radical members of the Dublin Society decide to go underground. Only at this stage too did they make their first tentative overtures for alliance to the Defenders. To succeed, the United Irishmen, with a hitherto fairly restricted social membership, needed a mass following. This came with increased Catholic militancy spreading, along with Defenderism, with Catholic fugitives from the 'Armagh Outrages' of late 1795, forced out by supporters of the new Protestant

[50] Duffy, *Soldiers, Sugar and Seapower*, pp. 217–40, 242–4, 257–63; PRO, CO 101/34, Houston to Portland, 30 July 1796; CO 101/35, Green to Portland, 12 July, 21 October, 1797; CO 106/12, Return of forfeited estates; MacMahon, *Narrative*, p. 128; CO 261/9, fo. 93.

Orange Order with the apparent connivance of local Ascendancy authorities.[51] Yet not until 1796 were determined approaches made to the French for assistance, and only in that autumn was a beginning made in the transformation of the Society into a military organisation to effect revolution. When a French expedition appeared in Bantry Bay in December 1796, they were still unprepared. Only in Ulster, at the opposite end of the kingdom, were military preparations far advanced. The United Irishmen and their Defender partners awaited the results of a French landing, and when the French failed to land because of bad weather the opportunity evaporated.[52]

The French appearance at Bantry Bay, however, enhanced prospects for a successful revolution by showing the feasibility of French assistance, so that the ranks of the United Irishmen swelled dramatically in the early months of 1797. The alarmed Ascendancy authorities began to strike back, purging the militia and forcibly disarming Ulster. By May 1797 members of the Ulster Society were urgently demanding a rising before they lost the capacity to act. The first half of 1797 has been regarded as the time when 'the United Irishmen might have produced their revolution with a minimum of foreign aid', but the extremists were held back by moderates within the Dublin society and the main Catholic delegates on the Executive, each urging restraint until the imminently expected invasion by the French or their Dutch allies occurred.[53]

This concern of much of the United Irish leadership to wait for a French landing contrasts starkly with the decision of the Grenada and St Vincent rebels to act by themselves thus taking the Caribbean authorities by surprise. The difference resulted from the fears of the Irish middling-class revolutionary leadership that if it let loose the Catholic peasantry then it might not be able to control them. The United Irishmen were prepared to offer the peasants the abolition of tithes and the reduction of taxes, but they had no wish for a major redistribution of property.[54] Wolfe Tone's second memorial to the French Directory in February 1796 sketched out the Society's ideal of a virtually bloodless palace revolution: with the French landing in sufficient force to persuade the existing Anglo-Irish ruling class to change sides rather than resist, so that a respectable and strong

[51] N. J. Curtin, 'The transformation of the Society of United Irishmen into a mass-based revolutionary organisation, 1794–6', Irish Historical Studies, 24 (1985), pp. 463–92; Elliott, Partners in Revolution, pp. 71–2, 95–6; E. Hay, History of the Insurrection of the County of Wexford (Dublin, 1803), pp. 39–40.
[52] Elliot, Partners in Revolution, pp. 79–115.
[53] Ibid., pp. 123–4, 127–33; W. J. MacNeven, Pieces of Irish History (New York, 1807), 'Memoir...delivered to the Irish Government', p. 189.
[54] MacNeven, Pieces, pp. 221–2; Elliott, Partners in Revolution, pp. 27–8; Wall, 'United Irish movement', pp. 133–4.

revolutionary government could be formed at once to maintain law and order. Another leader, Dr MacNeven, told his interrogators in 1798 that they sought a revolution like that of 1688, when a popular general landed with an army to act successfully and bloodlessly in conjunction with the British people. He 'only wished that French force that would cheque the Chounery [sic] of the Country... and give the New Executive Power time to form a provisional Government.'[55] In the West Indies to invite in the French revolutionary army was to invite social revolution, but in Ireland many United Irish leaders delayed their revolt in order to wait for the French army to *prevent* social revolution.

Commenting on such attitudes, a Dublin Ordnance Board official declared that, 'Their personal fears and their passion for finesse where force was necessary served Government'.[56] Delay occasioned many harmful consequences for the cautious conspirators. The Irish government had time to initiate countermeasures: savage intimidatory legislation and the formation of a loyalist yeomanry in 1796; the forcible disarming of Ulster in 1797, which severely damaged that province's ability to lead a rebellion and led to divisions and demoralisation within the movement. Demoralisation increased when the arms searches were extended to other provinces in early 1798, as the authorities frantically sought to prevent rebellion by depriving it of weapons before it began. Moreover the larger the United Irish movement grew and the longer it held back from acting, the more chance there was of informers emerging who betrayed the movement to the authorities.

There were Dublin United leaders, notably Lord Edward Fitzgerald and Arthur O'Connor from the Anglo-Irish elite, who pressed immediate revolt without awaiting the French, but Fitzgerald was unable to gain an ascendancy till March 1798 when the moderates were amongst those captured when the Leinster Provincial Committee meeting was betrayed by an informer. Yet even Fitzgerald was so nervous of success that he repeatedly postponed the date of a general rising till he too was caught on 19 May and the remaining Dublin leaders next day, so that the insurrection which broke out on 24 May was left without a head.[57]

When revolt at last began, it was a disorganised, spontaneous affair, less influenced by any plans of the United Irish leadership than by terror at the violent disarming of Leinster, which the authorities were now undertaking, and by escalating Catholic fears of being massacred by Orangemen. In this

[55] O'Brien, *Autobiography of Tone*, vol. II, appendix, pp. 383–95; MacNeven, *Pieces*, pp. 197, 204–5, 218–19; BL, Add. MSS 33, 106, fol. 80–v, Alexander to Pelham, 20 September 1798. The Breton peasant Chouans conducted a bitter civil war (*Chouannerie*) against the French Republic from 1793–6.   [56] BL, Add. MSS 33, 106, fo. 82.
[57] Roger Wells, *Insurrection: The British Experience, 1795–1803* (Gloucester, 1983), pp. 111–21, 128–36; Elliott, *Partners in Revolution*, pp. 150–1, 193–200.

it had perhaps more in common with the panic desperation of the Maroons of Jamaica than the careful calculation of the Grenada or St Vincent insurgents. This is not to deny the large part played by local United Irish organisations in the rebellion. It was not simply a wild Catholic peasant 'Chounery', although it was portrayed as such by those seeking to rally Protestants against it and by rebels of substance subsequently seeking exoneration. Even in Wexford, where United Irish organisation had long been considered weak and local leaders reluctant, recent research has suggested stronger organisation and greater United Irish input into the rebellion.[58]

United Irishmen, Defenders and other participants, however, took their decisions at a local level and largely according to local circumstances. Wexford proved the county most committed to the rising and a number of local factors have been adduced in explanation. It was highly politicised after two successive, closely contested county elections, and it was highly prosperous until recession (blamed on government malt taxes) hit its predominant barley and malt trade in 1797–8. Its ruling gentry were divided between organised pro-Ascendancy and pro-liberal power blocks (which led some into the Orange Order and others into the United Irishmen), and consequently unable to concert a uniform and restrained law enforcement policy and unable to control the growing extremism among the subgentry of Wexford's large Protestant community. This group, threatened already by the collapse of the middleman system of tenant farming which it had dominated, became increasingly more fearful of Catholic resurgency and used its access to the magistracy to press a harsh law-and-order policy extending to arbitrary house-burning and executions. This was bitterly opposed by the liberals and their allies in the increasingly politically confident ranks of the Catholic middle class, as well as by the Catholic peasantry increasingly terrified by this escalation of judicial violence and more attentive to United Irish and Defender propaganda. The result was the total collapse of traditional lines of authority and the old moral economy, and a rapid and mutual escalation of tensions until they erupted into reprisals and rebellion when news arrived of risings elsewhere.[59]

[58] Elliott, *Partners in Revolution*, pp. 196–8; BL, Add. MSS 38, 102, account by Thomas Handcock, fos. 10–11, 70–2; L. M. Cullen, 'The 1798 rebellion in Wexford: United Irishmen organisation, membership, leadership' in K. Whelan and W. Nolan (eds.), *Wexford: History and Society* (Dublin, 1987), pp. 248–95.

[59] For substantial recent re-examination of the Wexford rebellion in its local and wider context, see T. Powell, 'An economic factor in the Wexford Rebellion of 1798', *Studia Hibernica*, 16 (1976), pp. 140–57; L. M. Cullen, 'The 1798 rebellion in its eighteenth-century context' in P. J. Corish (ed.), *Radicals, Rebels and Establishments* (Belfast, 1985), pp. 91–113; K. Whelan, 'The religious factor in the 1798 rebellion in county Wexford' in P. O'Flanagan, P. Ferguson and K. Whelan (eds.), *Rural Ireland 1600–1900: Mod-*

Without overall leadership from the United Irish organisation, however, the risings lacked co-ordination and were suppressed more speedily than those in the Caribbean. The counties around Dublin which rose on 24–25 May were largely suppressed by 28 May, though some groups held out in more inaccessible areas till mid-July. Wexford rose on 26–27 May and after tough resistance was finally put down by early July. Antrim and Down rose in Ulster on 7–8 June but subsided after a week of sharp conflict. The belated arrival of Humbert's 1,000 French troops at Killala Bay on 22 August sparked a rising in hitherto quiescent County Mayo, neighbouring Sligo, and also in Longford and Westmeath, but this too collapsed when Humbert was cornered and surrendered on 8 September.

After the rebellion loyalists claimed £1,023,000 compensation for their losses (half from Wexford), while rebels are thought to have lost as much again. Between 25,000 to 30,000 deaths have been estimated; over seven-eighths were rebels, many summarily executed when caught in arms. Some 1,450 were convicted for insurrection in the eighteen months after May 1798: a third were sentenced to death (of whom perhaps a quarter were respited in 1798), some to flogging or imprisonment, and the majority to transportation or military service abroad. Most of the United Irish leadership was among the eighty-two state prisoners rounded up before the rebellion. Of these Lord Edward Fitzgerald died of wounds received in his capture, and after five others had been sentenced to death and four executed, the rest offered full confessions and in return were exiled, the twenty most important after detention for the remainder of the war. The last leader to be captured, as a French officer on a warship trying to land troops in October, was Wolfe Tone, who committed suicide to avoid sentence of execution.[60]

VI

The French Revolution affected the empires of all European powers. It led to revolts which destroyed France's Caribbean empire and Spain's American empire. The British empire too faced a revolutionary crisis between 1795 and 1798, which it overcame.

The British empire survived because the rebels failed to muster enough

ernisation and Change (Cork, 1987), pp. 62–85; Cullen, '1798 rebellion in Wexford', pp. 248–95, and K. Whelan, 'The role of the Catholic Priest in the 1798 rebellion in county Wexford', pp. 296–315, in Whelan and Nolan, *Wexford: History and Society*; and K. Whelan, 'Politicisation in County Wexford and the origins of the 1798 rebellion', in Gough and Dickson, *Ireland and the French Revolution*, pp. 156–78.

[60] The best recent account of the rebellion is Pakenham's *Year of Liberty*. For losses, see Pakenham, pp. 321–34, 392; MacDowell, *Ireland...1760–1801*, pp. 657–8, 675–7; Marianne Elliott, *Wolfe Tone, Prophet of Irish Independence* (New Haven, Conn., 1989), pp. 386–99.

strength to attain their ends. The French Revolution was an inspiration, but its practical help was a disappointment. Except in Ireland in late 1796, French aid was too late and too small for decisive effect, sufficient only temporarily to prolong resistance. French difficulties in financing and equipping complicated amphibious expeditions and getting them past Britain's stronger navy should not be underestimated, nor should weather factors which restricted departures and which disrupted the 1796 attempt. However, there was also lack of effective concert. At Dominica in June 1795 and Bantry Bay in December 1796 large French forces evaded British patrols, but arrived at the diametrically opposite place to that from which they could expect most insurgent support.

This was not for lack of information. Partly fear of the British navy led them to the shortest possible route, but perhaps even more it resulted from French determination to do things their own way and for their own purposes, rather than to be compliant auxiliaries for the rebels. Over Ireland they refused to be led by the United Irishmen, sought alternative contacts with the Defenders, and played Irish agents independently of each other. They were never completely committed to the United Irish programme because Irish independence was not essential to them. A destructive 'Chounery' or the subversion of Irish sailors in the Royal Navy would also effectively disrupt the British war effort and be less demanding on French resources to implement. In 1797 the French left preparations for a major invasion to their Dutch ally. Rather than landing themselves to set off the revolt, French policy switched to waiting for the Irish to rebel and then to send help. French interests moved elsewhere. Austria's unexpected collapse in 1796–7 opened new opportunities in central and southern Europe; the flight of the Director Carnot and the death of General Hoche in September 1797 removed the two French leaders most interested in Irish rebellion; and Bonaparte preferred to sail to Egypt in May 1798 rather than to Ireland.[61] Likewise in the Caribbean, Victor Hugues and the Guadeloupe French grew cool to raising rebellion when they found privateering more rewarding. When French forces next landed on a British colony – at Anguilla in November 1796 – it was to plunder rather than liberate.[62]

With French assistance so unreliable, it was even more important for the rebels to maximise domestic support by rallying all possible dissident groups to their cause. However, the new revolutionary popular politics

---

[61] W. B. Kennedy, '"Without any guarantee on our part". The French Directory's Irish Policy', *Proceedings of the Consortium on Revolutionary Europe* (1972), pp. 50–64; Elliott, *Partners in Revolution*, pp. 77–95, 102–7, 139–42, 152–62, 214–34.

[62] R. S. Johnston, *The Leeward Islands during the French Wars* (1932), part 1, pp. 14–15. One further attempt was made to raise Dominica in 1797 (*ibid.*, part 4, p. 8).

failed to overcome the old divisive politics sufficiently to create a united front. The Dominican revolt collapsed quickly when the Francophone white and mulatto rebels failed to attract either the Caribs (recently bought off by government) or the slaves. On St Vincent, Carib participation and early murder of Anglophone slaves alienated many of the latter from the rebellion. Very few of Jamaica's 256,000-plus slaves joined the Trelawney Maroons. In Ireland, the more the revolutionary movement developed into a Catholic mass-movement, the more Protestants of all sorts were frightened away, particularly when United Irish attempts to gain Catholic support, by exciting fears of Orange persecution, helped produce bloody sectarian conflict when the southern rebellion began. Presbyterian Ulster only belatedly and partially responded to the Leinster Outbreak, an outcome to which the surprised Irish Under-Secretary concluded that 'the Popish tinge in the rebellion and the treatment of France to Switzerland and America has really done much'.[63]

Much remains to be discovered of what motivated rebellion, neutrality or active loyalty in even the most dissident groups. Intertribal jealousy and military intimidation helped keep the three other tribes, who numbered over half of Jamaica's Maroon population, from joining the Trelawney Maroons.[64] The growth of commercial prosperity in the 1790s may have kept the minority of Francophone whites and free coloureds actively in the loyalist militia on Grenada (9.6 per cent of militiamen in April 1796) and St Vincent,[65] and confined the Dominican rebellion to the Francophone militia of only one district.

Without decisive French intervention, the rebellions were ultimately dependent on how much mass support they could gain from the largest groups within their populations: the Caribbean slaves and the Irish Catholic peasantry.

In the event, the slaves in the British colonies were unusually quiescent – sufficiently for Dundas to recruit twelve slave regiments which formed a third of the British army in the Caribbean by the early 1800s. David Geggus has recently posited massive white military presence during the French revolutionary era as the reason for the quiescence of Jamaica's slaves.[66] On Grenada and St Vincent the rapid British confinement to the capitals left slaves freedom to choose and many either voluntarily or under threat joined the rebels in the largest British slave insurrections of

[63] Cooke to Wickham, 2 June 1798, quoted in C. Dickson, *Revolt in the North. Antrim and Down in 1798* (Dublin, 1960), pp. 121–2. France's aggressive behaviour to sister republics offended Ulster republican sentiment. Irish divisions are explored in W. B. Kennedy, 'The Irish Jacobins', *Studia Hibernica*, 16 (1976), pp. 109–21.

[64] Geggus, 'Enigma of Jamaica', pp. 283–5; A. E. Furness, 'The Maroon War of 1795', *Jamaican Historical Review*, 5 (1965), pp. 33, 39–40.

[65] PRO, CO 101/34, fo. 215; CO 260/14, Meeting of HM's Council, 1 April 1795.

[66] Geggus, 'Enigma of Jamaica', pp. 288–99.

the period. Nevertheless, others stayed loyal and were formed into colonial Ranger battalions to combat the insurgents, and others still on Grenada can be seen as trying to keep out of the fighting, continuing plantation work or tending their provision grounds or squatting in abandoned houses and surviving by chewing sugar cane.[67] The Creolisation of established slaves and a massive influx of new slaves in the 1790s disrupted former patterns of revolt. Proximity to and understanding of white culture and of French revolutionary (and abolitionist) ideology were now the main destabilising factors, and skilled and domestic Creole slaves closest to whites and free coloureds the most likely to revolt, whereas the Grenada 'Eye-Witness' noted field slaves and particularly new slaves were the last to join the insurrection and many remained faithful. New slaves may have been cushioned against these rebellions by their incomprehension of the complexities of colonial politics and their ignorance of French, while many Anglophone Creole slaves had imbibed British Francophobia and were equally immunised against French doctrines. It is also possible that, as in Dominica in 1795, news spread that life for the emancipated slaves under revolutionary conscription on Guadeloupe was scarcely better than their former slavery.[68]

In Ireland many Catholics were also surprisingly quiescent. Munster played no part in the rebellion, nor did Connaught until the French landing three months later. Some priests were carried into the rebellion by local feeling, and a handful of gentry participated either willingly or under pressure, but the Catholic aristocracy, gentry and clergy generally stayed loyal and urged defence of 'constitution, the social order and the Christian religion' against atheist Jacobin republicanism. The United Irishmen claimed a membership of 300,000 early in 1798, but possibly far less than a third took part in the revolt. Many had joined the Society for socio-recreational purposes, or for insurance, or from a belief that a French landing would do their work for them, so that as the Carlow secretary later admitted, 'people in general were not aware that they would ever be brought into real action'. Many had also been demoralised by the government's savage disarmament campaign, so that there was much initial reluctance even amongst many participants.[69]

A major French landing or a major rebel victory over government

---

[67] R. P. Devas, *The Island of Grenada 1650–1950* (Grenada, 1965), pp. 144–5; Hay, *Narrative*, p. 128; Craton, *Testing the Chains*, pp. 189–90.

[68] An Eye-Witness, *Narrative*, pp. 11–12; Geggus, 'Enigma of Jamaica', pp. 291–2; PRO, CO 71/27, fo. 140.

[69] MacDowell, *Ireland…1760–1801*, p. 611; Whelan, 'The role of the Catholic Priest in the 1798 Rebellion', pp. 296–315; Cullen, '1798 rebellion in Wexford', pp. 188, 201, 258; Curtin, 'Transformation of the Society of United Irishmen', pp. 490–2; R. J. McHugh (ed.), *Carlow in '98. The Autobiography of William Farrell of Carlow* (Dublin, 1949), pp. 43, 50, 82–3.

forces might have roused more Catholics. The absence of the former left untested Wolfe Tone's assertion that the yeomanry and militia would defect when the French landed, so that the rebellion was in many areas a civil war between Catholic militia and Catholic rebels. In these circumstances the rebels were severely handicapped by their lack of military training and leadership and of arms and ammunition, particularly artillery and the expertise to handle it. Numbers and enthusiasm gained important local successes, particularly in Wexford, but they were not enough to achieve the really big victory necessary to carry the rebel forces irresistibly across county borders to rouse Catholics elsewhere to a victorious cause.[70]

The Caribbean revolts lasted longer than in Ireland because the non-slave insurgents had more experience with firearms and terrain better suited to prolonged resistance, but nowhere did insurgent morale stand up to prolonged set-backs so well as their opponents who had sufficient military discipline to recover from defeat, a preponderance of artillery and an often unrecognised ability to adapt to insurgent warfare (as by recruiting slaves and German *jaegers* as mobile light-infantry).

In this crisis the imperial government demonstrated a considerable number of strengths. Even its *ancien régime* nature as an aggregate of legislative entities, disliked by both the rebels and the centralising Pitt, proved a fortuitous advantage in producing different policies on Catholicism at the same time, separating the revolts and enabling government to deal with each in turn rather than simultaneously. In general the Royal Navy was able to isolate the revolts from decisive French assistance. Its victory at Camperdown in October 1797 decisively ended Dutch projects of invasion, and even when it failed to stop Hoche's expedition in 1796, fear of its intervention helped confuse that enterprise.[71] Otherwise, foreign assistance in both the West Indies and in Ireland was confined to ineffective small-scale forays which had the best chance of evading the British blockade, but the least chance to achieve much if they got through. Lastly, there was sufficient determination within Pitt's government to face up to each successive stage of the crisis, and, above all, sufficient support within the British nation to enable it to do so. Despite trouble in recruiting the 1795 expedition, enough troops were assembled to suppress the Caribbean revolts. Hoche's invasion attempt on Ireland may have swelled the ranks of the United Irishmen, but it also swelled those of the Irish yeomanry and the Orange Order, and when the invasion

[70] G. A. Hayes-McCoy, 'Insurgent efforts towards military organisation, 1798', *Irish Sword*, 3 (1957–8), pp. 51–6; C. Dickson, *The Wexford Rising in 1798* (Tralee, 1955), pp. 182–3.

[71] E. H. Stuart Jones, *An Invasion that Failed. The French Expedition to Ireland, 1796* (Oxford, 1950), pp. 107–61.

threat extended to Britain itself in 1797–8, it led to a patriotic upsurge which saw British militia regiments volunteering to go to Ireland to fight the rebellion. If at times there was considerable dissatisfaction with Pitt's government, it did not extend to a general refusal to fight to maintain the British empire.

7   Patriotism and the English state in the 1790s

David Eastwood

The last decade or so has seen a marked revival of interest in the way in which conservative opinion in Britain responded to the challenge of the French Revolution. If fraternal inquiries into British radicalism proliferated in the 1960s and 1970s, a good deal of scholarly attention in the 1980s was lavished on explaining the loyalist response to revolution. This shift in focus was foreshadowed in 1977 when Harry Dickinson argued, in the concluding section of *Liberty and Property*, that it is 'evident that the radicals had neither massive popular support nor an effectual political organization capable of seizing power; whereas their conservative opponents possessed considerable power and were ready to use it'. Dickinson went on to suggest that conservatives, rather than radicals, won the battle of ideas which raged in the 1790s.[1] Ian Christie went still further in his Ford Lectures for 1984, ending his discussion of 'The intellectual repulse of revolution', with the confident assertion that, 'in the 1790s, British publicists summoned up the lessons of history, of pragmatic experience, and of utility, in defence of the existing system of government. In so doing they appealed to and rallied the instinctive support of the great majority of the British political nation'.[2] Shortly before Christie delivered his Ford Lectures, Robert Dozier's *For King, Constitution, and Country* appeared, claiming to offer the first systematic treatment of the relationship between the British government and the loyalist movements of the 1790s.[3]

Reviewing recent writing in 1989 Harry Dickinson insisted that, 'it is

[1] H. T. Dickinson, *Liberty and Property: Political Ideology in Eighteenth-Century Britain* (London, 1977), p. 271. See also H. T. Dickinson, 'Popular loyalism in Britain in the 1790s' in Eckhart Hellmuth (ed.), *The Transformation of Political Culture: Germany and England in the Late Eighteenth Century* (Oxford, 1990), pp. 503–34. In preparing this chapter I benefited greatly from discussions and correspondence with Austin Gee. I am also grateful to Peter Ghosh, Joanna Innes and my fellow contributors for comments on an earlier draft.

[2] Ian R. Christie, *Stress and Stability in Late Eighteenth-Century Britain: Reflections on the British Avoidance of Revolution* (Oxford, 1984), p. 182. Professor Christie restates his position in his contribution to this volume, see pp. 169–87.

[3] *For King, Constitution, and Country: The English Loyalists and the French Revolution* (Lexington, Ky., 1983).

now being recognised that one of the most significant impacts of the French Revolution on British politics was the enormous boost it gave to popular conservatism'.[4] But if recent work has shifted the terms of debate by challenging the Whiggish certainties of an earlier consensus on the nature and strength of English radicalism, it has simultaneously raised new problems.[5] There has, for example, been a marked tendency to treat concepts such as 'loyalism' and 'patriotism' as if they were unproblematic. Although a few writers have subjected the language of conservatism and the activities of loyalists to careful scrutiny,[6] others have apparently been content to see popular patriotism as a straightforward response to a persuasive conservative ideology. In the same way the relationship between government policy and loyalist activity has generally been seen as direct and uncomplicated. A rather blunt understanding of the contours of debate in Britain in the 1790s and a crude conceptualisation of the relationship between government policy and loyalist activity is particularly characteristic of Robert Dozier's work. Dozier proceeds on the assumption that Edward Thompson, Gwyn Williams and Albert Goodwin have, so to speak, solved the problem of radicalism. English radicalism in the 1790s, Dozier concludes, was a blundering, somewhat inchoate, but genuinely revolutionary movement. He then goes on:

With the radical stimulus explained, the loyal response can now be understood. For the loyalists were not just the privileged classes in England, but hundreds of thousands of Englishmen in all ranks of life, who not only outnumbered the radicals but also were impressed with a view of the relationship between the individual and society which had implications as revolutionary as any doctrines synthesized by the radicals. Now that Goodwin has explained in detail what the radicals were attempting, we can see that their greatest immediate impact was the creation of the loyalists, people who voluntarily joined the system, sometimes led by but at other times leading the government.[7]

Such a view underestimates the ideological ambiguities of loyalism; exaggerates the uniformity, reliability and pervasiveness of popular patriotism; and ignores the highly problematic nature of the relationship between the government and the many, but varied, effusions of loyalism throughout the 1790s.

In what follows, I have tried to re-examine some aspects of the

---

[4] 'Popular conservatism and militant 1789–1815' in H. T. Dickinson (ed.), *Britain and the French Revolution 1789–1815* (London, 1989), p. 103.

[5] John Dinwiddy's suggestive contribution to this volume voices some other reservations about what he has called the new 'Dickinsonian consensus', see pp. 38–49.

[6] Amongst the more illuminating recent contributions are John Dinwiddy, 'England' in Otto Dann and John Dinwiddy (eds.), *Nationalism in the Age of the French Revolution* (London, 1988), pp. 53–70; T. P. Schofield, 'Conservative political thought in Britain in response to the French Revolution', *Historical Journal*, 29, 3 (1986), pp. 601–22; Robert Hole, *Pulpits, Politics and Public Order in England 1760–1832* (Cambridge, 1989), especially pp. 95–159.   [7] Dozier, *For King, Constitution, and Country*, p. x.

relationship between conservative ideology and popular patriotism in the 1790s, and, beyond that, I have attempted to look afresh at the interplay between loyalist activities and the state in order to try to evaluate their role in sustaining an essentially conservative polity during the era of the French Revolution. Dozier's volume ends by celebrating what he describes as 'the remarkable ability of the English to arrive at a consensus during times of stress and emergency', a view mirrored almost exactly in Ian Christie's Ford Lectures.[8] To speak of consensus, at least in the period before the breakdown of the Peace of Amiens, is somewhat fanciful. Rather than deal in such comfortable abstractions, we need to look in detail at sometimes delicate and frequently fragile relationship between conservative ideology, loyalist activities and government policy.

In the wake of the French Revolution the broadly based constituency which had supported moderate constitutional reform in Britain in the 1780s first fragmented and then dissolved. In the 1780s the language of reform had underpinned politically moderate but structurally ambitious programmes aimed at regenerating the British polity.[9] As the French Revolution inspired more specifically democratic reform movements in Britain, so both the language and programmes of the reformers (most notably, of course, parliamentary reform) became increasingly identified with popular radicalism. Even where the objectives of reformers remained constant, the changed configuration of politics in the 1790s invested both their projects and their rhetoric with a quite different political significance. As Burke put it in 1792 when opposing Grey's motion for a reform of Parliament: 'However upright the motives of the hon. gentlemen near him might be, they must necessarily, in order to succeed in their objective, unite themselves with some of the worst men in the kingdom.' A 'moderate or temperate reform' was, Burke argued, now quite impossible. Burke's views were echoed with, if anything, greater clarity by Windham.[10] In this process of political realignment, the constituency for moderate political reform all but disappeared.[11]

---

[8] *Ibid.*, p. 179; Christie, *Stress and Stability*, pp. 215–18.

[9] Ian R. Christie, *Wilkes, Wyvil, and Reform: The Parliamentary Reform Movement in British Politics 1760–85* (London, 1962), chs. 3–6; E. C. Black, *The Association: British Extra-Parliamentary Organization, 1769–1793* (Cambridge, Mass., 1963); Joanna Innes, 'Politics and Morals. The reformation of manners movement in later eighteenth-century England' in Hellmuth, *Transformation of Political Culture*, pp. 57–118; J. D. Binney, *British Public Finance and Administration, 1774–92* (Oxford, 1958); J. R. Torrance, 'Social class and bureaucratic innovation: the commissioners for examining the public accounts 1780–7', *Past and Present*, 78 (1978), pp. 56–81.

[10] *Parliamentary History*, 29 (1792), cols. 1323, 1325–6. For a similar view, see Arthur Young, *The Example of France a Warning to Britain*, 3rd edn (London, 1793), p. 58.

[11] Moderate reforming associations outside Parliament fragmented in the process. Manchester's Literary and Philosophical Society, which had been highly influential in the later 1780s, fell victim to harrassment and witch-hunts from the aptly named, 'Society to

Meanwhile conservative responses to the French Revolution explicitly affirmed both the utility and legitimacy of British public institutions. Antirevolutionary polemics tended to adopt one of two broad positions, arguing either that Britain had escaped the revolutionary crisis which had engulfed France because of the intrinsic superiority of its political and social institutions, or, more urgently, that British institutions and political culture must now be defended against a real and growing revolutionary threat both from within and without. Either way the avowed objective was the preservation of the established order within British society.

The essentially defensive nature of conservative ideology explicitly precluded the possibility of major institutional reform in response to any real or imagined revolutionary threat. Having defended the continuing effectiveness of British institutions in theoretical or polemical terms, it was hardly possible to deny it in practice by embarking on a thoroughgoing programme of political and administrative reform. As Arthur Young put it: 'We know that English practice is good – we know that French theory is bad.'[12] The British response to the Revolution should, in part at least, itself vindicate the ideological claims of conservatives. Thus, though the challenges of domestic radicalism and of the war led to a series of specific reforms and improvised innovations, they did not lead to a fundamental restructuring of the British state. The machinery of 'Pitt's Terror', although probably effective as a temporary deterrent, did not become institutionalised as a policy of systematic state violence; whilst political surveillance throughout the revolutionary period remained principally the responsibility of the Home Office, its network of informers and of local magistrates: the Alien Office, although significant, became neither the permanent nor the most pervasive agency of state surveillance.[13] Even wartime fiscal reforms did not long outlast the war.[14]

Put Down Levellers', see V. A. C. Gatrell, 'Incorporation and the pursuit of liberal hegemony in Manchester, 1790–1839' in D. Fraser (ed.), *Municipal Reform and the Industrial City* (Leicester, 1982), pp. 32–4. Even the open, essentially non-political, debating societies in London collapsed after 1792, see Mary Thale, 'London debating societies in the 1790s', *Historical Journal*, 32, 1 (1989), especially pp. 64–7.

[12] *The Example of France*, p. 85. For an almost identical sentiment, see Revd W. Finch, *A Sermon Preached Before the Oxford Loyal Volunteers* (Oxford, 1798), p. 8.

[13] Clive Emsley, 'The Home Office and its sources of information and investigation, 1791–1801', *English Historical Review*, 94 (1979), pp. 532–61; R. R. Nelson, *The Home Office, 1782–1801* (Durham, N.C., 1969), pp. 72–113; David Eastwood, '"Amplifying the province of the legislature": the flow of information and the English state in the early nineteenth century', *Historical Research*, 62 (1989), especially pp. 278–81; Roger Wells, *Insurrection: The British Experience, 1795–1803* (Gloucester, 1983), pp. 28–43.

[14] Richard Cooper, 'William Pitt, taxation, and the needs of war', *Journal of British Studies*, 22 (1982), pp. 94–103; P. K. O'Brien, 'Government revenue, 1793–1815 – a study in fiscal and financial policy in the wars against France', unpublished D.Phil. thesis (Oxford University, 1967); and his 'The political economy of British taxation, 1660–1815',

Yet if the British state was constrained by a semi-official conservative ideology, the twin threat of English radicalism and war with France posed a quite unprecedented challenge. Conservatism thus committed British institutions to proving themselves and their efficacy in a moment of deep and sustained crisis. In order to cope with the pressures of the 1790s a new public energy was required: a greater commitment on the part of traditional governing elites was imperative, and this would have to be coupled to systematic attempts to harness popular patriotism to the struggle against war and subversion. Whilst formally execrating democracy, the established order urgently needed mass support for and participation in the anti-revolutionary struggle. Volunteering, for example, implicitly acknowledged the central importance of popular participation without which the war on France and the campaign against subversion would become simply untenable. The problem of the 1790s thus became the creation of an accommodation between an elitist society struggling for survival and the broad mass of the people who, whilst denied a formal political role, nevertheless might possess the capacity either to make or to break an anti-revolutionary and anti-democratic state.

The strategy most frequently adopted to infuse new energy into the British state at this time of crisis was to welcome and to attempt to direct voluntary endeavour. When effectively harnessed, voluntary endeavour could constitute a major augmentation of the state's power and resources; giving government both at national and local level new capacity and new power without in any serious sense subverting the existing structure of authority within the state. Crucially, the struggles of the revolutionary period were struggles of nations in which the ultimately limited resources of *ancien régime* states would prove hopelessly inadequate. The human and material resources of nations would be mobilised by new methods and on an unprecedented scale. After the *levée en masse*, victory in the European theatre would only be possible for those states which could match France in their ability to mobilise the nation for victory, and those states such as Britain which maintained a radically anti-democratic stance were compelled to find mechanisms for matching the resources of a nation in arms. Whereas the French nation was to be mobilised by the *levée en masse* and patriotism interpreted in terms of the language of the

Economic History Review, 2nd series, 41 (1988), especially pp. 20–2; Sidney Buxton, Finance and Politics. An Historical Study 1783–1885, 2 vols. (London, 1888), vol. I, pp. 5–8, 117–18. The most significant financial legacy of the wars was a vastly inflated national debt, but this was itself a consequence of and a commentary upon the absence of major long-term fiscal restructuring during the war. The only fiscal innovation to outlast the war was Pitt's legacy duty on collateral successions to personal property imposed in 1796, Parliamentary History, 32 (1796), pp. 1026–32.

revolution,[15] in Britain the nation was to be mobilised by a variety of forms of voluntary endeavour and patriotism interpreted and indeed increasingly monopolised by the language of loyalism.[16]

The outbreak of Revolution in France triggered a war of ideas in Britain. The contours of this debate are now well mapped,[17] but it is important here to appreciate that the ideological debate took place at a variety of quite different levels, and it may well have been the less intellectually sophisticated productions which had the most immediate effect in the localities. Minor scribblers, voluble clergy and magistrates' disquisitions on the beauties of the English political system might have added nothing to the conservatives' intellectual case against radicalism, indeed in most cases they vulgarised it pretty shamelessly, but their pronouncements and publications did have a good deal of resonance locally and were therefore valued by the government. After preaching on the Christian duty of passive obedience and execrating Richard Watson's famous 1791 *Charge to the Clergy of Llandaff* which expressed limited sympathy for French aspirations to civil equality, the Oxfordshire clerical magistrate William Mavor actually wrote to Dundas asking whether the government would welcome publication of such exhortations to loyalism.[18] Dundas's reply aptly demonstrates the Home Office's enthusiasm for mobilising a broadly based campaign in defence of order and orthodoxy: 'It becomes the duty of every one capable of judging the advantages to be derived from our excellent Constitution to exert his endeavours for its support, especially at times like the present, when evil

---

[15] The literature here is, of course, vast, but the comparison between the British and French experiences is important. On France, see Colin Lucas, *The Structure of the Terror* (Oxford, 1973), especially chs. 4–9; S. J. Watson, *Carnot* (London, 1954), pp. 85–135; Norman Hampson, 'The French Revolution and the nationalization of honour' in M. R. D. Foot (ed.), *War and Society* (London, 1973). Some helpful comparisons are made in Clive Emsley, 'The impact of war and military participation on Britain and France, 1792–1815' in Clive Emsley and James Walvin (eds.), *Artisans, Peasants and Proletarians 1760–1860* (London, 1985), pp. 57–80.

[16] Two recent articles by Linda Colley touch on these themes in interesting ways: 'The apotheosis of George III: loyalty, royalty and the British nation 1760–1820', *Past and Present*, 102 (1984), pp. 94–129; and 'Whose nation? Class and national consciousness in Britain 1750–1830', *Past and Present*, 113 (1986), pp. 97–117.

[17] Most notably in Albert Goodwin's *The Friends of Liberty: The English Democratic Movement in the Age of the French Revolution* (London, 1979); but see also J. E. Cookson, *The Friends of Peace: Anti-War Liberalism in England, 1793–1815* (Cambridge, 1982); E. P. Thompson, *The Making of the English Working Class* (Harmondsworth, 1968), part 1; G. S. Veitch, *The Genesis of Parliamentary Reform*, new edn (London, 1965), chs. 5–14; Alfred Cobban (ed.), *The Debate on the French Revolution*, 2nd edn (London, 1960); and H. T. Dickinson, *British Radicalism and the French Revolution 1789–1815* (Oxford, 1985).

[18] Richard Watson, *A Charge Delivered to the Clergy of the Diocese of Llandaff June, 1791* (London, 1792). Watson's publication of this drew him into projected debates on the French Revolution, see Richard Watson, *Anecdotes of the Life of Richard Watson Written by Himself* (London, 1817).

minded people of different descriptions are employed in every part of the Country to overthrow it.'[19] The times thus demanded not passive but active subjects willing to use their energies in defence of order and property. Dundas's sentiments were faithfully echoed by Mavor who proclaimed: 'I think it the duty of the magistrate...to discourage all attempts at innovating on [sic] the Constitution of this Country, when that Constitution has been proved both in theory and in practice to be most excellent.'[20] When the government did not itself engineer effusions of loyalism, it was always sensitive to the potentially enormous advantage of encouraging all apparently spontaneous contributions to the anti-revolutionary crusade. Mavor himself went ahead and published one sermon as *Christian Politics* and his critique of Watson as *Vindiciae Landavenses*, and in 1798 published a further exhortation to proper patriotism, *The Duty of National Thanksgiving*.[21] Mavor's understanding of authentic Christianity was overtly political and austerely reactionary. Religion was, he insisted, 'genuine and real [only] when it teaches us to fear God – to honour the King – to obey the Magistrates, and to be ready for every good work'.[22]

The role of the clergy as an anti-revolutionary force is widely attested. Anglicanism did not fail the establishment.[23] In 1813 Mavor himself insisted on the effectiveness of the clergy as an anti-revolutionary force in the 1790s: 'If our constitution, to which we naturally cling, is to be preserved, it must be through the exertions of the clergy of the establishment, who frequently, under circumstances the most discouraging...have, with scarcely an exception, steadily persevered in inculcating submission to the laws.'[24] Some Anglican clergy were inclined to suggest

---

[19] Henry Dundas to William Mavor, 16 September 1792, Public Record Office (PRO), Home Office (HO) 42/21/548.

[20] William Mavor, *Vindiciae Landavenses: or Strictures on the Bishop of Llandaff's Late Charge* (Oxford, 1792), p. 11.

[21] William Mavor, *Christian Politics* (Oxford, 1793), and his *The Duty of Thanksgiving for National Blessings* (Oxford, 1798).   [22] Mavor, *Christian Politics*, p. 23.

[23] Classically in William Paley's 'Reasons for contentment, addressed to the labouring part of the British public' in *The Works of William Paley, D.D.*, 1 vol. (Edinburgh, 1827), pp. 567–70. Paley published 'Reasons for contentment' in 1791. See also Revd Thomas Zouch, *Address Delivered to the Clergy of the Deaneries of Richmond, Catterick, and Boroughbridge* (Newcastle-upon-Tyne, ?1792), especially pp. iii–iv; and Revd Thomas Armistead, *Sermon Preached at the Cathedral Church in Chester* (Chester, 1798). These themes are explored in the secondary literature, notably in Colley, 'Apotheosis of George III', pp. 120–1; Richard A. Soloway, *Prelates and People: Ecclesiastical Social Thought in England 1783–1852* (London, 1969), pp. 26–54; D. McClatchy, *The Oxfordshire Clergy, 1777–1869* (Oxford, 1960), pp. 202ff; Hole, *Pulpits, Politics and Public Order*, pp. 109–44, 160–73.

[24] *General View of the Agriculture of Berkshire* (London, 1813), pp. 96–7. Linda Colley has argued that during the French wars the clergy came close to being a national clerisy, training their congregations in loyalty and patriotism, and exhorting them to defend the realm; 'Whose nation?', p. 107.

that they had a kind of monopoly over the religion of patriotism, or that the established church was in some special sense invulnerable to the subversion of radicalism, but in fact they were often joined in their anti-radical polemics by dissenting ministers.[25] The voluntary endeavours of the clergy had an impact well beyond their own congregations or the readership for their published tracts. The 'Church and King' societies which sprang up to defend the union of throne and altar, were, in part at least, a popular efflorescence of the religiously embroidered conservatism enunciated from most pulpits. In this way, the loyalism of the clergy merged into and indeed sanctioned (even when it had not directly inspired) the raucous anti-radicalism of loyalist mobs.[26]

The 1790s saw an ever-flowing stream of anti-radical pamphlets. But if the state could rely upon a steady flow of volunteers to erect polemical barricades against the spread of radical and visionary ideologies, apparently spontaneous demonstrations of mass loyalism had to be more carefully nurtured. Collective voluntary actions in defence of the traditional order came not in a constant stream, but rather in waves breaking powerfully into the public arena and then losing their force and ebbing away until a new wave of popular patriotism broke. The 'Church and King' clubs doubtless gratified the authorities as symbols of anti-radical sentiment. Certainly magistrates were willing to stand aside in 1791, 1792 and 1794 when 'Church and King' mobs violently underscored popular hostility to English Jacobins.[27] But popular violence, although sometimes desirable as an emphatic demonstration of broadly based and passionate loyalism, was a volatile and potentially dangerous weapon in the campaign against subversion. Having established that crowd actions were not the monopoly of the English radicals,[28] the state ideally needed

---

[25] For an extreme statement of the Anglican case, see the sermon by Edward Tatham, Rector of Lincoln College, Oxford, *A Sermon Suitable to the Times* (London, 1792). Examples of the anti-Jacobin credentials of Dissent abound, see, for example, J. Hinton, *A Vindication of the Dissenters in Oxford* (Oxford, 1792), especially pp. 17–20; J. Dunkin, *History and Antiquities of Bicester* (London, 1816), pp. 182, 363–5; Bodleian Library (Bod. Lib.), Correspondence of John Dunkin, MS English letters, d. 38, fos. 31–2.

[26] Thomas Walker, *Review of Some of the Political Events which have Occurred in Manchester during the Last Five Years* (1794), pp. 17–18; J. H. Hinton, *Biographical Portraiture of the Late Rev. James Hinton* (Oxford, 1824), pp. 255–63, 360–5.

[27] See the complaints of Edward Jeffries, a delegate to the London Committee of Dissenters, Jeffries to Portland, 11 March 1795, PRO, HO 42/34/189; John Money, *Experience and Identity, Birmingham and the West Midlands, 1760–1800* (Manchester, 1977), pp. 223–9, 261–3; R. B. Rose, 'The Priestley riots of 1791', *Past and Present*, 18 (1960), pp. 68–88.

[28] Alan Booth, 'Popular loyalism and public violence in the north-west of England 1790–1800', *Social History*, 8 (1983), pp. 295–313. Mark Harrison has recently shown that between 1795 and 1804 'patriotic' crowd events in Bristol outstripped those with more radical overtones by 2:1 (and continued to do so until after 1825), 'The ordering of the urban environment: time, work, and the occurrence of crowds 1790–1835', *Past and Present*, 110 (1986), pp. 150–2. A similar case has been argued by James Epstein,

more reliable and more obviously constitutional demonstrations of popular support. It was this more restrained, but potentially more effective loyalism, that the Royal Proclamation of 21 May 1792 was designed to test and to awaken.[29] By 1 September 1792 some 386 loyal addresses had been received from counties, quarter sessions, boroughs and corporations promising still greater vigilance in the fight against radicalism in their own localities.[30] Typical was Hertfordshire Quarter Sessions which reaffirmed its intention to suppress all riotous and disorderly meetings, launched a campaign against sedition in a series of advertisements in county newspapers, and circularised all High Constables instructing them to be 'extremely attentive and vigilant' in enforcing the Spirit of the King's Proclamation.[31] The sheer number of Addresses was itself something of a propaganda coup for the government, and although merely returning a loyalist Address was in itself little more than a symbolic gesture, in so far as the process of responding to the Proclamation caused local authorities to look afresh at their strategies for surveillance and repression, it probably had a tangible longer term impact.[32]

The campaign to secure loyalist Addresses as tension mounted during the summer of 1792 was orchestrated by the traditional device of a Royal Proclamation, and formed part of an attempt to inject new urgency and energy into the fundamental constituent agencies of the state. The November of that year saw another distinct wave in the anti-radical campaign with the evanescent flourishing of the Loyalist Association Movement. A good deal of time has been devoted to trying to establish whether the Association for the Preservation of Liberty and Property against Republicans and Levellers (APLP) established at the Crown and Anchor Tavern, London, on 20 November 1792, was officially inspired or whether John Reeves was acting independently.[33] In fact, on the 19

'Understanding the cap of liberty: Symbolic practice and social conflict in early nineteenth-century England', *Past and Present*, 122 (1989), pp. 82–3.

[29] *The Parliamentary History of England*, 29 (1792), pp. 1476–7; *Annual Register...for the Year 1792* (London, 1799), Chronicle, pp. 158–61. Frank O'Gorman has recently suggested that the Proclamation was, to some extent, an attempt to measure public opinion, 'Pitt and the "Tory" reaction to the French Revolution 1789–1815' in Dickinson, *Britain and the French Revolution*, pp. 30–1.

[30] MS 'List of Addresses which have been sent to His Majesty between June and 1 Sept. 1792 in response to the Royal Proclamation', PRO, HO 42/21/478.

[31] Salisbury to Dundas, 1 July 1792, PRO, HO 42/21/9–10; cf. W. Temm to Dundas, 3 July 1792, PRO, HO 42/21/28.

[32] As in Oxfordshire, see Resolutions of a Special Meeting of the Oxfordshire Quarter Sessions, 21 December 1792, Oxfordshire County Record Office, Willoughby Papers, Wi X/21.

[33] Austin Mitchell, 'The Association Movement of 1792–3', *Historical Journal*, 4 (1961), pp. 56–77; D. E. Ginter, 'The loyalist association movement of 1792–3', *Historical Journal*, 9, 2 (1966), pp. 179–90; Dozier, *For King, Constitution, and Country*, pp. 55–75; Black, *The Association*, ch. 7.

November Mr Justice Ashhurst had delivered his uncompromising
Charge to the Grand Jury of Middlesex in which he inveighed against the
'monstrous and nonsensical' doctrine of equality, and insisted that the
maintenance of social subordination was crucial to the security of the
state. His peroration exhorted such members of the Grand Jury 'as are in
a private station, to endeavour by your example to discourtenance [*sic*] all
such unconstitutional tenets'. A day later the APLP was born, and a
number of loyalist associations printed and distributed Ashhurst's
Charge.[34] Ashhurst's judicial *Charge*, coupled with the equally urgent
Charge to the Grand Jury of Middlesex from the Chairman of the Quarter
Sessions, William Mainwaring, probably did as much to inspire the
formation of the 'Reeves Associations' as any covert action by
Whitehall.[35] Thus local government may well have played at least as
important a role as central government in inspiring the Loyalist
Association Movement. The debate about the inception of the loyalist
associations has served to hinder a proper appreciation of their actual
role. In practice they certainly were arm's length bodies rather than semi-
official instruments of government. Moreover, many associations clearly
did little more than meet, issue a manifesto or some other public
affirmation of loyalty to the King and abhorrence of 'seditious' ideas, and
perhaps organise a popular demonstration and a symbolic burning of
Paine's *Rights of Man* and perhaps Paine himself in effigy. Thereafter they
quickly faded away.[36] Again the net effect was to encourage and embolden
the forces of conservatism.

Some loyalist associations showed more imagination and resilience. The
East Kent and Canterbury Association proclaimed its aims as being 'to
enforce good Order and Government and support the Constitution as by
Law established; and more particularly to counteract the mischievous
attempts which had been made to poison the minds of the People, by
propagating false and absurd opinions inimical to and absolutely

---

[34] Mr Justice Ashhurst's *Charge to the Grand Jury for the County of Middlesex* ([Canterbury],
1792), was printed and sold by the East Kent and Canterbury Association for one penny
a copy, see Bod. Lib., Hope Adds. 731.

[35] William Mainwaring, *Charge to the Grand Jury of Middlesex* ([London], 1792). Both
Ashhurst's and Mainwaring's *Charges* were published by John Reeves as the first two
items in *The Association Papers* (London, 1793), part 1. Mainwaring was an energetic
chairman of the Quarter Sessions and had been involved with attempts to reform the
police and tighten Sabbath observance. He was also active in the Proclamation Society,
see L. Radzinowicz, *The History of the Criminal Law and its Administration since 1750*, 5
vols., (London, 1948–86), vol. II, pp. 195, 281; vol. III, pp. 186–7, 377–8.

[36] See, for example, *Jackson's Oxford Journal* (Oxford), 15 December 1792, 5, 12, 19, 26
January 1793. Dozier has recently estimated that around 1,500 loyalist associations were
formed between November 1792 and February 1793, and that they involved around
15,000 activist members. *For King, Constitution, and Country*, p. 62.

inconsistent with every principal [*sic*] of civil society'.[37] In its war against 'false and absurd opinions', the East Kent and Canterbury Association printed and circulated an extensive series of cheap populist pamphlets, amongst them Hannah More's *Village Politics*.[38] In this way some loyalist associations anticipated, albeit on a modest scale, the strategy of the Cheap Repository Tracts – although it is important to appreciate that neither Hannah More nor the subscribers to the Tracts conceived of their objects in simple anti-Jacobin terms, but rather as an attempt to redirect a broadly based 'reformation of manners' movement towards the particular problems of the 1790s, of which the most pressing happened to be to purge a corrosive 'Jacobin' morality.[39]

As loyalist associations faded from the public scene, not all of them disintegrated completely. The Reeves Association in London at least retained a skeleton committee whose members, after their 'so successful' appeal to patriotism in 1792, did not wish again to 'obtrude themselves on Public Attention, without strong reasons'.[40] By November 1795 the committee judged the situation to have deteriorated sufficiently to justify them in again calling for 'suitable' expressions of support for the King and the constitution and condemnation of seditious clubs, societies and newspapers. Accordingly, they published a proposed Address in *The True Briton* of 7 November 1795, and later in the month circulated copies of the Address to interested parties and to parishes.[41] Reeves's intention in resurrecting the machinery of the loyalist associations was to help create a climate of public opinion which would be sympathetic towards, or at the very least resigned to, a further instalment of repression:

I thought this a step, that would assist in preparing men's minds to support any strong measure the Government might be disposed to propose; and I took it, as on a former occasion, without any consultation or concert with anybody at Whitehall, for the same reasons, as on the former occasion, namely, that the Government might have all the benefit of it, if it produced any, and none of the disgrace, if such was the fate of it.[42]

---

[37] J. H. Stringer to William Pitt, 11 February 1793, PRO Pitt (Chatham) Papers, PRO 30/8/245, fo. 94. This theme was taken up in *The Annual Register for 1794*, 'History of Europe', p. 267.   [38] See Bod. Lib., Hope Adds. 731.

[39] Susan Pedersen, 'Hannah More Meets Simple Simon: tracts, chapbooks, and popular literature in late eighteenth-century England', *Journal of British Studies*, 25 (1986), especially pp. 84–7, 109–12.

[40] Reeves to Pitt, 10 November 1795, PRO 30/8/170, fo. 261.

[41] *Ibid.*, fos. 264–5; Reeves to Pitt, 18 November 1795, PRO 30/8/170, fo. 269.

[42] Reeves [to Pitt], 7 November 1795, PRO 30/8/170, fos. 259–60. Significantly, Reeves did not admit to Pitt his authorship of the sensational and ultra-royalist tract, 'Thoughts on English Government Addressed to the Quiet Good Sense of the People of England' (London, 1795), until 25 November, i.e. after he had attempted to revive a loyalist campaign, see Reeves to Pitt, 25 November 1795, PRO 30/8/170, fo. 271. For Reeves's subsequent trial, see *The Annual Register for 1796*, Chronicle, pp. 20–1.

Reeves clearly understood there to be a potentially useful division of labour between loyalist propagandists and government. Conservative ideologues could fly kites and promote repressive ideas which the government might subsequently adopt. Significantly, the *Annual Register* described the role of the loyalist associations as 'preliminary to, and co-operative with, those measures of government which the circumstances of the moment appeared to demand'.[43] Such an attempt to influence public opinion could work only if loyalist propagandists retained a good measure of autonomy, thereby acting as a kind of ideological outrigger to a conservative state.

By the spring of 1793 most loyalist associations were a spent force, but already a new and more important framework for voluntary endeavour was being established. Some associations, notably the East Kent and Canterbury Association, were as early as February 1793 inquiring into the kinds of measures adopted during the American war to supplement the military, and were urging the government to pass an act similar to 22 Geo. III *c.* 79 which would facilitate Volunteering as a means of augmenting the militia.[44] Critics of loyalist associations such as Arthur Young also urged the government to sanction the creation of a voluntary cavalry, or 'militia of property' in each county.[45] Young was explicitly critical of the strategies and effectiveness of most loyalist associations, ridiculing their 'faint declarations of loyalty, that mean anything or nothing, and will be forgotten in six months'.[46] Young envisaged a transformed loyalist movement which could offer *sustained* resistance to Jacobinism in all its

---

[43] *The Annual Register for 1793*, 'History of Europe', p. 3.

[44] Stringer to Pitt 11 February 1793, PRO 30/8/245, fo. 94. For the Volunteer movement during the American war, see H. C. Cardew-Rendle 'The Volunteer movement in the metropolis, 1779–1780', *Notes and Queries*, 166, 16 (April, 1934). I am grateful to Austin Gee for this reference.

[45] Young, *The Example of France*, pp. 139–42. Young originally floated his ideas in the *Annals of Agriculture*, 18, p. 495, in August 1792. It was an important aspect of Young's proposals that some 'gentlemen of fortune' should consent to serve not as officers but in the ranks of the Volunteer cavalry:

for had gentlemen accepted only the situation of officers, the spirit of entering the corps among yeomen, farmers &c. would have been much cooler; but when they saw their landlords, and men of high considerations in the neighbourhood, in the same situation, their vanity was flattered, and they enrolled themselves with great readiness, and the great object of property of such importance in case of revolutionary disturbance was thus secured.

M. Bentham-Edwards (ed.), *Autobiography of Arthur Young*, (London, 1898), pp. 205–6. Thus the protection of property and social hierarchy might entail a temporary tactical abandonment of the rank which property bestowed.

[46] Young, *Example of France*, pp. 146–7. Ginter, 'Loyalist association movement', pp. 187–8, argued that by their equivocal wording loyalist associations' Addresses were specifically designed to make it difficult for any men of rank and substance to refuse to sign, thereby maximising the associations' apparent support, but limiting their effectiveness as genuine purveyors of a counter-revolutionary ideology.

forms. Rather than loosely worded declarations, which even moderate reformers could endorse, he favoured direct action such as boycotting 'Jacobin' traders, raising subscriptions to bring the publishers of seditious libels to trial, and, crucially, subscriptions to support a voluntary militia.[47] The advantages of voluntary corps over the loyalist associations were many and obvious: they could be incorporated into a system of national defence; they of necessity had a longevity which few loyalist associations could rival; they explicitly extended the police resources of the state; and they mobilised a much broader social constituency than the loyalist associations.[48]

Given the groundswell of support for a voluntary force, it was hardly surprising that the response to the 'Plan of Augmentation of the Forces for Internal Defence', circularised to Lords Lieutenant on 14 March 1794, was swift and positive.[49] In Warwickshire a Volunteer corps was established and £2,900 was immediately pledged by sixteen subscribers to a fund to support the Volunteers.[50] When the Somerset Volunteers were established in April 1794, £4,273 10s was immediately subscribed by sixty-five people, and leading clergymen offered to receive voluntary contributions from their parishioners.[51] The system adopted in Devon was still more elaborate, and after £5,998 was initially pledged, the county was divided into districts, each with its own management committee made up from those in the area subscribing more than five guineas. A system of subscription by instalments was envisaged.[52] The localism of the Volunteers was both their principal strength and their major weakness. Their patriotism was articulated very much in civic or county terms, and many corps demonstrated a deep reluctance to serve beyond the confines

---

[47] Young, *Example of France*, pp. 146–7.
[48] For an authoritative treatment of the Volunteer movement see Austin Gee, 'Volunteering in Britain, 1793–1815', unpublished D.Phil. thesis (University of Oxford, 1989). J. E. Cookson, 'The English Volunteer movement of the French wars, 1793–1815: some contexts', *Historical Journal*, 32 (1989), pp. 867–91, also offers interesting insights. The earlier literature on the Volunteers is less satisfactory: J. R. Western, 'The Volunteer movement as an anti-revolutionary force', *English Historical Review*, 71 (1956), pp. 603–14; Dozier, *For King, Constitution, and Country*, pp. 138–71; and C. Sebag-Montefiore, *A History of Volunteer Forces* (London, 1908), all tend to simplify both the role and appeal of the Volunteers.
[49] PRO, HO 50/450; Parliamentary History, 21 (1794), pp. 91–7; S. Lambert (ed.), *Reports from the Committee of Secrecy: House of Commons Sessional Papers*, vol. xciii, p. 51; Peter Bloomfield (ed.), *Kent and the Napoleonic Wars* (Kentish Sources X, Kent Archives Office, 1987), pp. 139–42; M. Y. Ashcroft, *To Escape the Monster's Clutches. Notes and Documents Illustrating the Preparations in North Yorkshire to Repel the Invasion Threatened by the French in 1793*, 15 (North Yorkshire Record Office Publications, 1977), p. 10.
[50] Warwick to William Pitt, 21 April 1794, PRO 30/8/245, fos. 108–9.
[51] Thomas Knatchbull [to Pitt], 9 April 1794, PRO 30/8/255, fos. 115–18.
[52] PRO 30/8/244, fos. 192–3.

of their county or locality.[53] This kind of patriotism operated at a subnational level perfectly consonant with the decentralised traditions of the English polity. Thus in terms both of their structure and the limits of their patriotism, the Volunteers reinforced rather than subverted the essential structure of the English state.[54]

The manner in which the Volunteers combined patriotism, public service and economy was particularly welcome to the government, and the government's enthusiasm for the scheme survived throughout the 1790s despite growing evidence of the limited effectiveness of the Volunteer corps. In 1798 Dundas wrote to Wilberforce that,

There can not be a doubt of the wishes of Government to bring forward the zeal and exertions of the country in every possible shape; at present I am not aware of anything cheaper (if really efficient) can be resorted to than the system of volunteer corps and yeomanry corps to which every encouragement is given.[55]

Before the Peace of Amiens the Volunteers had grown into a force whose paper strength exceeded 300,000, and only after the renewal of hostilities when the Amiens agreement collapsed did the government's disillusionment with the system of Volunteers become sufficiently acute to lead to the abandonment of the idea of Volunteering and to the eventual creation of the Local Militia.[56] But the defects of Volunteers were apparent well before the Napoleonic era. Many corps had exhausted their financial reserves by 1796, and raising new subscriptions proved difficult and sometimes impossible. The Bolton Volunteer Corps, raised in 1794, was supported by voluntary subscriptions until 1796, but thereafter was forced to apply to the government to pay expenses, allowances, and other basic costs.[57] Such financial difficulties were not uncommon, and Henry Dundas's circular of 5 March 1798 announced that government funds would be available to all corps formed before 15 January 1798 where

[53] See, for example, John Child to Dundas, 8 March 1798; William Blakeney to Dundas, 17 March 1798; Marquis of Bute to Dundas, 20 March 1798, all in PRO HO 50/40 (unfoliated).

[54] There was enthusiasm for Volunteering even in Scotland, where a system of Lords Lieutenant and Deputy Lieutenants was imposed in 1794. Opposition to the idea of a militia in Scotland (which had been intense during the American war) also declined, and Volunteering helped pave the way for the establishment of a militia in Scotland in 1797; see John Robertson, *The Scottish Enlightenment and the Militia Question* (Edinburgh, 1985), pp. 150–1.

[55] Henry Dundas to William Wilberforce, 29 January 1798, A. M. Wilberforce (ed.), *Private Papers of William Wilberforce* (London, 1897), p. 92.

[56] J. W. Fortescue, *The County Lieutenancies and the Army, 1803–14* (London, 1909), pp. 3–119; R. Glover, *Britain at Bay, Defence Against Bonaparte, 1803–14* (London, 1973), pp. 44–6; S. C. Smith, 'Loyalty and opposition in the Napoleonic wars: the impact of the Local Militia, 1807–1815', unpublished D.Phil. thesis, (Oxford University, 1984), especially pp. 42–126.

[57] Peter Rasbotham to Earl of Derby, 22 February 1798, in PRO HO 50/40.

original voluntary subscriptions had been exhausted and government aid appeared 'indispensably necessary'.[58] Interestingly, even such subventions from central government did not dilute the essential localism of many corps. Four days after Dundas's circular, the Derby Corps of Volunteers happily availed itself of government assistance on the strict understanding that 'it shall in no event be called upon to serve beyond the limits of its own Borough, agreeably to the terms of its original enrolment and to the expectation of the original subscribers'.[59]

The spirit of patriotism harnessed by the Volunteers was a delicate flower requiring the most careful nurturing. Whilst Volunteers were distinctly resistant to being deployed away from their home area, inaction in the locality could also lead to disaffection. If Volunteers were underused the enthusiasm for Volunteering and subscriptions could ebb away. In Worcestershire 'owing to the length of time this business [of embodying the Provisional Cavalry] has in a manner lain dormant, people in the County have been led to the belief that Government had relinquished the idea of making any use of this Force, and to consider a muster only as a needless tax upon themselves'.[60] When the heady brew of the voluntary spirit turned sour amidst recriminations of its having led to 'needless taxes', the limits of popular patriotism had clearly been reached. The Volunteers, although imbued with far more life and staying power than the loyalist associations, ultimately lost energy and vision. To characterise this as an English *levée en masse*, even though the term was in contemporary usage, is to risk misunderstanding both the ethos and the political context of Volunteering. It flowed not from a systematic patriotic ideology (as did the French Terror), but rather from a set of patriotic enthusiasms. And like all enthusiasms, its passion was eventually spent.

Loyalists' moderate success in mobilising popular patriotism enabled them to redeploy elements of the language and some of the rhetorical idioms of radicalism in defence of the constitutional order. It became a commonplace of conservative polemics to juxtapose radicals' theoretical construction of abstract 'rights of man' with what loyalists were increasingly disposed to call the '*real* rights of man'.[61] It was these (largely undefined) real rights which the constitution upheld, and these rights were presented as part of a nexus of social order and social obligations, of

---

[58] For a copy of Dundas's circular see PRO 30/8/244, fos. 227–9.
[59] Mr Heathcote to Dundas, 9 March 1798, in PRO HO 50/40.
[60] Thomas Cockes to Dundas, 2 March 1798, in PRO HO 50/40; cf. Cookson, 'English Volunteer Movement', pp. 868–9.
[61] For a brief, but useful discussion see Dinwiddy, 'England', pp. 62–4; also Hugh Cunningham, 'The language of patriotism, 1750–1914', *History Workshop Journal*, 12 (1981), pp. 8–33.

duties and rights, of deference and paternalism.[62] The assertion that the existing socio-political order bestowed effective liberties on all Englishmen became a commonplace in conservative circles. In 1798 the Brentford Armed Association was assured of their crucial role in helping to 'maintain social order, moral duty, the laws, the liberties, and the Rights, yes, the violated RIGHTS OF MAN'.[63] And if the language of patriotism succeeded in redefining radical notions of the 'rights of man', Volunteering offered a loyalist variation on the theme of fraternity. Volunteers were 'a part of that system of true and genuine fraternity, which, from one extremity of the Kingdom to the other, has united the best and bravest of our countrymen in the common cause ... to the support of that magnificent and venerable fabric, THE CONSTITUTION OF ENGLAND'.[64] Thus 'liberty' and 'fraternity' both had their analogues in the conservative catechism.

By making the strategically necessary claim that the existing order explicitly recognised and respected the rights of all, conservatives were left with a tactical dilemma in devising means for demonstrating that this was really so. The institutions of the English state were unmistakably elitist, and serious political reform was now ruled out on both prudential and ideological grounds. Moreover, even if the threat posed by the English Jacobins did not lead to any significant or sustained increase in the repressive resources of the state, it did lead the government to use essentially limited repressive powers with unprecedented rigour.[65] Surveillance and repression could be presented as the unhappy but unavoidable consequences of war and sedition, but if stability was to be maintained in the longer term, the government had also to present another, more indulgent and understanding face. The years of 'Pitt's Terror' were also the years of 'Speenhamland', and if the central

---

[62] *Dialogues on the Rights of Britons*, 2nd edn (London, 1792); Charles Wilson, *The Authority of Government and Duty of Obedience* (Durham, ?1793); Anon., *A Few Minutes Advice to The People of Great Britain on Republics* (Bristol, 1792), especially pp. 6–12; Richard Cecil, 'The true patriot' (first printed 1798) in Thomas Preston, *Patriots in Arms. Addresses and Sermons in Praise of the Volunteer Movement* (London, 1881), pp. 169–86; Mavor, *Duty of Thanksgiving for National Blessings*, pp. 12–13.

[63] George Henry Glasse, *Sermon Preached before Members of the Brentford Armed Association* (Brentford, 1798), p. 10.

[64] *Ibid.*, pp. 13–14. See also, Revd Henry Gabell, *A Discourse Delivered on the Feast Day in February*, 2nd edn (London, 1799), especially pp. 17–18.

[65] For a balanced account, see Clive Emsley, 'An aspect of Pitt's "Terror": prosecutions for sedition during the 1790s', *Social History*, 6, 2 (1981), 155–84; and his, 'Repression, "Terror" and the rule of law in England during the decade of the French Revolution', *English Historical Review*, 100 (1985), pp. 801–25; and John Ehrman, *The Younger Pitt*, 2 vols. (London, 1969/83), vol. II pp. 385–440. The state's aims and methods emerge as more overtly repressive in F. K. Prochaska, 'English state trials in the 1790s: a case study', *Journal of British Studies*, 13 (1973), pp. 63–82.

government was associated with state trials, informers and recruitment offers, local government offered a politically necessary counterpoint in the form of Bread Scales and loud exhortations to the rich to limit their bread consumption in order to ease the plight of the poor.[66] Expressed in these terms, the argument is too schematic, the juxtaposition of stick and carrot too obvious to be credible. The reality was more complex, and it was Pitt himself, after all, who in 1796 made the most generous of all wartime proposals on poor relief.[67] But there is a point of substance here, and it is that the most serious threat to the conservative order in Britain in the 1790s would have come from a radical politicisation of the plight of the poor, from food rioters in England following their French counterparts into the temples of Jacobinism. That most, although not all, food riots reflected the frustrations of temporary hardship rather than any deep-seated ideological alienation from the governing elite was crucial to the survival of that elite.[68] A fusion of popular hardship and political radicalism (along French lines) might have led to an explosion of a force sufficient to shake the foundations of the state itself.

Attacking the material causes and attenuating the political consequences of poverty thus came to be regarded as an indispensable element in the conservative strategy. As Sir Thomas Bernard put it: 'To the patriot, who wishes to deserve well of his country, I could prove that from the increase of the resources and virtues of the poor, the Kingdom would derive prosperity, – the different classes of society, union – the constitution, stability.'[69] This preoccupation with the material and moral condition of the poor became more urgent as social conditions worsened in the crisis of 1795–6. The single most important response to the deepening poverty of the mid-1790s came in the form of vastly increased poor rates. The shift towards a more systematic and a more generous

[66] The literature on the wartime treatment of poverty is vast. The argument of this paragraph is developed at greater length in David Eastwood, 'Governing rural England. Authority and social order in Oxfordshire, 1780–1840', unpublished D.Phil. thesis (Oxford University, 1985), especially pp. 74–91.

[67] For details of Pitt's proposals and the largely hostile response they brought forward, see PRO 30/8/307–8; also J. R. Poynter, Society and Pauperism. English Ideas on Poor Relief, 1795–1834 (London, 1969), pp. 62–76.

[68] The most authoritative study is now John Bohstedt's, Riots and Community Politics in England and Wales, 1790–1810 (Cambridge, Mass., 1983); but see also Eastwood, 'Governing rural England', pp. 217–23 and John Stevenson, 'Food riots in England 1792–1818' in John Stevenson and R. Quinault (eds.), Popular Protest and Public Order (London, 1974), pp. 33–74. A more obviously politicised interpretation is argued in three important articles: E. P. Thompson, 'The moral economy of the English crowd in the eighteenth century', Past and Present, 50 (1971), especially pp. 79–88, 74–107; and Roger Wells, Dearth and Distress in Yorkshire 1793–1802 (York, 1977); and his 'The revolt of the south-west: a study in English popular protest', Social History, 6 (1977), pp. 713–44.

[69] James Baker, The Life of Sir Thomas Bernard (London, 1819), pp. 9–10.

policy of public relief in the wake of the 1795 crisis was unmistakable.[70] Nevertheless enhanced public provision of relief did not crowd out charitable responses, and voluntary subscriptions in support of the poor remained significant.[71] Indeed magistrates in some parts of the country articulated a positive preference for meeting the needs of the poor from voluntary subscriptions rather than compulsory poor rates. On the Wirrall in 1801 'voluntary' subscriptions in support of the poor became almost a public duty as magistrates circulated a resolution from petty sessions asserting:

That liberal, voluntary subscriptions, by the landowners of each parish, for the purpose of making such provision [i.e. to relieve the poor] will be less oppressive, and more grateful to the feelings of the Magistrates, than imposing heavy rates on upon the respective townships...and therefore such subscription [sic] shall be immediately entered into.[72]

The attempt to meet the needs of the poor, at least in part, from voluntary subscriptions was hardly new, nor was it a spectacular success.[73] But subscriptions in relief of the poor in the 1790s enabled subscribers to demonstrate both charity and patriotism. Subscriptions to relieve the poor were, like subscriptions in support of Volunteer corps, a form of alternative taxation, but in the context of the 1790s subscriptions retained an air of being spontaneous effusions of patriotic generosity, and at least

[70] Magistrates' intention in the period after 1795 was to try to guarantee minimum family incomes, and in so doing they effectively committed ratepayers to a major increase in expenditure on poor relief, see Oxfordshire County Record Office, Quarter Sessions Records, QSM II/2, Epiphany 1795; Buckinghamshire County Record Office, Quarter Sessions Minute Book 1792–6, QSM/10 fo. 332. The effect in Oxfordshire was that expenditure on poor relief increased by around 750 per cent in the six years after 1795, see Eastwood, 'Governing rural England', p. 103. 'Optimists' such as Professor Christie tend to underestimate the extent to which the structure of the old Poor Law was changed during the war, and understate the importance of magistrates' willingness to commit new public resources to the alleviation of poverty and the management of the poor, Stress and Stability, pp. 94–123. It was, after all, quite conceivable that the state could have limited or even diminished its commitment to the poor, as indeed was urged by Malthus in the difficult years after 1798.

[71] For subscriptions see Jackson's Oxford Journal, 10 January, 18 July, and 1 August 1795; for charity, see F. M. Eden, The State of the Poor, 3 vols. (London, 1797), vol. I, pp. 458–65. In establishing minimum family incomes rather than a strict system of entitlements to public relief, magistrates were inviting overseers to incorporate the poor's income from charitable sources into their assessments of entitlement to public relief.

[72] Cheshire County Record Office, Correspondence relating to Poverty, QAX 6/5, printed copy of 'Resolutions entered into at a Meeting of the Inhabitants of the Hundred of the Wirrall convened by Magistrates'; cf. an earlier resolution of Hertfordshire magistrates in 1795, W. J. Hardy (ed.), Hertford County Records, 10 vols. (Hertford, 1905–57), vol. viii, p. 451.

[73] Over the war years as a whole, inflation probably more than wiped out the value of increased charitable giving.

implied taxation by consent.[74] Again, whilst the voluntary response was not sufficient in itself, it formed a part of the total response and helped demonstrate the elite's perception of the reality of the crisis facing the poor. If, as Roger Wells amongst others has suggested, there was a real danger of popular insurrection in the 1790s, then the effectiveness of responses to poverty must have played a decisive role in retarding a radical politicisation of poverty.[75]

But practical patriots such as Sir Thomas Bernard envisaged a more systematic response to the material and moral demands of poverty than waves of subscriptions. The times demanded a practical response to the plight of the poor which, by articulating the elite's recognition of its social responsibilities, by implication also reaffirmed the poor's duty of obedience. In 1796 Bernard joined the Bishop of Durham and William Wilberforce in establishing the Society for Bettering the Condition and Increasing the Comforts of the Poor (SBCP).[76] A number of the leading lights of the SBCP had been active in the earlier Proclamation Society formed to give effect to George III's Proclamation against Vice and Immorality of 1787, but by 1796 they saw the need for a less socially exclusive society which directed its endeavours not so much towards the elevation of public morality in general, but addressed the material and moral plight of the poor more directly.[77] The SBCP concentrated on distributing straightforward pamphlets containing 'practical' schemes: plans for soup kitchens, subsidised village shops, friendly societies, and cheap nutritious recipes for the poor were much in vogue.[78] At times the ideological underpinnings of such paternalism was anything but subtle: 'Industry will make a man a purse and frugality will find him strings for

---

[74] From the first wave of 'patriotic' subscriptions, leading Whigs expressed profound reservations as to their real inspiration and political effects. Sheridan argued in the Commons in 1794 that subscriptions resulted not from strictly voluntary acts, 'but from the express requisition of the secretary of state; and this was followed by an advertisement in the public papers, worded in a manner that seemed to indicate that those who did not join it, had views that were hostile to the constitution', *Parliamentary History*, 21 (1794), p. 84. Sheridan had in mind Dundas's general circular on subscriptions to fund Volunteer corps, but the Whig case had a much wider potential application.

[75] For a different interpretation see, Roger Wells, *Wretched Faces: Famine in Wartime England 1793–1801* (Gloucester, 1988).

[76] *Reports of the Society for Bettering the Condition and Increasing the Comforts of the Poor*, 7 vols. (London, 1798–1817), vol. I, pp. 262–4; Baker, *Life of Thomas Bernard*, pp. 9–23.

[77] On the Proclamation Society, see Joanna Innes's authoritative essay, 'Politics and Morals'. The SBCP has not been so imaginatively explored, but see Poynter, *Society and Pauperism*, pp. 91–8.

[78] *First Report of the Society for the Bettering the Condition and Increasing the Comforts of the Poor* (London, 1797), pp. i, v–vi, appendix, pp. 1–6; see throughout the *Reports of the Society*. For similar 'practical' schemes see Eden, *State of the Poor*, vol. II, pp. 491–632; and for an indication of the influence of the SBCP in the localities, see John Foley, *Charges Delivered to the Grand Jury at the General Quarter Sessions for the County of Gloucester* (Gloucester, 1804), p. 58.

it ... let the poor man find his way to the cheapest market on Saturday, to a place of Divine worship on Sunday, and like an honest man, go to his labour on Monday.'[79] Such trite aphorisms say much about the aspirations of those who coined them, and incidentally underlined the essentially practical Evangelicalism of the SBCP's leadership. Their original manifesto of 17 December 1796 had argued that 'in proportion as we can multiply domestic comforts, in the same degree we may hope to promote the cause of morality and virtue', and in so doing the SBCP hoped its efforts would contribute significantly 'to national security'.[80]

In the face of war, shortages and sedition, even traditional forms of charity acquired a new political significance. If private charity could no longer hope to match public relief in terms of the scale of resources it redeployed towards the poor, it retained an important role in defining the network of social obligations which underpinned the political order. Charity created 'more reciprocity of good-will and friendship between different classes in society ... [thereby] teaching [the poor] the virtue of those gradations of rank and condition which our creator has thought fit to establish'.[81] The nexus of power relations which so often constitute the impetus to charitable action could hardly have been more explicitly enunciated. Viewed in this way, wartime charity amounted to a form of political insurance.

But if charity played a part in holding back a revolutionary tide, it did not follow that agencies such as the SBCP can be easily accommodated within a Burkean tradition. In their practical Evangelicalism men such as Thomas Bernard, William Wilberforce and Arthur Young identified a crisis facing the English state in the 1790s, but tended to locate that crisis in the realm of public morality rather than in the world of politics: it was a crisis of manners rather than a crisis of institutions. In 1797 Wilberforce was inclined to see England's distemper 'as a moral rather than a political malady'.[82] A political crisis might be postponed by a vigorous assertion of the coercive powers of the state, but only by moral regeneration would the nation escape the kind of convulsion which had engulfed the French state. The Evangelicals could agree with Burke that the corrosive influence of Enlightenment rationalism must be countered by an assertion of Christian belief, but they went well beyond Burke's assertion of reasonable

---

[79] *Reports*, vol. II, appendix 6, p. 285.   [80] *Ibid.*, vol. I, p. xxiv.
[81] Baker, *Life of Thomas Bernard*, pp. 30–1.
[82] W. Wilberforce, *A Practical View of the Prevailing Religious System of Professed Christians ... contrasted with Real Christianity* (London, 1797), p. 422; cf. the much more hysterical but morally similar analysis in John Bowdler, *Reform or Ruin: Take Your Choice!* (London, 1797). For a discussion of Christian moral attitudes in the 1790s, see Richard A. Soloway, 'Reform or ruin: English moral thought during the first French republic', *Review of Politics*, 25 (1963), pp. 110–28; and his, *Prelates and People*, pp. 26–45.

Christianity. What the 1790s demanded was not 'reasonableness', which too often shaded off into a latitudinarian compromise with 'Reason',[83] but passion. The counterpoint to Jacobinism must be not moderate Anglicanism but Christian mission: a mission directed in part against an increasingly pervasive 'Jacobin morality'.[84] Granted this framework of analysis, one of the more serious developments of the 1790s in the long term was a further fragmentation of the evangelical movement which would see a good deal of its potential energy dissipated in inter-denominational factionalism.[85]

The revived preoccupation with the 'reformation of manners', symbolised by the formation of the SBCP, helped provide a context for magistrates and others to renew their campaigns to police sabbath observance and confront vagrancy and licentiousness.[86] There was nothing new in these kinds of attempts to try to superimpose 'polite' values on plebeian culture, but in the 1790s, with moral degeneracy identified as a symptom of radicalism, official and semi-official movements for moral reform had specifically political connotations. Jacobinism, and Godwinianism for that matter, offered models of society in which new moral and religious systems became both symptoms and agents of political change. Confronting new and more obviously individualistic systems of morality and reasserting traditional religious and cultural values became an essential means of protecting the integrity of traditional social institutions, and defenders of the English state came increasingly to claim for it a moral primacy over its French (i.e. revolutionary) counterpart.[87]

My purpose in this chapter has not been to deny the importance of limited

---

[83] See John Gascoigne, 'Anglican latitudinarianism and political radicalism in the late eighteenth century', *History*, 71 (1986), pp. 22–38; and Hole, *Pulpits, Politics and Public Order*, pp. 145–59.

[84] See V. Kiernan's important and too frequently overlooked article, 'Evangelicalism and the French Revolution', *Past and Present*, 1 (1952), pp. 44–56.

[85] W. R. Ward, *Religion and Society in England 1790–1850* (London, 1972), pp. 1–52; David Hempton, *Methodism and Politics in British Society 1750–1850* (London, 1985), pp. 55–80; B. Semmel, *The Methodist Revolution* (London, 1974), ch. 5.

[86] The campaign by Oxfordshire magistrates in the early 1790s to enforce the 'due observance of the Sabbath' and to punish vagrancy and decadent street theatre could be paralleled in most other counties; see Oxfordshire County Record Office, Sessions Records, QSM II/2, Trinity 1791, Epiphany 1792; Sessions Minute Books, QSM I/5, Epiphany 1791, Easter 1792, and 5 September 1795; QSM I/6, Trinity 1798.

[87] See, for example, John Bowles, *Reflections on the Political and Moral State of Society at the Close of the Eighteenth Century* (London, 1800). For most opponents of radicalism the publication of Tom Paine's *The Age of Reason* (part 1 of which appeared in 1794) was deeply significant, identifying revolutionary and radical ideas unequivocally with irreligion. Godwin and Mary Wollstonecraft symbolised both in print and in fact the kind of radical subversion of traditional morality of which conservatives complained. In the first edition of the *Anti-Jacobin* in 1798, Wollstonecraft was presented as the epitome of 'Jacobin morality'; see Emily Lorraine de Montluzin, *The Anti-Jacobins 1798–1800* (London, 1988), pp. 13–14, 67–8.

reforms within the structure of the English state in the 1790s, but rather to construct an analytical framework which helps explain why the English state was able to confront the manifold challenges of that revolutionary decade without embarking on a thoroughgoing programme of political and institutional reform. Within the evolutionary history of the English state, the 1790s are best seen as a decade of revival, with government at all levels drawing renewed energy from tides of patriotic enthusiasm. The state succeeded in meeting the problems of sedition, recruitment, public finance, public order and poverty in partnership with voluntary initiatives emanating from an essentially practical patriotism. Had loyalism not translated, albeit imperfectly, into voluntary programmes, the state would have been compelled to confront an essentially French revolutionary threat by essentially French revolutionary means. As it was, loyalists took it upon themselves to transform expressions of affection for British traditions into actions which extended the authority and resources of the state. The principal consequence was a greater public energy on the part of the social elite.

The number of active magistrates rose significantly during the 1790s, and without this increase in available manpower neither the Quarter Sessions nor the County Lieutenancies would have been able to meet the demands placed upon them.[88] Even an overcommitted public servant such as Sir Joseph Banks was willing to take time away from the promotion of science to serve as High Sheriff of Lincolnshire in 1794 and to organise both a political association in London and a Volunteer corps in Lincolnshire.[89] In 1795 William Paley reaffirmed the dependence of the English polity on the civic energies of the wealthy and the privileged by suggesting that in no other country did civil institutions so constantly demand that private wealth should acknowledge its public responsibilities. 'With us a great part of the public business of the country is transacted by the country itself: and upon the prudent and faithful management of it, depends, in a very considerable degree, the interior prosperity of the nation and the satisfaction of great bodies of the people.'[90] Without the dramatic increase in its human and material resources, Britain would in all probability, like her Prussian and Austrian counterparts, have found itself

---

[88] L. K. J. Glassy and Norma Landau, 'The commission of the peace in the eighteenth century: a new source', *Bull. Institute Historical Research*, 45 (1972), pp. 262–3; Norma Landau, *The Justices of the Peace, 1679–1760* (Berkeley, Calif., 1984), p. 395; David W. Howell, *Patriarchs and Parasites. The Gentry of South-West Wales in the Eighteenth Century* (Cardiff, 1986), pp. 145–6.

[89] H. B. Carter, *Sir Joseph Banks* (London, 1988), pp. 305–6, 390. In 1788 Banks had declined to serve as High Sheriff on account of his other public commitments, but in the very different circumstances of 1794 he felt he had no alternative, and went on that year to produce his *Outlines of a Plan of Defence against a French Invasion*.

[90] Assize sermon preached at Durham, 29 July 1795, 'On Our Duty to God and Man', in *Paley's Works*, p. 614.

eclipsed by the superior energy and resources of revolutionary France. If we pursue the counterfactual a little further, it is not entirely fanciful to suggest that the likely consequence of military defeat, mutiny, unassuaged poverty and inadequate public revenues, would have been political and financial bankruptcy. Not, of course, a 'French (style) Revolution' in England, but an *English* revolution because of France.

In a broader perspective the effect of the 1790s might have been to retard the progress of political and institutional reform in Britain. The claims to power of an anti-democratic state had been apparently vindicated. The impetus for reform which had flowed from the Economical Reform Movement and had been so influential on Pitt in the 1780s was dissipated and to some extent even repudiated in the 1790s. Men such as Wyvil were isolated from, and sometimes attacked by, former sympathisers.[91]

The political lesson of the 1790s was simple: substantial reform was unnecessary, and Tory adoration of the gothic beauties of the Constitution could translate into a kind of politics which retained credibility in the post-revolutionary era.[92] Whiggism, at least in its visionary reforming guise, was marginalised as unnecessary and unEnglish. The degree to which the new Tory establishment had repudiated substantial structural reform was amply demonstrated in the post-war years as the pre-war system was painstakingly re-established, more or less irrespective of the social and economic cost.[93] Only in the 1830s did committed reformers recover the initiative, and by then the inspiration was no longer the radicalism of the revolutionary era, but a blend of Benthamite utilitarianism, classical economy, and political opportunism under the aegis of a rejuvenated Whiggism, and given a new urgency by the French Revolution of 1830.

---

[91] Young, *The Example of France*, pp. 54–8; Ashcroft, *To Escape the Monster's Clutches*, pp. 12–14; John Dinwiddy, *Christopher Wyvil and Reform 1790–1820* (York, 1971).

[92] David Eastwood, 'Robert Southey and the intellectual origins of romantic conservatism', *English Historical Review*, 104, 411 (1989), pp. 308–30.

[93] Boyd Hilton, *Corn, Cash, Commerce* (Oxford, 1977), pp. 3–97; J. E. Cookson, *Lord Liverpool's Administration, 1815–22* (Edinburgh, 1975), chs. 1–3; Thompson, *Making of the English Working Class*, chs. 15 and 16.

8   Conservatism and stability in British society

Ian R. Christie

I

The great storm which swept over southern England on the night of 15–16 October 1987 prompts a reflection on parallels between natural and political events, which have a certain bearing on the present theme. Everywhere that wind of hurricane force wrought destruction among the trees in the southern English countryside. Yet there were some which survived. They withstood the gale because of some inner toughness, strength of root, integrity of fibre, health of timber, absence of areas of rot and weakness – rot and weakness which, in less fortunate specimens, manifested themselves in wind-torn branches broken clean off the stem, or the whole tree wrenched from its roots and thrown to the ground. Without too much straining of metaphor, we may think in these terms of France and Britain in the early 1790s. The weaknesses, the internal divisions, the bottled-up discontents of French society led from 1789 onwards to revolutionary disruption. Britain on the other hand, though not without some areas of dissonance, nevertheless had the tensile strength to remain largely impervious to the storm of revolution. The purpose of this chapter is to outline in summary terms what seem to have been the salient elements of that power of resistance.

Late eighteenth-century British society comprised an enormous range of groups of differing social and economic status, from the common labourer at the bottom of the pile, whose wage might be no more than six to eight shillings a week, insufficient to support a family, to the wealthiest of the landed aristocracy with incomes of £30,000 to £40,000 a year. It contained within itself many subcultures, among which the nonconformist churches are perhaps some of the most familiar. But despite sectional loyalties, and the conflicts of interest and the group solidarities to which they sometimes gave rise, important structural features within the national society ensured that polarisation never developed to an extent which might lead to fatal upheavals. While there can be no question but that insurrectionary elements lurked here and there in England at the time of the French Revolution,[1] there was no great number of totally alienated people likely to accept their lead – no mass of tinder for their spark to kindle into a flame. The most compelling evidence for the conclusion that the majority of Englishmen were loyal to the established order is to be found in the circumstances of the years around 1797 to 1804. It has been estimated that at that period one in six, or even one in five, of all adult males were enrolled in Volunteer corps or other defence forces or the regular army. Over 400,000 men then had arms in their hands, but there is no evidence that any significant number of them thought to turn these arms against the state.[2]

Underpinning this situation lay a complex of social and economic factors making for social and political stability in Britain, the relative importance of which is very difficult to assess, but the combined effect of which seems beyond doubt.

II

In the first place British society was a society not sharply divided between confronting aristocratic and plebeian groups. Whilst the argument that it was an 'open society' must not be pressed too far – Lawrence and Jeanne Stone present solid grounds for recognising the existence of a very stable and fairly exclusive group of big landowners at the top level of society[3] – nevertheless this argument has elements of truth, especially if one considers the whole social hierarchy. Contemporary commentators noted the almost infinite gradations of economic and social status between one group and the next above it, such that the people in any one grade were not sharply set apart from the one above them and, moreover, could hope by emulation and material success to elevate themselves into their ranks;

[1] Roger Wells, *Insurrection: The British Experience, 1795–1803* (Gloucester, 1983).
[2] See, for instance, the account of the Devon Volunteers' willingness to fight for King and country, but determination to hand in their arms rather than act as a police force against rioters in 1801, in John Bohstedt, *Riots and Community Politics in England and Wales, 1790–1810* (Cambridge, Mass., 1983), pp. 50–1. Despite the reputation for disorder of Manchester, there was a massive enrolment of Volunteer militia, who were generally deemed reliable, between 1798 and 1804; *ibid.*, pp. 82–3, 114–16. The historian of that depressed class of the 1800s, the handloom weavers, has expressed scepticism about the rumours of sedition among them (Duncan Bythell, *The Handloom Weavers* (Cambridge, 1969), pp. 207, 210). On the popular conservative reaction in the north-east after 1791, see H. T. Dickinson, *Radical Politics in the North-East of England in the Later Eighteenth Century* (Durham County Local History Society, 1979), pp. 17–20. For a very thorough reappraisal of the social interreactions set up by the food shortages of 1795–6 and 1800–1, partly contesting but in places supporting the lines of argument in this chapter, see Roger Wells, *Wretched Faces. Famine in Wartime England, 1793–1801* (Gloucester, 1988).
[3] Lawrence Stone and Jeanne Fawtier Stone, *An Open Elite? England 1540–1880* (Oxford, 1984).

and various later historians have concurred in recognising the importance of this circumstance.[4]

In so far as upward mobility was possible and a feature of the system, the meaningful process at work was not the sudden jump from low down to the top of the social tree, but stage-by-stage advancement. Sudden jumps did occur: witness the rise of the billiard-saloon attendant, Robert Mackreth, to wealth as a financier and to the social accolades of knighthood and membership of the House of Commons, or the professional progress to the office of Lord Chancellor of John Scott, the son of a merchant in a small way of business at Newcastle. But these cases were relatively few. Of just under 2,000 Members of Parliament, whose biographies appear in the late eighteenth-century section of *The History of Parliament* covering the years 1754–1790, only about twenty self-made men of wealth had a parentage so obscure as to be untraceable or of so low a social status as tradesman or shopkeeper.[5] However, the number was increasing towards the end of the century. The subsequent section of *The History of Parliament* for the years 1790–1820 records well over 100 self-made men, many of whom had built up fortunes from relatively nothing: these represented over 5 per cent of the 2,143 men returned to Parliament during this period.[6] In both periods there were also Members of Parliament who had made the ascent from a less lowly starting-point, sons of fathers who had established themselves among the middling ranks of society, for instance as clergymen, as well-to-do bankers and merchants, or as provincial attorneys.

What contributed far more to social cohesion than the openings for the occasional high-flyer was the infinitely easier facility for upward movement over a relatively few steps on the social ladder – as it might be, from master craftsman to shopkeeper, from shopkeeper to ownership of a small business, from this perhaps to the ranks of schoolmasters, attorneys, ministers of religion, and so on. Even a limited extent of advancement of this kind could have a significant effect in channelling off energies and aspirations which might, if thwarted, have flowed in the direction of political discontent. François Crouzet's examination of the origin of the

[4] Esther Moir, *Local Government in Gloucestershire, 1775–1800* (Bristol, 1969), p. 73; Historical MSS Commission, *Verulam MSS*, p. 164, cited in Ian R. Christie, *Stress and Stability in Late Eighteenth-Century Britain: Reflections on the British Avoidance of Revolution* (Oxford, 1984), p. 57; Roy Porter, *English Society in the Eighteenth Century* (Harmondsworth, 1982), p. 64; Stone and Stone, *An Open Elite?*, p. 408; Harold Perkin, *The Origins of Modern English Society* (London, 1969), pp. 22–5.

[5] Sir Lewis Namier and John Brooke, *The History of Parliament. The House of Commons, 1754–1790*, 3 vols. (London, 1964), vol. I, pp. 103–7, vol. III, pp. 89–90, 415–16.

[6] R. G. Thorne, *The History of Parliament. The House of Commons, 1790–1820*, 5 vols. (London, 1986), vol. I, pp. 278, 290–1.

industrialists during the Industrial Revolution suggests that while overall the number of industrialists of working-class origin was small, engineering, a rapidly expanding sector, offered exceptional opportunities; and he remarks:

In the secondary metal trades of Birmingham and Sheffield, entry was also easy; an overwhelming majority of firms were very small, capital requirement was low, the system of renting room and power was widespread, and second-hand machinery could be bought cheaply, especially in times of depression. So there was a high degree of mobility between 'superior workmen' and 'small masters'.

Crouzet also observes that many entrepreneurs of 'lower middle-class' origin were 'self-made', and in social and economic terms some of them stood close to the working class and may have passed an early period of their lives as manual workers. Most industrialists, he notes, came from the middling classes; thus, within this sector of society the opportunities for upward mobility were significant, as was the consequent contribution to social and political stability.[7]

Even in government service an element of this sort of upward mobility was to be found. For instance, while the plums of the military profession went to the sons of aristocrats and gentry and to men who belonged to 'service' families who had managed to secure the backing of a patron, there was a not insignificant group of ex-rankers who found their way into at least the junior ranks of the officer corps. One scholar has remarked that it was 'greater in numbers than is generally realized'. Of such men, who had originally enlisted as private soldiers and had achieved success as senior NCOs, some 200 were commissioned during the 1739–48 war, and perhaps as many again got commissions during the Seven Years War.[8] The incidence of such commissions in the late eighteenth century has not received similar scholarly attention, but it seems likely that the practice of commissioning NCOs may even have been accelerated by the pressure to expand the army after 1792.

This pattern of gentle gradations and a movement between them constituted perhaps an unique quality of English society towards the end of the eighteenth century – a quality which moved a French apologist for events across the Channel to write in 1793: 'You have not amongst you that shocking inequality which disfigured human society in France.'[9]

[7] François Crouzet, *The First Industrialists: The Problem of Origins* (Cambridge, 1985), especially pp. 85, 90, 92–4, 99–115, 129.

[8] J. A. Houlding, *Fit for Service. The Training of the British Army, 1715–1795* (Oxford, 1981), p. 105, and for specific examples, p. 103. Houlding here relies mainly on J. Hayes, 'The social and professional background of the officers of the British army, 1714–63', unpublished M. A. Thesis (London University, 1956) – no comparable study has been made for the period of the revolutionary and Napoleonic wars.

[9] *The Monthly Review or Literary Journal Enlarged*, 13 (1794), p. 62.

Perhaps not the least important corollary and consequence of this phenomenon – facilitated also by the absence of any hierarchy of legal privilege such as existed in most continental countries – was the degree of cultural assimilation which it made possible, indeed encouraged, reaching down from the landed elite through the lesser gentry to the professions and to larger sections of the business class. As Lawrence and Jeanne Stone have remarked: 'The great strength of the...elite was its success in psychologically coopting those below them into the status hierarchy of gentility.'[10]

Co-optation by the landed elite from echelons below them at the political level is a question which the Stones do not discuss, but it is a significant element in the whole picture. Their concentration on the tenure of landed estates leads to the conclusion that in general, so far as their samples are representative, wealthy merchants formed only about 6 per cent of the elite landowners.[11] But this finding leaves a material consideration out of account: it is also important to examine the numbers of merchants in the political arena of the House of Commons if one is to gain a meaningful picture of their impact and their participation in the governing of the country. The proportion of Members of Parliament who were merchants was already well in excess of 6 per cent by the middle of the eighteenth century. In 1761 fifty merchants were elected – approximately 9 per cent – and the number rose slowly but steadily through the rest of the century. In 1780 it was seventy-two (approximately 13 per cent), and by 1790 eighty-seven (nearly 16 per cent).[12] Work in hand on the social classification of Members of Parliament through the period 1715–1820, though not yet sufficiently advanced to permit the report of definite conclusions, suggests that if sons of merchants sitting in the House of Commons who were 'first-generation' country gentlemen are taken into account, the infiltration into the House of men who were not members of the established elite was even larger – and larger by a substantial amount – than these figures indicate. Looked at from this angle the degree of 'openness' of the 'Open Elite' has a rather different appearance than when the attempt is made to measure merchant infiltration simply in terms of the ownership of great estates.

Psychological co-optation perhaps penetrated further in some respects than Lawrence and Jeanne Stone allow for, and here a further subtle cultural factor may have been at work. Dr Linda Colley has drawn attention to the surprised observation of a Venetian diplomat in the mid-

[10] Stone and Stone, *An Open Elite?*, p. 409.   [11] *Ibid.*, p. 403.
[12] For these figures, see Sir Lewis Namier, *England in the Age of the American Revolution*, 2nd edn (London, 1961), p. 254, n. 4; Ian R. Christie, *The End of North's Ministry, 1780–1782* (London, 1958), p. 180; Thorne, *House of Commons, 1790–1820*, vol. I, p. 318.

eighteenth century on the 'linguistic unity between plebeian and patrician', so different from the situation in his own land.[13] There can be little doubt that a powerful underlying influence promoting this state of affairs came from the constant recitation in public of the standard texts of the Church of England, the Elizabethan Prayer Book and the Authorised Version, readings of which (apart from the sermons) were heard regularly by the church-going sections of the lower ranks of the populace.[14]

Apart from this fostering of a national tongue superimposed above regional dialects, the Church of England and the various dissenting groups which flanked it had some moral effect in promoting the stability of the realm, although the extent to which this was so is difficult to assess and may in the past have been overestimated. The established church was in some disarray, its organisation on the ground inadequate especially in the industrialising areas of the north, its personnel lacking in numbers and sometimes poor in morale; and even in the late eighteenth century there was a considerable element of the population in the lower levels of society which had ceased to be attached to it to any active degree. The nonconformist churches, by now becoming influenced by the evangelical movement, and the spearhead of that movement, Wesleyanism, as yet counted only a relatively small proportion of the population among their adherents, and were much less influential than they were to become in the mid-nineteenth century.

Nevertheless, given all these limitations, for many people their church or chapel and the congregation to which they belonged provided an established familiar reassuring framework for their lives, one which very speedily after 1789 began to generate an abhorrence of the Revolution in France because of its hostility to church establishments and the degree of atheism which came to be associated with it. In some areas clergy of the established church took a lead in working up popular agitation against men whom they bracketed as heathen Unitarians and Jacobins – Joseph Priestley in Birmingham was merely the most prominent of their victims. Evangelicalism may have been a force making for stability in various ways. The members of evangelical congregations were concerned about mutual welfare in time of need, so supplementing, indeed sometimes supplanting the facilities of the Poor Law so far as their brethren were concerned. The mental and moral disciplines which these congregations imposed made for material success. And the evangelical mission working

[13] Linda Colley, 'Whose nation? Class and national consciousness in Britain, 1750–1830', *Past and Present*, 113 (1986), p. 97.

[14] Not that this necessarily meant the disappearance of dialects. Cf. for instance the concern to explain the Yorkshire Association of 1780 in West Riding speech (Ian R. Christie, *Myth and Reality in Late-Eighteenth-Century British Politics and Other Papers* (London, 1970), p. 275).

within the confines of a theological system may have channelled off into socially 'safe' activity reforming energies which, in a purely lay environment and with lay objectives, might have been potentially much more disruptive both socially and politically.[15]

Other important political conditions had evolved in company with the development of this peculiar structure of society in Britain. One very basic circumstance was the underlying implication behind the concept of English liberty, and the fact that within this tradition Britain had never developed the trappings of a police state. True, in one sense the state had a monopoly of force. There was a standing army. It was not, however, an instrument of arbitrary power but one which existed with the sanction of the representatives of the people, and which was bound to operate within the margin of the law. In fact, throughout the eighteenth century, the army, when policing riots, acted within even narrower limits than that – for both the bad drafting of the Riot Act of 1715, and the casuistry with which the lawyers treated it, created a very general impression that the arms carried by soldiers 'were to be used not to disperse a mob but only in the last resort in self-defence'.[16] Successive secretaries-at-war, the executive subministers responsible for detaching troops to deal with riotous situations, in their overcautious directives denied the right of the troops to act at all unless actually ordered to do so by a civil magistrate, and conveyed the impression that, whatever the circumstances, to act without such an order would be illegal and render them liable to criminal proceedings for death or injury caused by their actions.[17] The moral pressure against adoption of a purely coercive role by the military is also evident from the reluctance of magistrates to call them in, and from the way officers of units detached to restore public order would intervene and mediate with leaders of mobs, often exerting sufficient moral influence to defuse a situation which might otherwise have ended in human tragedy.[18] It is not surprising that mobs were often contemptuous of soldiers sent to police riots.[19]

No effective civilian police force existed in Britain in the eighteenth century. Moreover, the nation's rulers were not prepared to entertain the idea of creating one: when the Earl of Shelburne suggested in the House of Lords at the time of the Gordon Riots of 1780, that a metropolitan force should be set up on the French model, his proposal fell on deaf

---

[15] Christie, *Stress and Stability*, ch. 7. Cf. John Rule, *The Labouring Classes in Early Industrial England, 1750–1850* (London, 1986), pp. 162–5.

[16] Tony Hayter, *The Army and the Crowd in Mid-Georgian England* (London, 1978), pp. 9–12.   [17] *Ibid.*, pp. 12–15, 31–3.

[18] *Ibid.*, pp. 170, 182–3; Bohstedt, *Riots and Community Politics*, pp. 56–8.

[19] Hayter, *The Army and the Crowd*, p. 29.

ears.[20] This attitude reflected the overwhelming prejudice of Englishmen against the creation of any force which might become a danger to English liberty. The psychological effect of this absence of any such coercive force is difficult to assess, but there can be little doubt that it was of profound significance, and the uninhibited politicking and public demonstrations which were a regular feature of life in London bear witness to its consequences. Men were not terrorised and therefore were not alienated. Far otherwise – the integration of 'the people' into the national community was a feature of life in this island which impressed foreign observers. It was evident in the lively interest shown by the man in the street in public affairs. Such an interest was displayed not only by shopkeepers and craftsmen; it could be found even lower down in the scale, as an Irish visitor to London pithily remarked: 'Every coal-porter is a politician and vends his maxims in public with all the importance of a man who thinks he is exerting himself for the public service; he claims the privilege of looking as wise as possible, of talking as loud, of damning the ministry and abusing the king, with less reason than he would his own equal.' Arthur Young was amazed at the contrasting political apathy of the public in France when he passed through Clermont in the summer of 1789.[21] The German pastor Moritz remarked of the English scene in the 1780s: 'When one sees how the lowliest carter shows an interest in public affairs; how the smallest children enter into the spirit of the nation; how everyone feels himself to be a man and an Englishman...as good as his king and his king's minister...it brings to mind thoughts very different from those we know when we watch the soldiers drilling in Berlin.'[22]

It was not just a matter of feeling, but also of role. Another circumstance, as at least one shrewd contemporary observer noted, was that the parliamentary electoral system in England contributed effectively to foster civil relationships between members of the upper and the lower ranks in society.[23] This point has recently received increasing emphasis. Some recent scholarship points to the conclusion that by the end of the eighteenth century the potential – if not the actual – involvement of 'the people' in the electoral system was considerably greater than has hitherto been realised. From 1780 onwards an increasing number of constituencies began to be contested. The thirty-three borough constituencies with the largest electorates embraced some two-thirds of the total electorate, and it was in these that most of the contests fought to a finish regularly

[20] Lord Edmond Fitzmaurice, *Life of William, Earl of Shelburne*, 2nd revised edn, 2 vols., (London, 1912), vol. II, pp. 60–1.   [21] Christie, *Stress and Stability*, pp. 59–60.
[22] Quoted in Porter, *English Society* p. 119. Cf. the comment by von Archenholz, cited *ibid.*, p. 273.
[23] *The Works of William Paley, DD, and an Account of the Life and Writings of the Author*, by the Revd Edmund Paley, AM, 4 vols. (1983), vol. III, p. 258, cited in Christie, *Stress and Stability*, p. 54.

occurred.[24] To these instances contests which were aborted after the holding of canvasses have to be added, since the canvass gave the elector an initial opportunity to state his choice, and the result was often determined by the expression of these options. To the problem posed for the statistician by this phenomenon there is added that of the intermittent and abstaining voters. Faced with the difficulty of enumerating the total electorate in these circumstances one scholar has advanced the general conclusion that, 'the total electoral pool must consequently have been far greater than the measured size of the electorate. In the early nineteenth century it must have contained well over one million individuals.'[25] In some large boroughs the electorate included a substantial proportion of the resident adult males, and the social composition extended well down the social spectrum. An analysis of one selected group of such electorates yields the conclusion that retailers made up approximately one-fifth of the voters, skilled craftsmen over one-third, and that about 14 per cent were unskilled labourers.

Under these conditions a sense of participation was evident, and the mores of elections reinforced this. The same scholar has noted that the conduct of elections, especially in boroughs, was deliberately keyed to 'the politics of communal involvement'. There was a stress on liberties and the freedom which guaranteed their independence, but an emphasis also on the need to show respect to opponents: 'The language of liberty was carefully rehearsed amidst a real awareness of the fragility of social discipline and the need to preserve the social order.' The contribution of all this to the political stability of the nation was unmistakable.[26]

III

Moving on from socio-political to socio-economic circumstances, it can be argued that a fundamental factor making for political and social stability in Great Britain towards the end of the eighteenth century was the country's expanding economy and the increasing prosperity widely distributed through many sections of the population. The fact that there were major sectors of depression, particularly among the agricultural labourers of the south, that there were periods of hardship due to bad harvests in 1795–6 and again in 1800–1, and occasional recessions in particular areas of the economy, is no refutation of this conclusion; for

---

[24] J. A. Phillips, 'The structure of electoral politics in unreformed England', *Journal of British Studies*, 19 (1980), pp. 92–5; and see his study, *Electoral Behaviour in Unreformed England, 1761–1802* (Princeton, N.J., 1982).

[25] Frank O'Gorman, 'The unreformed electorate of Hanoverian England: the mid-eighteenth century to the Reform Act of 1832', *Social History*, 11 (1986), p. 38.

[26] *Ibid.*, pp. 35–52; and see his very full exposition of these lines of argument in his excellent study, *Voters, Patrons and Parties: The Unreformed Electorate of Hanoverian England, 1734–1832* (Oxford, 1989).

those circumstances do not negate the indications of the general upward trend in many people's economic situations in the period of the French Revolution, a phenomenon which is indicated by numerous kinds of converging evidence. It was not until after the period with which we are here concerned, that is from about the beginning of the Regency, that more widespread general deterioration of the economic situation of working people set in.[27]

There are first the comments of political and administrative observers, who were directly concerned in one way or another with elucidating the state of the economy, notably the commercial negotiator, William Eden, Lord Auckland and the government statistician, John Rickman. Then there are the direct descriptions by contemporaries of the transformations which were being effected in various localities. Arthur Young, for instance, left accounts of developments, sometimes striking, even exciting, at Tamworth in Staffordshire and Mistley in Essex, and a similar impression comes from the descriptions given by John Wesley and by Josiah Wedgwood of the Staffordshire potteries. To Wesley, who had travelled time and again through west Staffordshire on his missionary circuits, and to whom the poorest folk were a primary concern, it was as if 'the wilderness [had] literally become a fruitful field'. Towards the end of the century, so Wedgwood recorded, the craftsmen who lived and worked there were earning wages on an average nearly twice as high as their predecessors of a generation before. Other contemporary descriptions by British or foreign travellers attest how housing and industrial settlement transformed the scene – for example, in such districts as south Wales, or Birmingham, or the Warmley area east of Bristol. One scholar has observed, with specific reference to Birmingham, Sheffield and Lancashire, that, 'despite the prevalence of low-quality accommodation for large numbers of eighteenth-century artisans, there are indications that some artisan groups lived in rather better houses, which they sometimes owned themselves'. The upward thrust of a burgeoning industrial economy, especially the expansion going on in textiles and metallurgy, was well tuned to deal with the growth of population, providing increasing numbers of people with jobs and with housing often superior to what was available in backward, less developing agricultural areas, such as, for instance, Lincolnshire, which so depressed Colonel John Byng when he travelled through it.[28]

[27] The contrast between the years before and after about 1810 emerges noticeably from comparison of Dr John Rule's study, *The Experience of Labour in Eighteenth Century Industry* (London, 1981), and chs. 1–5 of his judicious survey, *The Labouring Classes*. Dr Roger Wells's *Wretched Faces*, filling a hitherto total lacuna in the literature, now provides a definitive account of the famine years 1795–6 and 1800–1.

[28] Christie, *Stress and Stability*, pp. 69–77; Rule, *The Labouring Classes*, pp. 91–6.

Figures for wage earnings in the late eighteenth century are fragmentary and have to be assembled from such miscellaneous sources as travellers' reports and clergymen's notes, in addition to the very few business archives which survive for this period. And yet, incomplete though this evidence may be, it gives strong support to the conclusion that increasing numbers of people were disposing of larger family incomes than before as a result of industrialisation. At the very least, on average there was little decline. One substantial analysis by Professor M. W. Flinn made in 1974 shows that, overall, the real purchasing power of wages in a selected group of eighteen categories of employment was roughly maintained during the last forty years of the century: although prices went up, on average wages more or less kept pace.[29]

Much of the scholarship touching on agriculture points to abysmally low wage rates for farm workers during the later Hanoverian period; but certain reservations need to be made for the years of the French wars. In general, agricultural wages followed the general upwards trend, more or less doubling between 1790 and 1810.[30] There are clear indications that in the north of England the growing competition for labour between industry and agriculture pulled up agricultural wage rates.[31] In the south, and also in some outlying areas like Cumberland, the shortage of manpower created by war between 1793 and 1815 had a similar effect.[32] Labourers' incomes – as distinct from *wages* – benefited in the south from the various modes of supplementation from public funds, now known by the general name of the Speenhamland system. Undoubtedly life was hard, simple and without amenities for numbers of people in the rural districts. Even so, the difficulty of making generalisations, of judging to what degree it might be thought intolerable, is illustrated by the Reverend Gilbert White's description of his parish of Selborne in the 1780s. Having remarked, 'we abound with poor', he immediately continued, 'poor, many of whom are sober and industrious and live comfortably [*note that phrase*] in good stone or brick cottages, which are glazed, and have chambers above-stairs: mud buildings we have none'.[33]

Using the admittedly low wage level of the farm worker or the general labourer as a basis of comparison, figures can be culled from various

---

[29] Christie, *Stress and Stability*, pp. 78–80; M. W. Flinn, 'Trends in real wages, 1750–1850', *Economic History Review*, 2nd ser., 27 (1974), p. 408. John Rule sees a more general tendency in the literature towards this conclusion in respect of the years up to the 1790s (*The Labouring Classes*, pp. 31–4).

[30] Bohstedt, *Riots and Community Politics*, table 3, p. 185.

[31] *Ibid.*, pp. 184–5; Christie, *Stress and Stability*, pp. 79–80; Pamela Horn, *Life and Labour in Rural England, 1760–1850* (London, 1987), p. 9; Bythell, *The Handloom Weavers*, p. 45.

[32] A. H. John, 'Farming in wartime, 1793–1815' in E. L. Jones and G. E. Mingay (eds.), *Land, Labour and Population in the Industrial Revolution* (London, 1967), pp. 32–4.

[33] Cited in Horn, *Rural England*, p. 9.

sources to show that in many spheres of industry workers in the 1790s were able to command pay two or three times as high. Moreover, there were some groups, for example the craftsmen in the government shipyards and copper workers in areas of the north-west who could add substantially to their wages by various perquisites. One historian has described the two decades after 1788 as Lancashire's 'golden age' for weavers, though this description perhaps requires qualification, especially for the period after 1806.[34] The Lancashire cotton-spinning industry furnished good earnings to its workers in the 1790s – one explanation perhaps for the tardy development of trade combinations in this region. To quote my summary in print elsewhere: 'Mule cotton-spinners might earn between 30s and 38s a week during the 1790s.' And again: 'Analysis of the wage books of fourteen leading firms of textile printers towards the close of the century indicates that the highest paid journeymen were receiving £103 per annum and the lowest over £51.'[35] This, incidentally, was at a time when, in the textile centre of Norwich, a wage of 12s a week (about £31 a year) was judged sufficient for a local family to live on 'comfortably'.[36] The growing demand for textile pattern designers, and for people to execute hand-painted decoration on pottery and chinaware, opened up new opportunities for men and women with particular artistic skills to win earnings at even higher rates than ordinary craftsmen. Working people's family incomes were also significantly increased as industry surged forward, by the far more numerous opportunities for daughters and sometimes wives to add appreciable sums to the household earnings. Servants attached to large households also seem to have fared pretty comfortably at the end of the eighteenth century. The lists of domestic wages and the household bills for Lord Braybrooke's establishment at Audley End in Essex, which make possible comparisons between the beginning and the middle years of George III's reign, indicate significant increases of wages as well as increases of 'hidden wage' in the form of food and drink consumed, and suggest that the domestic staff of this household at any rate enjoyed a comfortable standard of living. Although this is only one instance, it

---

[34] The level of earnings of weavers in this period is particularly difficult to judge, because many combined weaving with the running of a small farm, others were content to earn a conventional rather low income for three or four days work a week only, and yet others were part-time workers (including women and children). In the mid-1780s weavers working for Samuel Oldknow averaged 17s 7d a week for fancy muslins down to 12s for plain calico and 9s for coarse linen: the information adduced by Dr Bythell implies that at this period takings could have been pushed up to at least twice these levels by men who were willing to work a full six-day week. See the discussion in Bythell, *The Handloom Weavers*, especially pp. 44, 45, 59, 115, 118, 131–3. The description 'golden age' is in Rule, *Labouring Classes*, p. 94; but see Bohstedt, *Riots and Community Politics*, ch. 6.

[35] Christie, *Stress and Stability*, pp. 80–2, quotation at p. 82.

[36] C. B. Jewson, *Jacobin City. A Portrait of Norwich in its Reaction to the French Revolution, 1788–1802* (London, 1975), pp. 4–5.

seems unlikely that it was greatly out of line with other similar households. Another aspect of the advancing prosperity of the population shows itself in the degree of upward mobility which was a further consequence of early industrialisation in the 1780s and 1790s, as some skilled craftsmen, exploiting the 'ecological niches' of the expanding economy, established themselves as members of a managerial class or launched their own independent business ventures.[37]

The same story of increasing widespread prosperity is indicated by various other converging lines of evidence. Statistics of output adjusted in relation to population suggest that 'between 1780 and 1800 total output was expanding twice as fast as population and industrial output was increasing three times as fast as population'.[38] Where it is possible to use customs and excise figures as indicators the evidence is inescapable, that per head of population increasing quantities of commodities in common use were being absorbed by the domestic market. The nature of these goods – for instance, tobacco, soap, candles, beer, printed fabrics – makes it clear that these increasing quantities were being distributed among wide sections of the public; they were not simply contributing to a higher living standard of a small privileged minority.[39] Yet another indication that conditions were improving for many people towards the end of the eighteenth century is afforded by what has been referred to as an 'efflorescence' of popular leisure.[40]

The two major contemporary analyses of the general pattern of incomes in England which we have available for this period, one for 1759, the other for about 1803, again reveal how the proportion of people in poverty at the base of the social pyramid was shrinking in relation to total population, and larger numbers of people were rising into the ranks of those whose earnings gave them at least a modest degree of comfort and prosperity. Using a rough and ready rule-of-thumb in comparing these tables, one can conclude that whereas six families out of seven fell below such a level of earnings in 1760, only three in four fell below it in 1803; and it is possible that these figures are too pessimistic.[41] One historian's analysis suggests that between 1750 and 1780 the number of households in the middle income range (£50 and £400) rose from 15 per cent of the population of England to 20 or even 25 per cent, and the indications that this trend continued are unmistakable.[42]

Yet another line of investigation – population growth – supports this optimistic interpretation of the condition of England in the last two

---

[37] Christie, *Stress and Stability*, pp. 82–7.   [38] *Ibid.*, p. 88.

[39] *Ibid.*, pp. 87–9.

[40] Rule, *Labouring Classes*, pp. 214–26, description cited at p. 226.

[41] Christie, *Stress and Stability*, pp. 90–2.

[42] D. E. C. Eversley, 'The home market and economic growth', in Jones and Mingay, *Land, Labour and Population*, p. 221.

decades of the eighteenth century. Dr E. A. Wrigley has argued effectively that whereas in earlier centuries any significant spurt in population soon brought its nemesis in unacceptably high levels of prices of provisions, this did not occur in the Hanoverian period. In the past this self-regulating mechanism had always worked to damp down any tendency to a population explosion, having its effect chiefly on rates of marriage and so of procreation. There are some indications that this process was at work in France in the late eighteenth century, where grain prices advanced much more severely than in Britain and where a slowing up of the rate of increase of population was evident.[43] Such a well-informed observer as Malthus expected the same thing to happen in England. In fact, as Wrigley shows, it did not, and he provides various elements of an explanation. From about 1730 onwards there was an increased expectation of life, and though he does not mention it, one obvious factor here was the development, long before Jenner, of successful inoculation against smallpox. Also the fertility rate was rising. But he picks out as the most crucial factor, 'earlier and more universal marriages'. Between the last quarter of the seventeenth century and the beginning of the nineteenth century women's age at first marriage 'dropped by about 3 years from 26 to 23 years, while the proportion of women surviving throughout the child-bearing period who never married fell from a figure of perhaps 15 per cent at the beginning of the period to no more than half of its initial level towards the end of the eighteenth century'. In the past the incidence of marriage had always demonstrably been linked with the extent of economic opportunity – couples did not found a household unless conditions were sufficiently favourable. This ethos, Wrigley writes, can be traced as still operative well into the nineteenth century; and it follows that the high rate of marriage and the early age of marriage in the reign of George III correlate clearly with favourable economic conditions. Wrigley sums up his argument thus: 'At the end of the eighteenth century suddenly prices no longer rose nor did real wages fall as was to be expected from past experience. Rising numbers were no longer incompatible with rising individual prosperity, a change which was one of the most fundamental defining characteristics of the Industrial Revolution.'[44]

All these circumstances suggest that in late eighteenth-century Britain, opportunities were opening up for a significant proportion of the lower classes to have a slightly more prosperous life than before. This is not to deny that a good deal of hardship still existed, especially in country districts, or that there was a worsening of the situation for many people after 1815, beyond the period with which this chapter is concerned. But in

---

[43] Olwen Hufton, *The Poor of Eighteenth-Century France* (Oxford, 1974), p. 16.

[44] E. A. Wrigley, 'The growth of population in eighteenth-century England. A conundrum resolved', *Past and Present*, 98 (February 1983), pp. 121–50, quotations at pp. 131, 137.

the revolutionary decade at the end of the eighteenth century, whatever may have been the difficulties created at times by harvest failures or recessions in various trades, it is as inappropriate to attribute any serious threat of insurrection or the creation of a revolutionary frame of mind to economic circumstance as it would be to attribute such phenomena in this country to the depression of 1929–31.

So far as the poor at the bottom levels of the social structure were concerned, there is little doubt that the English Poor Law – and to a less extent its Scottish equivalent – helped to defuse what might otherwise have been a serious source of discontent. The system in England, firmly bedded upon the parish structure, and with unified corporations of the poor operating with enhanced efficiency in a number of the larger towns and cities, was based on what a leading northern Justice of the Peace described in 1793 as 'a very extensive and important branch of the law'.[45] It was a branch to which considerable attention was given both by Parliament and by social reformers and philanthropists.

Without equivocation or ambiguity, this body of law placed on the ratepayers of all parishes or urban Poor-Law incorporations a responsibility for the maintenance of the poor.[46] So far as the aged and infirm without other means of support or family help were concerned, this meant either constant contribution to maintenance with doles for the purchase of food and payment of rent, allowances for repairs such as the rethatching of cottages, and perhaps assistance with such part-time employment as spinning or pig-keeping that the pensioner could manage; or else the provision of board and accommodation in an institution sometimes described not as a workhouse but, more accurately, as a house of care. Despite occasional serious scandals due to poor supervision and unchecked mismanagement, conditions in these establishments generally seem to have been tolerable and the diet provided adequate – more adequate, indeed, than that officially prescribed under the reformed nineteenth-century Poor Law after 1834.

So far as the able-bodied were concerned, the Poor Law was quite categorical. Work was to be found for them if at all possible, and if employment using their own skills was out of the question, then parish work would be required in return for maintenance. This might be, for instance, labour in repairing the roadways in the parish, or, if nothing else offered, cultivation of the garden attached to the workhouse or house of care, as a contribution to the maintenance of themselves and their fellow paupers. Children whose parents could not maintain them were to be found work, if possible being apprenticed to some trade.

---

[45] G. B. Hindle, *Provision for the Relief of the Poor in Manchester, 1754–1826* (Manchester, 1975), p. 112.
[46] For what follows, see the more detailed account in Christie, *Stress and Stability*, ch. 4.

While this represented the central core of the activity undertaken by the Poor Law authorities, it by no means comprised the whole of the range of their responsibilities. More particularly in the southern agricultural districts, where there was no competition from industry to force up wages, and when disastrous harvests sent wheat prices soaring, guardians of the poor found themselves increasingly driven to adopt one method or another to subsidise the inadequate wages paid to agricultural labourers – the so-called Speenhamland system. In time of war the guardians also faced additional demands to those normally generated by the uncertainties of economic circumstance. Both the pressing of sailors and the embodying of the militia threw heavy extra burdens on their funds, through the need to support the wives and children of breadwinners who had been suddenly withdrawn from their employments and often sent far away from the district where they lived. Attention also had to be given to support for the widows and orphans of sailors and soldiers who died on active service. A very marked increase in the total of poor-rate expenditure after 1795 indicates how the system was responding to need.[47]

In times of real crisis the relief afforded by the Poor Law was supplemented by charity on a massive scale. This might be, as in the Ironbridge district in 1795–6 and in 1801, in discharge of obligations undertaken by major employers to cover the needs of their imported workforce when necessary.[48] On a great estate, relief might be an automatic exercise in paternalism: the painter Joseph Farington, visiting the Duke of Devonshire's seat at Chatsworth in the dearth year of 1801, recorded: 'Many pensions of £5 a year are allowed to poor people in this village and in the neighbourhood by his Grace whose goodness is extensively felt.'[49] Municipal leaders in Manchester organised massive aid in the form of soup charity in 1799 and 1800, and also in the sale of foodstuffs at subsidised prices.[50] In 1801, at Wrest Park in Bedfordshire, and at Wentworth Woodhouse in Yorkshire, and no doubt elsewhere, the estate managers organised relief supplies of barrels of Scotch herring and distributed them at a subsidised price.[51] Also, in times of bad harvest, landowners intervened to ensure that any reserve supplies of grain held by their tenant farmers were made available.[52] The philanthropist Sir

---

[47] Bohstedt, *Riots and Community Politics*, p. 19.
[48] Christie, *Stress and Stability*, pp. 115 and 122, n. 55.
[49] Quoted in Horn, *Rural England*, p. 35.
[50] Bohstedt, *Riots and Community Politics*, pp. 95–7.
[51] Horn, *Rural England*, p. 52; Sidney Pollard and Colin Holmes (eds.), *Essays in the Economic and Social History of South Yorkshire* (Barnsley, S. Yorks, 1976), p. 51.
[52] Christie, *Stress and Stability*, p. 153; Bohstedt, *Riots and Community Politics*, pp. 52, 98–9, 205, 206; O'Gorman, *Voters, Patrons and Parties*, pp. 52–3 (on the activities of the Grosvenors at Chester). In February 1796, in a speech against Whitbread's labourers' wages bill, Thomas Coxhead, MP, assured the House from his own knowledge that the

Frederick Morton Eden estimated that in the crisis year 1795–6 more was spent on relief of the poor by way of charity than was expended through the Poor Law system itself.[53]

Charity apart, in very many ways the Poor Law organisation of late eighteenth-century England played a vital part as a welfare service. Had it not been in operation, then the degree of desperation and disaffection that might have been generated can only be guessed – at least the contrasting situation in France, where there was no comparably effective secular Poor Law suggests that it would have been formidable and destabilising.[54]

Social stability rested in part on the degree of assurance felt by many sections of the community in the availability of support in time of need from friendly societies or workmen's combinations. These were of no avail to such very poverty-stricken ranks of the populace as the general labourers, who could not afford even the most modest subscriptions, but they were a help to wage earners higher up the scale in all sorts of callings, and indeed also in sections of society such as shopkeepers and minor clergy. Friendly societies, although usually relatively small in size and locally based, typically comprising some fifty to a hundred members, existed in such large numbers that, overall, they provided contingent support in case of need to a very significant proportion of the population. Eden calculated in 1801 that there then existed some 7,200 societies with a membership of about 648,000 and an annual financial turnover of almost £500,000.[55]

No determinate line can be drawn between the friendly societies pure and simple and the trade combinations of the eighteenth century. The latter commonly, if not universally, included benefit functions among their activities – the provision of unemployment or sick pay, and defrayment of funeral expenses – but were also concerned to bargain with their employers from such strength as they could command over conditions of employment, particularly wages, working hours and the closed shop; and this could entail the use of society funds to provide strike allowances if disputes proceeded to such extremes.

A good deal of recent scholarship has pointed to the relative success of these embryo trade unions in defending and advancing the interests of

farmers and gentry of Worcestershire were as forward in relieving the poor as those of any other county (Thorne, *House of Commons, 1790–1820*, vol. III, p. 519).

[53] Christie, *Stress and Stability*, p. 122.

[54] For a brief outline of the starkly contrasting situation in France, based on Olwen Hufton, *The Poor of Eighteenth-Century France*, see Christie, *Stress and Stability*, pp. 120–1.

[55] Sir F. M. Eden, *Observations on Friendly Societies...* (London, 1801), pp. 6–9, cited in Christie, *Stress and Stability*, p. 128.

their members, particularly in respect of wage-rates.[56] This activity took place – and the need for it was felt – not so much among new categories of employment being opened up by the Industrial Revolution, where for the time being at any rate the levels of profit and the rates of reward were relatively good, but among older established crafts and groups of relatively skilled workers, such as those in the clothing and building trades.

Such activity was carried on despite the considerable formal restrictions and prohibitions which had found their way on to the statute book. The dice were loaded against effective invocation of the law by employers, and even when leaders of strikes were prosecuted, magistrates and judges often tended to show forbearance in dealing with them. The Acts against labour combinations which were put on the statute book in 1799 and 1800 made little difference. The argument in favour of their ultimate repeal in 1824 was that they had been almost entirely ineffective, and this is indeed borne out by the facts.

IV

It will be evident that the conclusions outlined in this chapter are in important respects irreconcilable with those adduced by Dr Roger Wells in his contribution to this volume.[57] The problem here is, perhaps, one of achieving the correct balance in judging the respective momentum of cohesive and of disintegrating tendencies in British society in the 1790s. It would seem that its resolution will require further research and consideration. That elements of the population suffered extreme distress at times during this period is undeniable. That there were some British revolutionaries committed by emotion and intellect to a French-style transformation of the British polity is also undeniable. What seems much more dubious is that resulting discontents and agitations were sufficiently acute or on such a scale as to raise any serious challenge to the existing social and political order.

On the contrary this survey suggests that, by the last decade of the eighteenth century, an extremely complex interlocking set of conditions – political, social, economic – had become established in Great Britain, which created a situation in which antagonisms between class and group interests, and discontent with the established order never developed to the level of intensity at which a serious threat of revolution was likely to emerge. Rather, these conditions to some extent fostered a sense of

[56] For a more detailed account, on which this passage is based, see Christie, *Stress and Stability*, ch. 5. Cf. Rule, *The Labouring Classes*, pp. 255–66.
[57] See pp. 188–226, below.

opportunities for mutual advantage pursued in common, and, more broadly, opened up prospects for material improvement – prospects which perhaps were more open in the second half of the eighteenth century than they were either in the previous or the subsequent decades. Also the situation was one in which various bonds and networks of mutual assistance – some public, some private – operated to provide a machinery to defuse tension and to reduce the potential for disaffection likely to lurk within any human society.[58] Other still more intangible factors also probably played a part in determining British attitudes towards France in the 1790s. A series of wars – 1740–8, 1756–63, 1778–83 – had sharpened the sense of national antagonism and stimulated emotions of patriotism and national feeling at the popular level.[59] While a minority of intellectuals welcomed the early stages of the French Revolution, seeing in it French emulation of the English Revolution of 1689, much of this enthusiasm soon withered in face of the Revolution Militant after 1793. Furthermore, the ideology of the Revolution and the consequences to which this led soon came under heavy destructive attacks from numerous critics, of whom Edmund Burke was merely the best known and one of the most trenchant in rhetorical style.[60] The instinct of the people coincided with the thought of the critics of the Revolution. After an intensive examination of over 600 riots in England and Wales in the years 1790–1810, one scholar observes: 'If the public actions of hundreds of crowds can be taken as more representative of the English common people than the elusive activities of revolutionary conspirators, revolution was not imminent in this period.'[61] In this decade of crisis and war beginning in 1789 the overwhelming majority of the British people were loyal – loyal to the King, whose popularity and whose status as a symbol waxed with the passing years; loyal to the system of government under which they lived; and, it may be said, loyal to themselves, in that they felt themselves in some sense partners and participants in the affairs of the country and the nation to which they belonged.[62]

---

[58] See, for instance, the analysis in Bohstedt, *Riots and Community Politics*, ch. 1.
[59] See, for instance, the discussion in Linda Colley, 'The apotheosis of George III: loyalty, royalty and the British nation, 1760–1820', *Past and Present*, 102 (1984), pp. 94–129, and 'Whose nation?', pp. 97–117.
[60] T. P. Schofield, 'Conservative political thought in Britain in response to the French Revolution', *Historical Journal*, 29, 3 (1986), pp. 601–22; 'English conservative thought and opinion in response to the French Revolution, 1789–1796', unpublished Ph.D. thesis (University of London, 1984); H. T. Dickinson, *Liberty and Property. Political Ideology in Eighteenth-Century Britain* (London, 1977), ch. 8; Christie, *Stress and Stability*, ch. 6.
[61] Bohstedt, *Riots and Community Politics*, p. 222.
[62] Linda Colley, articles cited, n. 59 above; O'Gorman, *Voters, Patrons and Parties*, especially ch. 4.

9   English society and revolutionary politics in the 1790s: the case for insurrection

Roger Wells

I

After a quarter of a century's debate, Edward Thompson's identification of revolutionary Englishmen engaged in insurrectionary plottings in the aftermath of the notoriously repressive Gagging Acts of 1795, has been accepted – perhaps grudgingly – by historians concerned with the 1790s. For example, Professor Dickinson in his *British Radicalism and the French Revolution*, an Historical Association study aiming to 'critically summarise research on some of the central themes and key episodes of history', devotes one quarter to 'The Revolutionary Underground'.[1] If the principal historical outlines of revolutionary groupings – the United Britons, the United Scotsmen, the United Englishmen and the United Irishmen – and their alliances, have been established,[2] problems remain, notably over their hypothetical chances of success. This remains central to the bigger problematic, namely explaining non-revolution in Britain in the epoch of the French Revolution.

The magnitude of the latter question is reflected in Professor Christie's choice of topic when invited to give the prestigious Ford Lectures in 1984. His search for 'a comprehensive answer' to the problem, comprised an analysis of British 'political, social... [and] economic interconnections' which 'displayed a sort of disordered cohesion'. This simultaneously absorbed and withstood the massive strains generated by the ideologically motivated war, on a global stage, the disequilibriums galvanised by relatively rapid economic change, and the challenge from democratic ideology germinating the first working-class movement for the political dismantling of the British *ancien régime*. Christie gently observed that

---

[1] H. T. Dickinson, *British Radicalism and the French Revolution 1789–1815* (Oxford, 1985).
[2] The main empirical studies are: Albert Goodwin, *The Friends of Liberty: The English Democratic Movement in the Age of the French Revolution* (London, 1979), especially ch. 11; J. Ann Hone, *For the Cause of Truth. Radicalism in London 1796–1821* (Oxford, 1982), ch. 2; Marianne Elliott, *Partners in Revolution: The United Irishmen and France* (New Haven, Conn., 1982); Roger Wells, *Insurrection: The British Experience, 1795–1803* (Gloucester, 1983).

historians' concentration on 'popular radicalism' in the nineties, may have 'swayed them in the direction of assuming...the nation's susceptability to revolution...[was] more real' than 'factors on the other side of the equation' actually warrant.[3] Other historians have also recently, and legitimately, explored forces fiercely operative in sustaining the establishment, notably loyalism, and Dr Colley has, for example, emphasised the central role of the apotheosis of the monarch himself. George III's 1809 Golden Jubilee witnessed the climax to this development.[4] But Colley's time-scale reveals distortions which can derive from theses which transcend the critical decade, the nineties themselves. George's deification *also* involved bullet-proofing the state-coach – in 1796[5] – a telling fact, which she does not mention. Although Christie's specific question of 'revolution...avoidance' *is* addressed to 'during the 1790s', his analysis is sustained by *juxtaposed* evidence from across a sixty-year period, 1750–1810; for example, he insists, and in the present volume apparently maintains, that a 'buoyant economy' created economic opportunities, and 'between 1750 and 1800 more people were faring better than before, and the general outlook was one of optimism and reasonable hope for material gain'. 'Despite occasional fears and alarms,' he continues, 'economic conditions provide a cogent explanation why...there was no danger of revolution in the 1790s.'[6]

Such juxtapositions seriously distort the realities of experiences in the decade. It is difficult to express the apocalyptic tone of the nineties. Here we have a central nation, England, with at best semi-integrated peripheries, Wales, Scotland and above all Ireland, locked in a war which increasingly looked unsustainable and unwinnable. Yet, defeating revolutionary France, and restoring the Bourbon monarchy, were presented as the sole guarantors of English society, and its *ancien régime*. A French victory was projected as the precursor of a democratic revolution imposed by a foreign power, assisted by indigenous egalitarians, successfully dubbed Jacobins, after the authors of the most violent episode in the French Revolution itself. The imagery orchestrated by the British state in perhaps the first prolonged campaign to identify a national interest, was a world on the brink of being turned upside down. The issues of war, and the fitness of the existing establishment literally to rule in the traditional way, were enormously divisive. If the governing oligarchy drew

[3] Ian R. Christie, *Stress and Stability in Late Eighteenth-Century Britain: Reflections on the British Avoidance of Revolution* (Oxford, 1984), pp. 1, 54, 70–1, 79, 83–4, 215.
[4] Linda Colley, 'The apotheosis of George III: loyalty, royalty and the British nation 1760–1820', *Past and Present*, 102 (1984).
[5] *Cambridge Intelligencer*, 28 May 1796.
[6] Christie, *Stress and Stability*, pp. 92–3; and ch. 8 of this volume, 'Conservatism and stability in British society'.

closer together – epitomised by the conjunction of the Portland Whigs with Pitt to comprise a conservative front in 1794 – even the ruling class remained divided; the Foxite rump's consistent opposition to war, and growing belief that only limited political reform to embrace a broader spectrum of the population could pre-empt indigenous revolution, was an eloquent expression of that division. Democratic ideology also divided opinion among the burgeoning middling ranks, and the rapidly expanding proletariat; every local community experienced those divisions, expressed in the parlance of 'aristocrats' and 'democrats'. Ideological penetrations also bitterly divided other organisations, among them, the Methodist Connexion, the English Roman Catholic hierarchy, and the agencies of local government from corporations down to the humblest village vestry. These divisions were expressed and reinforced over Pitt's many novel innovations, from fiscal measures, manning the armed forces, and above all – political repression. Identification of the need for political reform, moderate or radical, was closely aligned to the issue of war or peace. There is also an assumption that support for political reform virtually disappeared in the late nineties, while loyalism became overwhelmingly dominant, as the nation – bar an ineffectual minority comprising the 'Friends of Peace' – drew together in the face of repeated diplomatic and military reverses, as the French swept across Europe, landed in Wales, invaded Ireland, and intensified the real threat of invading England herself.

II

If we concentrate on the 1790s, or rather the period up to the armistice of October 1801, we encounter a decade punctuated by crisis upon crisis. First, that of 1792–3, where the opening loyalist campaign popularised and orchestrated by the Reevite Associations, galvanised a radical backlash, as Anglo-French relations collapsed, coterminously with the horrific September massacres, the execution of Louis XVI, and climaxed by the declaration of war; the economy faltered owing to inevitable mercantile uncertainties, and coincided with the first foretaste of the serious subsistence problems which plagued the nineties. The second, of 1794–6, was characterised by the growth of organised plebeian political radicalism, and the repression commencing with the Gagging Acts, played out against a background of eighteen horrendous months of famine, and periodically intense public disturbances. The war effort was compromised by military defeat and serious diplomatic reverses as the allies split. The third, of 1797–8, saw a dangerous combination of attempted and actual invasions of Wales and Ireland, the devastating naval mutinies, financial collapse and industrial recession, a massive groundswell of peace demands, and finally the Irish Rebellion. Austria's withdrawal from the war was only partially compensated for by naval victories at Camperdown and Aboukir Bay. The final crisis, of 1799–1801, saw military defeat in the European theatre, and but one belated major naval victory, in April 1801; while Pitt struggled to effect the Act of Union, his government finally collapsed ostensibly over the hoary question of Catholic emancipation: this precipitated the political paralysis in the form of George III's prolonged bout of insanity from February to May 1801: famine returned with unparalleled violence, now combined with serious industrial recession. The situation spawned a massive crisis of confidence in Pitt's government; strong petitioning for peace by previously stalwart supporters of the war preceded Addington's desperate peace initiative, but even that was played out against a background of the seeming certainty of invasion over the summer of 1801.

Each of these recurrent crises generated the disorder which characterised the decade, and the cement identified by Christie as the binding, cohesive element, disintegrated under the *cumulative* impact. This can be established by an alternative analysis of the key components of Christie's Ford Lectures, namely the economy, religious developments as opposed to 'church' history, loyalism, popular patriotism and deference, the dissemination of democratic ideology rather than simply organised radicalism, and the actual degree of stability in the countryside – that assumed bastion of the *ancien régime*. Here we re-assess the structural weaknesses in the *English* 'establishment... not only the centres of official power... but rather the whole matrix in which power is exercised',[7] and finally focus on its experiences in the final crisis of the period, that of 1799–1801.

III

The war's complex and contradictory economic impact was complicated by further major dislocations generated by the famines of 1794–6 and 1799–1801. Unprecedented mobilisation essentially postponed an embryonic employment crisis until 1815. If all industries supplying the artefacts of war were powerfully stimulated, this injection of demand peaked in 1797.[8] War seriously compromised overseas trade, rendering demand at best volatile, notably for textiles, thereby recurrently depressing

---

[7] The words are those of Henry Fairlie, *The Spectator*, 1985, cited in *The Observer*, 12 March 1989.
[8] C. K. Harley, 'British industrialisation before 1841; evidence of lower growth during the Industrial Revolution', *Journal of Economic History*, 92, 2 (1982), p. 283; J. L. Anderson, 'A measure of the effect of British public finance, 1793–1815', *Economic History Review*, 2nd ser., 28 (1974), p. 616.

entire regional economies. Occasionally, especially in 1800, exporters of other major commodities, including Sheffield and Birmingham metals, experienced collapses in foreign demand.[9]

The agrarian sector, by contrast, benefited handsomely from general price inflation, further stimulated by recurrent subsistence crises. Profits maximised between 1792 and 1802, and the resultant heavy and multifarious investment in agriculture is well known. The marked intensification of farmers' consumerist mentality inflated demand for rural service industries, located both in the countryside and the market towns.[10]

Neither mobilisation nor economic conditions combined to produce significant labour shortages during the first phase of the war; only the armed forces suffered serious manpower difficulties. Both armed forces, but especially the army, drew disproportionately on the less and unskilled sectors of the proletariat, and those least securely employed. Farmworkers came squarely into the latter category, and many sought escape through enlistment. Rural labour shortages were either mythical, or very ephemeral and localised. With the odd exception of major constructions, shortages of unskilled labour in industrial or urban locations, are rarely encountered. Shortages occurred almost exclusively in skilled trades, and even then in extraordinary, local circumstances.[11] Economic factors were responsible for throwing the adverse direct impact of technological change on sectors of the skilled work force. The apparently limitless potential of machinery and structural change extended the threat of seemingly revolutionary industrial innovations, to *destabilise* entire communities, notably in West Country and Yorkshire woollens, and northern cottons.[12]

[9] Revd Pawson to Rhodda, 28 March 1793, and to Atmore, 12 January 1801, John Rylands Library (JRL), Methodist Church Archives (MCA), PLP. 82-9-4; 82-17-1; *Cambridge Intelligencer*, 18 March 1797; *British Magazine* (January 1800), p. 108; *Salisbury and Winchester Journal*, 2 February 1801; *Monthly Magazine*, 9 (June 1800), p. 515; Roger Wells, 'The revolt of the south-west 1800–1: a study in English popular protest', *Social History*, 6 (1977), pp. 714–16.

[10] B. A. Holderness, 'Prices, productivity and output' in G. E. Mingay (ed.), *The Agrarian History of England and Wales* (1750–1850), vol. VI (Cambridge, 1989), especially pp. 187–9; A. H. John, 'Farming in wartime: 1793–1815' in E. L. Jones and G. E. Mingay (eds.), *Land, Labour and Population in the Industrial Revolution* (London, 1967), pp. 28–47; Roger Wells, 'Tolpuddle in the context of English agrarian labour history 1780–1850' in John Rule (ed.), *British Trade Unionism 1750–1850. The Formative Years* (London, 1988), pp. 106–7.

[11] Clive Emsley, *British Society and the French Wars 1793–1815* (London, 1979), pp. 31–2, 52–3, 82–5; Wells, 'Tolpuddle', pp. 101–7; W. A. Armstrong, 'Labour I: rural population growth, systems of employment, and incomes' in Mingay, *Agrarian History*, pp. 702–5; L. D. Schwarz, 'Conditions of life and labour in London c. 1770–1820, with special reference to East London', unpublished D.Phil. thesis (University of Oxford, 1976), especially pp. 91–2, 99–104; *Monthly Magazine*, 11 (January 1801), p. 580; F. O. Darvall, *Popular Disturbances in Regency England* (Oxford, 1934), p. 38, n. 4.

[12] J. Smail, 'New languages for labour and capital; the transformation of discourse in the early years of the industrial revolution', *Social History*, 12, 1 (1987), especially pp. 53–7,

The marked resort to trade unionism was fuelled by technological change, and more broadly, by sustained inflation which galvanised parallel reactions by many workers, including country craftsmen and even farm-workers. If Christie correctly identifies this phenomenon, he underestimates the scale of militancy, and exaggerates the degree of success. Even in London, where trade unionism embraced 'every trade requiring skilled labour' in a 'constant struggle' to win wage increases adequate to the 'advanced and advancing price of necessaries... they were unable fully to accomplish their purpose', experiences shared by their counterparts 'in some other places'. Finally, whatever the advances of trade unionism amongst the skilled, and a few other groups, most proletarians, including the largest occupational group, farm-labourers, were painfully unsuccessful or unable to engage in collective bargaining.[13]

Detailed analysis of the two famines of 1794–6 and 1799–1801 in fact belies Christie's confident, 'there never was any crisis of subsistence'; ironically, his acceptance that the detailed exposition of the famines' recurrent impact filled 'a hitherto total lacuna in the literature' on the nineties, is not permitted to alter his almost surreal optimistic perception of working-class living standards.[14] The degrees by which the latter were undermined came from the enormous cumulative pressures of food price-rises in excess of 100 per cent across periods of sixteen and twenty-two months respectively: these were aggravated by regionalised hypercrises, when the food supply disintegrated. There can be no doubt that the second famine was immeasurably worse than the first, not least because it was accompanied by a severe industrial recession, the product principally – though not exclusively – of a collapsed home market for manufactures. Nor was the rural proletariat preserved; early in 1801, Mrs Fremantle 'visited all the poor' in her Buckinghamshire village, and recorded that 'some are truly starving and look the picture of death'. Recession, soaring living costs, and escalating local and national taxation, hit the non-

62, 66, 71; *Commercial and Agricultural Magazine*, 1 (October 1799), pp. 215–17; A. J. Randall, 'The shearmen and the Wiltshire outrages of 1802; trade unionism and industrial violence', *Social History*, 7, 3 (1982); Randall's 'The philosophy of Luddism; the case of the west of England woollen workers c. 1790–1809', *Technology and Culture*, 1 (1986); Roger Wells, *Dearth and Distress in Yorkshire, 1793–1802* (York, 1977), pp. 37–8.

13 Christie, *Stress and Stability*, ch. 5 and especially pp. 124, 145, 149; Wells, 'Tolpuddle', pp. 106–7, 113–14; D. Mills, *Francis Place 1771–1854: The Life of a Remarkable Radical* (Brighton, 1988), p. 171; D. E. Brewster and N. McCord, 'Some labour troubles in the 1790s in north-east England', *International Review of Social History*, 13 (1968); Roger Wells, *Wretched Faces: Famine in Wartime England, 1793–1801* (Gloucester, 1988), pp. 168–74.

14 Christie, *Stress and Stability*, p. 151; Christie, 'Conservatism and stability', especially n. 27.

agrarian middle classes too. The London bourgeoisie spoke of the 'Miseries of the Middle ranks', and in some cities subscriptions were launched for 'relieving the lower class of tradesmen and householders'.[15]

My analysis of these famines, published in 1988, underestimated notably the amount of disease, especially during the second. Fevers and other epidemics were more pronounced in 1800, and especially 1801–2; 'a very sickly time' was reported from Leeds in February 1800, and many anticipated that 'some very malignant disorder will break out among the poor and carry great numbers to eternity by reason of their want of proper food'. The extraordinary hot summer of 1800 was central to additional mortality deriving from the 'organic pollution of water and food', with the 'epidemic of the month' of August comprising 'Disorders of the bowels', namely dysentery. 'Continual fevers'[16] were, however, in places, including London, the cause of a 'very unusual degree' of prolonged illness, and typhus persisted beyond its customary autumnal season, and was still prevalent in mid-1801; by then 'aliopathetic disease' was also rampant in victims who showed 'no symptoms of fever'. Smallpox in 1800 was also 'uncommonly prevalent and fatal'. The year 1800 has been identified as one of the ten eighteenth-century years of crisis mortality in London, temporarily reversing the trend whereby the massive metro-politan excess of deaths over births reduced after the mid-1760s. From late 1800, and during the whole of 1801, 'fevers' – almost certainly typhus – struck hard in many industrial regions, and Midland and northern towns; it still raged in Leeds, Liverpool and Sheffield, as late as January 1802. Disease, notably forms of influenza, which were lengthy and unpleasant, but not markedly fatal, occurred in many rural regions. Moreover, there is some evidence that the medical profession – possibly in league with the government – covered up the details. In 1800–1 certain London doctors represented their struggles 'with an unprecedented degree of hunger, anxiety[17] and fatigue' among patients, which drove up mortality rates; medics also reported that 'the administration of drugs is farcical... To such feeble, hungry and emaciated wretches'. Doctors were attacked for 'indiscretion, in thus revealing the extreme wretchedness of the poor', and

---

[15] A. Fremantle (ed.), *The Wynn Diaries*, 3 vols. (Oxford, 1940), vol. III, p. 34; Petitions, London parishes, November 1800, *Journal of the House of Commons*, 55, pp. 797–9, 827–8, 864; *Monthly Magazine*, 11 (1801), p. 537; Wells, *Wretched Faces*.

[16] A comprehensive contemporary term for 'typhus and synochus'; *Medical and Physical Magazine*, 3 (1800), pp. 393–5.

[17] According to one doctor, the 'principal pre-disposing cause of...typhus', was the 'lamentable deficiency of the common articles of nourishment', aggravated by 'the gloomy and depressed state of mind, which parents at least must experience, when, surrounded by a hungry offspring, they find themselves unable to satisfy their urgent demands for bread'; *Monthly Magazine*, 10 (1800), pp. 343–5; cf. 11 (1801), p. 167.

admitted that they had 'enlarge[d] more perhaps than is consistent with the proper bounds'.[18]

Newly consulted sources reveal further instances of deaths through starvation during the second famine, while Malthus himself confirmed 'that a considerable number ... would have actually starved', but for the Poor Law. There seems to be little doubt that the higher estimated mortality for the earlier famine derives from the impact of the 1794–5 winter, the third hardest in the entire century; there were 'many instances of sudden death, after exposure to cold', numerous victims of 'remarkably severe and obstinate coughs', and 'a very sickly Time' was reported from 'every where else'.[19]

IV

This famine-induced enhancement of the customary uncertainties of life in later eighteenth-century England increased resort to traditional discourse, imagery and morality; informed by Christianity, they also embraced popular, pagan survivals. The Bible and the ultra-popular almanacs, were major sources of reference, the ultimate theoretical authority, for many, including that considerable sector of the proletariat whose at best, rare church attendance, was not religious indifference. War, the violent overthrow of social structures, institutions and governments, the prevalence of disease and pestilence, and above all – famine – are powerful biblical themes indicative of divine wrath. A critical corollary of these unique circumstances in the 1790s was greater resort to religion for interpretation, explanation and consolation.[20]

[18] *Medical and Physical Magazine*, 3 (1800), pp. 109–10, 117–19, 298–300, 393–5, 408; 5 (1801), pp. 97–8, 145, 194–5, 298–307, 217–20, 411–12, 509, 588–91; 7 (1802), pp. 38, 54, 95, 148, 255–6; J. Landers, 'Mortality, weather and prices in London, 1675–1825; a study of short-term fluctuations', *Journal of Historical Geography*, 12, 4 (1986), especially pp. 350, 353, 355–9; R. Willan, *Reports on the Diseases of London (1796–1800)* (London, 1801), pp. 281–2, 290–5, 329; medical reports in the *British Magazine* (August 1800), pp. 138–9; (September 1800), p. 250; and the *Monthly Magazine*, 10 (1800), pp. 342–5, 457; 11 (1801), pp. 16–18, 60, 107, 537; 12 (1801), p. 160; Pawson to Atmore, and Marsden, 24 February 1800 and 9 January 1802, JRL, MCA, PLP.82-16-2; 82-18-2; Wells, *Wretched Faces*, pp. 69–70.

[19] For example, the Southampton inquest on infants aged two and three, which returned a starvation verdict in April 1801; *Salisbury and Winchester Journal*, 20 April 1801; *Monthly Magazine*, 5 (March 1801), p. 138; Willan, *Diseases of London*, pp. 76–7; Pawson to Atmore, 19 March 1795, JRL, MCA, PLP.82-11-1.

[20] W. H. Oliver, *Prophets and Millenialists* (Auckland, 1978), p. 174; J. C. D. Clark, *English Society 1688–1832: Ideology, Social Structure and Political Practice during the Ancien Régime* (Cambridge, 1985), pp. 43, 87; R. Richardson, *Death, Dissection and the Destitute* (Harmondsworth, 1987), pp. 7, 11; J. Walsh, 'Religious societies; Methodist and evangelical, 1730–1800', in W. J. Shields and D. Wood (eds.), *Studies in Church History*, vol. XXIII (Cambridge, 1986), p. 301; A. W. Smith, 'Popular religions', *Past and Present*, 40 (1968), pp. 182–5; D. B. Valenze, 'Prophecy and popular literature in

The principal historical debates embracing religious developments during the nineties, have been distorted by covering much longer periods. For example, the study of the decade alone could never have even suggested Halévy's thesis of Methodism as the key antidote to revolution. Conversely, the nineties would sustain elements of arguments hinging on the 'chiliasm of despair', on condition that the context of despair extends to major economic dislocations, including those experienced regionally, as well as the defeat of organised radicalism. In March 1794, one Methodist minister said that the Yorkshire revival was 'at present...a tenfold blessing, when poverty & deep distress are on every side, on account of the badness of trade'.[21] The failure of the massive increase in rural poverty, ushered in by the 1794–6 famine, to decline thereafter in the country's premier southern and eastern cornlands, also coincided with a rapid expansion in the numbers of registered dissenting and independent meeting-houses and ministers, in parts of these regions, including their 'astonishing explosion' in the diocese of Salisbury between 1797 and 1799. But there was no unfailing relationship; the Wesleyans experienced a statistically small, but nevertheless absolute fall in membership in the worst economic crisis of 1799–1801, though this was possibly compensated for by sectarian growth.[22]

Edmund Burke's speedy identification of the threat implicit in democratic ideology to the Anglican Church, its theology, doctrine and dogma, was taken up by several Bishops, who soon added the new fashion of atheism. Anglicanism's 'political theology' was crucial. The Bishop of Exeter ordered his clergy to 'animate their fellow citizens in the defence of their country' against the internal and external threats, and several of his episcopal colleagues made no bones about the necessity for the clergy's 'proportionate zeal...in every crisis of constitutional difficulty'. The nominal omnipresence of the Church of England and its sermons on the great Anglican *political* anniversaries, when the divinity of governance

eighteenth-century England', *Journal of Ecclesiastical History*, 29, 1 (1978), pp. 76–7, 80, 89. I have to thank my colleague, historian of religion, Dr Peter Bishop, for discussing biblical issues with me.

21 E. P. Thompson, *The Making of the English Working Class* (Harmondsworth, 1968), pp. 411–30; D. Luker, 'Revivalism in theory and practice; the case of Cornish Methodism', *Journal of Ecclesiastical History*, 37, 4 (1986), pp. 604, 608–12, 617; Pawson to Benson, and Atmore, 12 July 1793 and 21 March 1794, JRL, MCA, PLP. 82-9-9; 82-10-3.

22 D. J. Jeremy, 'A local crisis between establishment and nonconformity; the Salisbury preaching controversy, 1797–9', *Wiltshire Archaeological and Natural History Magazine*, 61 (1966), pp. 63–4; D. W. Lovegrove, *Established Church, Sectarian People. Itineracy and the Transformation of English Dissent 1780–1830* (Cambridge, 1988), pp. 38–40, 142–3, 146; R. Currie, A. Gilbert and L. Horsley, *Churches and Churchgoers; Patterns of Church Growth in the British Isles since 1700* (Oxford, 1977), p. 42; David Hempton, *Methodism and Politics in British Society 1750–1850* (London, 1987), p. 34; J. Kent, 'The Wesleyan Methodists to 1849' in R. E. Davies, A. R. George and E. Gordon Rupp (eds.), *A History of the Methodist Church in Great Britain* (London, 1978), vol. II, pp. 271–2.

was stressed, gave it the theoretical apparatus to fulfil this role.[23] But its capacity to deliver was undermined by many factors, including endemic non-residence, rife pluralism, antiquated parochial structures, which militated against attendance notably in the faster growing towns, and the increasingly densely populated industrialising regions. Even in the more stable rural farming heartlands, the enrichment of clergy through generous tithe commutations under enclosure acts, put them at an increasing remove from most parishioners, as did their expanding role as magistrates.[24]

The Anglican Church was the sole denomination which failed, and failed abysmally, to exploit enhanced populist resort to religion, and indeed the scanty statistical evidence suggests that their congregations declined in the nineties. Only a relative handful of clergy were evangelical,[25] and they germinated colleagues' ire on occasion.[26] Most Anglicans remained indifferent to the exhortations of the handful of energetic Bishops, and were as baffled at their rivals' successes, as they were horrified at their vehement criticisms. Anglicans hit back lambasting the *de facto* secession of the Methodist Connexion, the low social origins and ignorance of many dissenting ministers, the democratic tendencies of Calvinism, and, of course, castigating dissent was a traditional mode of seeking preferment.[27] In aggregate, press, pamphlet and pulpits, fuelled

[23] J. C. D. Clark, *Revolution and Rebellion in England in the Seventeenth and Eighteenth Centuries* (Cambridge, 1986), p. 111; and his *English Society*, pp. 158–60, 200, 249; S. Barrington, *A Charge Delivered to the Clergy of the Diocese of Durham at the Primary Visitation* (Bath, 1792), especially p. 6; H. R. Courtenay, *A Charge Delivered to the Clergy of the Diocese of Bristol at the Primary Visitation of Henry Reginald Lord Bishop of Bristol* (Bristol, 1796), pp. 5, 7; H. R. Courtenay, *A Charge Delivered to the Clergy of the Diocese of Exeter* (Exeter, 1799), p. 18; J. Buckner, *A Charge Delivered to the Clergy of the Diocese of Chichester at the Primary Visitation of that Diocese in the Year 1798* (London, 1799), especially pp. 38–9; *The Arminian Magazine* (1795), pp. 200–3.

[24] W. R. Ward, 'The religion of the people and the problem of control, 1790–1830' in C. J. Cuming and D. Baker (eds.), *Studies in Church History*, vol. VIII (Cambridge, 1972), p. 237; George (Tomline) Pretyman, *A Charge Delivered to the Clergy of the Diocese of Lincoln* (London, 1800), p. 23; E. J. Evans, 'Some reasons for the growth of English rural anti-clericalism, 1750–1830', *Past and Present*, 66 (1975); W. R. Ward, 'The tithe question in England in the early nineteenth century', *Journal of Ecclesiastical History*, 16, (1965), pp. 70–4; B. Walker, 'Religious changes in Cheshire 1750–1850', *Journal of Ecclesiastical History*, 17 (1966), p. 78; F. C. Mather, 'Georgian churchmanship reconsidered; some variations in Anglican public worship 1714–1830', *Journal of Ecclesiastical History*, 36 (1985), pp. 266–76, 282.

[25] V. Kiernan, 'Evangelicalism and the French Revolution', *Past and Present*, 1 (1952), p. 45.

[26] See the interchange between the *Anti-Jacobin Review*, 5 (1799), pp. 361–71, and the *Gospel Magazine*, 4 (1800), pp. 8–9. Cf. Mrs Reynolds to William Frend, 19 July 1800, in F. Knight (ed.), 'Letters to William Frend', *Cambridge Antiquarian Record Society*, 8 (1974), p. 44.

[27] *Gospel Magazine*, 1 (1796), pp. 360, 363–4; 2 (1797), p. 79; *Report from the Clergy of a District in the Diocese of Lincoln…[re] the State of Religion* (London, 1799), p. 9; Cursitor, *A Letter to the Lord Bishop of Lincoln respecting the Report from the Clergy*

fierce interdenominational conflict. The very successes of Methodism, Dissent and Millenarianism, rendered them targets of Anglican attacks in general, and particularly reflect alarm over the perceived socio-political dangers in the growth of non-Anglicanism, which constituted a serious dilution of church and state.

These attacks added to the Methodist leadership's difficulties. The revivals, which were spectacular evidence of success, also brought their problems, notably the 'considerable degree of irregularity and apparent confusion', which commonly overwhelmed ministers by getting 'beyond all bounds of decency'. In fact, revivalism bitterly divided Methodist ministers. More importantly the numbers of even medium-term converts recruited at revivals were very modest: many – especially the 'most noisy converts' – soon 'concluded there is nothing in religion'.[28]

The Connexion's principal geographical foci were on industrialising regions, and urban locations, including London, and the movement attracted many from precisely that huge artisanal and petty entre-preneurial sector of society which also provided the strongest support for the popular democratic movement. There is no doubt that a significant proportion of Methodists sympathised with that ideology, as revealed by the trustee debate, and the number of pastors, and not just Kilham, who advocated political reform and opposed the war before 1794–5. Indeed, the Methodists were as divided over these two key issues as their host communities. The need to contain the anti-war, and especially the seething democratic component of the Methodist movement, became crystal clear with intelligence of intended statutory intervention against itinerancy, mooted first in 1795–6, which threatened the Connexion's very existence. From 1795 Conference passed many formal declarations of loyalty, none more so than the sycophantic address in direct response to the Irish Rebellion, demanding prayers for 'KINGS AND ALL THAT ARE IN AUTHORITY'.[29]

(London, 1800), pp. 14–15; S. Horsley, *A Charge of Samuel Lord Bishop of Rochester to the Clergy of His Diocese Delivered at the Second General Visitation* (London, 1800), p. 19; Pretyman's *Charges* (London, 1800 and 1803); W. H. Reid, *The Rise and Dissolution of the Infidel Societies in the Metropolis* (London, 1800), pp. 45–6; *Anti-Jacobin Review* (October 1798), p. 439; Jeremy, 'Salisbury preaching controversy', pp. 73–5; Clark, *English Society*, pp. 230, 260; Lovegrove, *Sectarian People*, p. 126.

[28] Walsh, 'Religious societies', pp. 288–9; S. Mews, 'Reason and emotion in working-class religion, 1794–1824' in D. Baker (ed.), *Studies in Church History*, vol. IX (Cambridge, 1972), p. 365; T. Entwisle, *Memoir of the Reverend Joseph Entwisle*, 9th edn (1869), pp. 110–2, 124, 179–80; J. MacDonald, *Memoirs of the Rev. J. Benson* (London, 1822), pp. 259, 278–81, 284–5, 299; *The Arminian Magazine* (October 1795), pp. 519–21; *Methodist Magazine*, 21 (1798), pp. 175–7, 240–5; 22 (1799), pp. 409–13; Pawson to Benson, 27 June 1794; Benson to his wife, 22 June 1795, JRL, MCA, PLP.7-9-8; 82-10-8.

[29] B. Semmel, *The Methodist Revolution* (London, 1974), pp. 100, 128; P. Stignant, 'Wesleyan Methodism and working-class radicalism in the North, 1791–1821', *Northern*

In this climate, Kilham's expulsion became a certainty after he refused to accept the supreme power of Conference and their support for Pitt's political stances. Kilham's use of Paineite metaphors was compounded by his admitted 'republican principles'.[30] But Wesleyan satisfaction that the secession purged their radicals – a perception endorsed by some historians – is wide of the mark. Moreover, the fragmentative quality of the Kilhamite division, is rarely stressed. While there was a close relationship between the centres of the New Connexional strength and the powerhouses of the popular democratic movement, Kilham did not simply remove radicals from the main Methodist movement. The Revd Pawson mused over 'such a Government man' as a Mr Waterhouse 'of Halifax...should be a Kilhamite', and another 'who is just come amongst' the Wesleyans, 'should be a [parliamentary] reformer'. The Wesleyans rightly worried over the 'undercurrent of radicalism [which] remained in the connexion' from 1798, and members of each connexion commonly went to hear each other's preachers. The fact that 'chiefly minorities' only seceded, where congregations formally split, should not obscure the divisive impact of either Kilham's incessant campaigning in 1797–8, or the ferocity of disputes at both the local and national levels. The Revd Benson opined that Kilham was a 'vile...slanderer', while Kilham 'said in Leeds he "would never be quiet until he has turned the whole world upside down"'. It all contributed to unnerve loyal Wesleyan ministers: as the Revd Entwisle wearily concluded, 'I think that the people in some places are almost mad'.[31]

The secession facilitated Wesleyan claims to have weaned people 'from political debates', and 'in the most perilous times of the State, have been an essential service in maintaining subordination and loyalty'. Dissenters, aggressively evangelical on the ground, were forced into parallel defensive political posturing, emphasising their 'political quietism', while ordering their flocks to be 'obedient to magistrates and submissive to all lawful authority': their teachings 'warn against the pernicious principles of PAINE'.[32]

Ironically, while the major religious organisations competed in self-

---

History, 6 (1971), p. 101; Hempton, Methodism and Politics, pp. 62, 68–9; Clark, English Society, pp. 239–40; Methodist Magazine, 21 (1798), pp. 546–9; Pawson to Benson, 25 April 1793, and Atmore, 22 December 1792, 19 March, 15 July 1795 and 24 February 1796, JRL, MCA, PLP.82-8-10; 82-9-6; 82-11-7, 17; 82-12-6.

[30] Kilham to the Revd J. Brodie, 12 January 1795, JRL, MCA, PLP.64-36-6.

[31] Stigant, 'Wesleyan Methodism', pp. 103–5; Hempton, Methodism and Politics, pp. 68–70; Benson to his brother, 8 November 1796; Pawson to Benson, 13 April 1797: Bunting diary, 1799–1801, JRL, MCA, PLP.82-13-6; 7-9-13: diaries box; Entwisle, Memoir, pp. 148–9, 151, 156–8; Methodist Magazine, 25 (1802), p. 226.

[32] Cursitor, The Bishop of Lincoln, pp. 20–1; Evangelical Magazine, 10 (1802), preface; Lovegrove, Sectarian People, pp. 123–4, 127, 265; W. Kingsbury, An Apology for Village Preachers (Southampton, 1798), especially pp. 8–9, 12, 21, 31, 41.

presentation as the agencies for order and political subservience, their initiatives in aggregate were socially divisive. Anglicans were allegedly reduced to 'the language of fear', while Methodist splits enabled 'Deists [to] laugh at us and Christianity'. The divisiveness is most clearly revealed by the commonly fierce conflict directly generated in many localities. Hampshire Anglican clergymen claimed that itinerant dissenting ministers aimed at 'a new Government', and their counterparts at Market Harborough, accused Dissenters of arming 'in opposition to the Measures of Government'. New dissenting initiatives, including field preachings, are known to have been mobbed in Hampshire, Hertfordshire and Sussex, but relatively few were recorded, not least because such as were reported to Whitehall served only to enable the Home Secretary to 'display...a complete lack of sympathy for the Dissenters'. Dissenters were subjected to the illegal withholding of licenses, and withdrawal of poor relief, and also occasionally sacked: they sometimes successfully retaliated, as in the preservation of a puritanical Sabbath in one Berkshire village, through a judicial ruling against Sunday cricket.[33]

Claims by Methodist and nonconformist apologists that their activities disciplined their converts, *thereby* also producing quietism and loyalism, are simply not supported by the evidence from the nineties. Among the many manifestations of disorder, which expose the fact that even Methodists could not control their people, were the 'wild and strange proceedings' following a Methodist revival at Birmingham. 'Some of the new converts have gone off with other womens husbands; others have turned whores, others thieves...but whether they will make 200 or not' was an open question.[34] The Kingswood colliers, and Cornish miners, repeatedly given as exemplars of Wesleyans' claims, continued their riotous traditions. Both groups were involved in the intense protests over food in 1795, 1796, 1800, and again in 1801. Identical observations should be made for several West Riding communities where the Methodist revivals were strongest; trade unionism and industrial militancy among the skilled trades throughout, achieved notoriety by 1802. Moreover, West Yorkshire remained a powerhouse of the democratic movement; some activists were recruited to the insurrectionary United Englishmen,

---

[33] *Cambridge Intelligencer*, 12 September 1797 and 27 September 1800; *Gospel Magazine*, 3 (1799), pp. 428–9; *Evangelical Magazine*, 8 (1800), pp. 555–6; 10 (1802), pp. 247–8; *Methodist Magazine*, 21 (1798), pp. 253–4; Entwisle, *Memoir*, p. 153; Revd Densham, Petersfield, to Revd Eyre, 5 June 1799, 14 January, 2 and 6 October 1800, Dr Williams Library (DWL), New College Manuscripts (NCM), 41/46, 58, 74–5; printed notice, 20 May 1794, and endorsement, British Library (BL), Althorp papers (Alt), G.16; R. H. Martin, 'Evangelical Dissenters and Wesleyan-style itinerant ministries at the end of the eighteenth century', *Methodist History*, 16 (1978), p. 180; Lovegrove, *Sectarian People*, pp. 106, 115–16, appendix A.

[34] Pawson to Marsden, 18 May 1796, JRL, MCA, PLP.82-12-13.

including members of both the Old and New Connexions.[35] Non-Anglican religious enthusiasts, drawn from the lower end of the social spectrum, and known to have led popular protests even in the countryside, included a past living-in farm servant who was crowd spokesman to Northamptonshire authorities, over the militia issue in 1797, and about subsistence problems in September 1800. In fact, political loyalties and views among the Wesleyans remained as volatile as those of the population at large. In the crisis of mid-1797, Pawson observed that, 'We have a public prayer every Wed[nesday]...for the Safety of the Nation, but very few attend it. The prejudice against the Ministers of State seems to run high indeed'.[36]

The capacity of nonconformists to exercise forms of social control over their membership, was compromised further by the religious fragmentations of the later nineties.[37] If the dynamic religious response in the nineties impresses, and the numbers engaging ephemerally with organised religion far exceeded the numbers presented statistically,[38] the country was not evangelicalised; the situation mortifying the Anglican clergy of Manchester and Salford in December 1796 – 'that at least two thirds of the inhabitants...absent themselves from Sunday services', a calculation which 'included...Dissenters of all kinds' – persisted. At the very turn of the century, the Methodists and evangelical Dissenters who made the greatest impression, experienced many logistical and especially financial problems, aggravated by both the general increase in poverty, and its vast swelling to embrace the middling ranks during the second famine.[39]

Conversely, but not compensatory, were the multifarious and intensifying millennial impulses, generated by events. The eighteenth-century millenarian tradition, intensified into a 'millennial culture', partially revealed by the huge boom in 'prophetical publishing', and was initially

---

[35] See below, n. 83.
[36] Pawson to Marsden, and to Benson, 18 May 1796, and 1 June 1797, JRL, MCA, PLP.82-12-13; 82-13-10; Hempton, *Methodism and Politics*, pp. 101–2; Wells, *Wretched Faces*, pp. 99–101, 110–8, 132, 173; 'South-west', pp. 722–3; Isted to Spencer, 17 September 1800, BL, Alt, G.39.
[37] W. R. Ward, 'Swedenborgianism: heresy, schism or religious protest?' in D. Baker (ed.), *Studies in Church History*, vol. IX (Cambridge, 1972), p. 303; Luker, 'Revivalism in theory and practice', p. 606; R. Carwardine, *Transatlantic Revivalism: Popular Evangelicalism in Britain and America 1790–1865* (Westport, Conn., 1978), p. 106; Reid, *Infidel Societies*, pp. 44, 54.
[38] Of the population 0·85 per cent were Methodists.
[39] *Cambridge Intelligencer*, 10 December 1796; Lovegrove, *Sectarian People*, pp. 97–102; letters to Eyre from Densham, 8 February 1798 and 5 September 1800, and Revd Buffrey, 11 February 1799, DWL, NCM, 41/20, 41, 69; Pawson to Benson, 6 May 1796; Clarke to Brogie, 26 March 1801; Benson to Marsden, 18 June 1806, JRL, MCA, PLP.82-12-12; 25-2-5; 7-10-8; MacDonald, *Memoirs*, p. 351; *Methodist Magazine*, 25 (1802), pp. 336–8. 343–6.

stimulated by the falls of the French monarchy and the papacy, further inflated by war, threatened invasion and indigenous insurrection, and above all galvanised by famine. Famine was central to the first prophecies of especially Joanna Southcott, and her use of the issue was crucial in her release from Devon obscurity and projection on to the national stage in 1801.[40] Prophets in the nineties continued to draw heavily on apocalyptic biblical passages, to produce a 'flexible predictive mechanism', postulating disorder and perennial crisis as the prelude to the ultimate, catastrophic scenario, about to *occur on earth*. Millenarianism, while not class specific, was particularly attractive to the poor and oppressed, because it promised an imminent release from earthly trials. The common and scarcely concealed political message, was that all were equal before God, but the wealthy were responsible for war, the resultant severe socio-economic dislocations, including 'enormously increased' poverty.[41]

Many of the people responsible for the emergent radical culture were religious, and responded positively to millennial messages. Moreover, major prophets engaged in the political arena. Richard Brothers predicted that George III would lose his throne for making war on the French. Millenarianism is powerfully present in Spence's writings, and Dr McCalman has demonstrated the vigour of this alternative, principally but not exclusively proletarian culture, in subterranean London. During a thunderstorm in June 1795, sixty men, women and children, huddled together in a pub, in anticipation of the start of the millennium: 'every one in the room knew something of Brothers' prophecy...There was a general feeling and expression of alarm'. Once Brothers progressed to identify himself as the Prince of the Hebrews, and 'entirely credibly' to demand George III's crown, his arrest and incarceration were understandably precautionary. Others making millenarian claims in London were arrested and interrogated by intelligence officers. The millenarian posturing of Bannister Truelock persuaded James Hadfield of his divine orders to assassinate the King in May 1800; Truelock and Hadfield frequented pubs used by known insurrectionaries. Hadfield may have been an epileptic, but the timing of both his and Truelock's manifestations of religious mania – which led the former to be acquitted of high treason, and the latter to evade prosecution – was *after* their respective arrests.[42] Millenarianism

---

[40] Oliver, *Prophets*, p. 43; Joanna Southcott, *The Strange Effects of Faith* (London, 1801), books 1 to 4, especially pp. 5, 7, 18, 23, 39, 77, 132–3; book 7 (1802), pp. 10–11. For the local subsistence situation at this moment, see Wells, 'South-west', pp. 717–20.

[41] Oliver, *Prophets*, pp. 19–23, 34, 44–5, 118, 177; J. F. C. Harrison, *The Second Coming; Popular Millenarianism 1750–1850* (London, 1979), pp. 64–6; James K. Hopkins, *A Woman to Deliver Her People; Joanna Southcott and English Millenarianism in the Era of Revolutions* (Austin, Tex., 1982), pp. 82, 114, 141–2.

[42] Hopkins, *Joanna Southcott*, pp. 170, 173; Harrison, *The Second Coming*, especially pp. 68, 78–9, 210–11; Malcolm Chase, *The People's Farm: English Radical Agrarianism 1775–1840* (Oxford, 1988), pp. 48–9; Ian McCalman, *Radical Underworld. Prophets, Revolutionaries*

induced an attitude that powers were about to be released, unstoppable by human agencies, which encouraged the fearful apathy and inertia encountered in the pub, or the concept that the second coming could only be accelerated by the action of the individual, as revealed by Hadfield's case. Millenarianism in the nineties conclusively demonstrates, that in addition to the social divisiveness of resort to religion, ultimately that resort contained fundamentally destabilising ingredients. This is at a considerable remove from Professor Christie's admittedly cautious interpretation of the 'good order' promoted by the 'churches' – an analysis which neither does justice to the social divisiveness of religious developments, nor even mentions Millenarianism.[43]

V

If the history of organised popular radicalism is too well known to require rehearsal here, a number of important considerations must be adduced. First, the increased resort to petitioning in the later eighteenth century, by voters and the unfranchised in both parliamentary and non-parliamentary boroughs, suggests 'a substantially larger political nation' than traditionally assumed.[44] Secondly, historians' orthodox urban and industrial geography of radical organisation, obscures radicalism's diffusion to the market-towns and villages. Rural England was not isolated as is so commonly assumed. Closely interdependent hierarchies of market-towns, each with their hinterlands, provided a web for the constant interchange of goods and people, including artisans on the tramp.[45] Some market-towns, which were parliamentary boroughs, important centres for Dissent, and hosted manufacturing industry, including Maidstone, had organised radical groupings; so too did other parliamentary boroughs, both with and without important manufacturing, including Hertford, Tewkesbury, Banbury and Chichester, and other towns, among them Godalming, High Wycombe and Spilsbury. Some, however fleetingly, opened communi-

and Pornographers in London, 1795–1840 (Cambridge, 1988); Wells, Wretched Faces, pp. 147–9; Cambridge Intelligencer, 8 November 1800.

43 Christie, Stress and Stability, ch. 8, 'The churches and good order', especially pp. 186, 208.

44 J. A. Phillips, 'Popular politics in unreformed England', Journal of Modern History, 52 (1980), especially pp. 601–4, 607–9, 614, 622–3.

45 Roger Wells, 'Rural rebels in southern England in the 1830s' in Clive Emsley and James Walvin (eds.), Artisans, Peasants and Proletarians 1760–1860 (London, 1985), pp. 26–8; R. A. Leeson, Travelling Brothers (London, 1979); A. Everitt, 'Country, county and town; patterns of regional evolution in England', Transactions of the Royal Historical Society, 5th ser. (1978), pp. 92–6; R. Schofield, 'Traffic in corpses; some evidence from Barming Kent' (1788–1812)', Local Population Studies, 33 (1984), pp. 50–2; P. Clark, 'Migration in England during the late seventeenth and early eighteenth centuries', Past and Present, 83 (1979).

cations with the London Corresponding Society. Even a spa-town like Tunbridge Wells catering for the very wealthy, and therefore 'the worst place for Democrats', contained a society, formally established as late as 1797 but still operative in 1801.[46] Some market-town societies liaised with others formed in villages, and a handful of the latter also had direct London Corresponding Society contacts.[47] Moreover, apparently non-organised democrats, were widely dispersed in towns and villages. Many villages had a core of locally notorious democrats, but they are rarely encountered in the sources, not least because they were generally circumspect, and indeed vulnerable.[48] The opposition press and radical tracts percolated these local networks, and were claimed to have induced political disaffection among the 'lowest of the Farmers & Common People'; 'there is no great difficulty', asserted Lord Sheffield from the heart of his Sussex fiefdom, 'in exciting sedition and mischief among the ill-disposed who are to be found in all communities'.[49] Events and experiences in the decade, notably in the villages, greatly inflated the numbers of the ill-disposed.

Thirdly, trade unionism not only escalated in the nineties, as we have seen, but became increasingly involved with populist politics. Unionists

[46] Mary Thale (ed.), *Selections from the Papers of the London Corresponding Society 1792–1799* (Cambridge, 1983), pp. 77, 81–2, 86, 346–7, 364, 380, 412–13; Wells, 'Rural rebels', pp. 26–8; J. A. Phillips, *Electoral Behaviour in Unreformed England* (Princeton, N.J., 1982), pp. 40–1, 89, 110, 124 and n. 31; Everitt, 'Country, county and town', p. 92; and his 'The pattern of rural Dissent in the nineteenth century', *Department of English Local History, University of Leicester, Occasional Papers*, 4 (1972), p. 67, n. 2; *Sussex Weekly Advertiser*, 19 October 1795; London Corresponding Society (LCS) General Committee reports, 2 July, 10 September, 28 and 29 October 1795; incomplete list of places contributing to the state prisoners' relief fund in 1801, Public Record Office (PRO), Privy Council (PC), 1/23/A38; 1/3526; R. Spillman, Banbury, to the Home Office, 25 August 1793, PRO, Home Office (HO), 42/26.

[47] J. Payne, Welford, Northamptonshire, to Earl Spencer, 25 May 1794, BL, Alt, G.16; LCS committee reports, general, and executive, 10 and 21 September 1795, and northern district, 25 January 1796, PRO, PC, 1/23/A38.

[48] D. Neave, 'Anti-militia riots in Lincolnshire, 1757 and 1796', *Lincolnshire History and Archaeology*, 11 (1976), p. 25; *Sussex Weekly Advertiser*, 26 April 1802 and 16 January, 1804; *Reading Mercury*, 23 June, 28 July, 4 August 1794, 7 and 14 May 1810; J. Ayres (ed.), *Paupers and Pig Killers: The Diary of William Holland a Somerset Parson 1799–1818* (Harmondsworth, 1986), p. 51; Hugh Cunningham, 'The language of patriotism', *History Workshop Journal*, 12 (1981), p. 16; John Burgess, letters home from the USA, 18 September and 29 October 1794, in D. S. and P. M. Burgess (eds.), *The Journal and Correspondence of John Burgess 1785–1819* (privately printed, Ditchling, 1982), pp. 88–96; P. Lucas, *Heathfield Memorials* (London, 1910), p. 105; S. Isted to Earl Spencer, 12 July 1794, BL, Alt, G.16; *Cambridge Intelligencer*, 19 April 1798.

[49] The radical *Cambridge Intelligencer* could be purchased from outlets in at least forty-five market-towns across the country; see issue of 17 February 1798. Letters to Reeves from R. Sparrow, Suffolk, 13 December 1792; J. H. Stringer, and W. Deedes, both Canterbury, 17 January and 2 February 1793, BL, Add, MSS 16922, fos. 81–2; 16924, fos. 106–7; 16925, fos. 11–12; *Sussex Weekly Advertiser*, 3 September, 10, 24 and 31 December 1792; *Kentish Gazette*, 15 January 1793; Thompson, *Making of the English Working Class*, p. 201.

were addressed by anti-war campaigners, with dire – and oft-realised – predictions of war-induced slumps. The London Corresponding Society used the powerful metropolitan unions' organisations to distribute its literature, and warned these organisations that the Gagging Acts might stop normal industrial negotiations; an 'Executive Committee' of union leaders representing at least ten trades, circulated petitions against the Bills.[50] Many friendly societies, including those in Birmingham, were fronts for union branches. Knowledgeable contemporaries correctly asserted that democrats were not simply active in the unions and friendly societies, but used them for semi-covert politicisation; several unions – or groups of unions in certain constituencies – petitioned Parliament against the Combination Acts. The petitions castigated the legislation's legal aspects, the powers accruing to employers, and above all the seeming incapacity to fight for higher wages, when workers presently 'earn by their daily labour barely sufficient to maintain themselves and families'. The state's statutory initiative against trade unionism served only to facilitate persuading unionists of the paramountcy of the democrats' case, and indeed, many work-places were theatres for politicisation.[51]

Trade-union vitality is but one element of a vigorous plebeian culture; taverns provided key foci commonly through the ubiquitous 'free and easies' – popular neighbourhood clubs. Evidential snippets provide the occasional glimpse into this opaque world of labourers, artisans, and a leaven of marginalised middle-class folk, and not solely in London. Issues of the day were discussed, newspapers read, and the considerable outpourings of the subterranean press consumed; celebrations of Bastille Day symbolise the anti-establishment tone of these seminaries. However, this world, with its formally organised components, union branches, friendly and remnants of political societies, and its unorganised, informal veneer, retained a capacity for mobilisation at the local level, and through connections past and present, on a broader stage. That indefatigable campaigner for universal suffrage, Major Cartwright, used the concept of 'Town Associations' to denote these cultural foci. In late 1800 and early 1801, Cartwright launched an essentially secretive programme to mobilise these associations as the core of a petitioning movement for peace and

---

[50] Address 'To the manufacturers and other inhabitants of Nottingham', *Nottingham Journal*, 3 March 1793; Wells, *Wretched Faces*, p. 138; R. A. E. Wells, *Riot and Political Radicalism in Nottinghamshire in the Age of Revolutions, 1776–1803* (Nottingham, 1984), p. 22; Thale, *London Corresponding Society*, pp. 204–5. LCS bills, n.d., but November/ December 1795, BL, Place newspaper collection, vol. XXXVII, fos. 93, 97.

[51] C. Behagg, 'Customs, class and change; the trade societies of Birmingham', *Social History*, 4 (1979), pp. 400–1; Reid, *Infidel Societies*, p. 20; *Cambridge Intelligencer*, 22 and 29 June, 20 July 1799; *The Times*, 11, 19, 20, 21 and 27 June, 2 July 1799, 1 and 22 July 1800; *Journal of the House of Commons*, 55, pp. 645–6, 648, 665, 672, 707, 712, 730, 744, 749, 755–6, 765–6, 770–2, 776, 785, 792; Wells, *Insurrection*, pp. 52–3.

political reform, which he hoped would thereafter solidify in the form of a new 'Union', constituting 'a National Opposition' party.[52]

Claims that the anti-democrats won the argument in the internal ideological war in the nineties look decidedly unconvincing in this context, and indeed at the more theoretical level do not survive Professor Dinwiddy's penetrating revisionism in this volume. Nor should the relative paucity of state prosecutions for political offences be seized upon as evidence of very limited worker-politicisation.[53] Overnight or twenty-four hour commitment of radicals given to impromptu public denunciations of arms of the state 'was the common custom... about London', and elsewhere. Giving provincial radicals a taste of the local judiciary's powers under the resuspensions of habeas corpus was officially recommended on occasion. In contrast, some Benches notoriously turned a blind eye.[54]

Our detailed knowledge of the principal riotous episodes in metropolitan and provincial England, may obscure greatly enhanced social tensions during the nineties, notably in London. The King's coach was bullet-proofed after it was attacked again in February 1796, and on subsequent state processions to Westminster, the Guards were backed by the 'whole police of London and Westminster', comprising 2,000 constables. George III's drives to the theatre commonly provoked impromptu street protests, as did Pitt's appearance anywhere, even in Cambridge. London was recurrently covered in radical graffiti 'written in large characters, upon the walls of... houses at almost every corner', and virtually any incident could galvanise protesting crowds. Parts of London, notably but not exclusively St Giles, were virtually beyond the pale of normal policing, and on occasion the Volunteers were mobilised to throw a *cordon sanitaire* round the aristocratic West End. From April 1798 – in part a response to knowledge that insurrectionary cadres intended to fire the capital – 'a very strong patrole' did nightly duty 'at the head of the New River' where pipes drew off London's water supply. In 1799 a vicar wore 'an unpowdered wig because clergymen could not pass along the

---

[52] McCalman, *Radical Underworld*, pp. 83, 92, 113–15, 118, 122–4; Wells, *Insurrection*, pp. 195–7; *Monthly Magazine*, 11 (January 1801), p. 86; 12 (September 1801), pp. 114–15; *British Magazine* (July 1800), p. 59; *Cambridge Intelligencer*, 10 August 1799; *Anti-Jacobin Review* (October 1798), p. 478; (March 1799), p. 157; Cartwright to Wyvill, 31 December 1800; Wyvill to Fox, 5 February and 29 April, and to Cartwright, 1 May 1801, in C. Wyvill (ed.), *Political Papers*, 6 vols. (York and Richmond, 1794–1804), vol. IV, pp. 559–75; vol. VI, pp. 102–5, 138–40, 226–30, and editorial notes, pp. 234–7.

[53] H. T. Dickinson, *Liberty and Property: Political Ideology in Eighteenth-Century Britain* (London, 1977), especially pp. 271–2; Clive Emsley, 'An aspect of Pitt's "Terror": prosecutions for sedition during the 1790s', *Social History*, 6, 2 (1981); John R. Dinwiddy, in ch. 2 of this volume, 'Interpretations of anti-Jacobinism'.

[54] *Cambridge Intelligencer*, 7 April and 19 May 1798; A. Graham to J. King, 26 December 1800, PRO, HO, 42/55; Wells, *Nottinghamshire*, pp. 2–3.

streets without being insulted'. Upper-class residents mused that '*knowing people predict all sorts of horrors...many...things that make one quite nervous*'; 'God knows how long this calm may last.'[55]

VI

Several important facets of loyalism identified by historians look decidedly shaky when examined exclusively in the context of developments in the nineties, none more so than the supposed strength and duration of the populist variety, initially launched by the Reevite Associations.[56] The movement was conceived and born in the unique jingoistic crisis of 1792–3, when French promises to export their democratic revolution at bayonet point, were followed by war declarations by a regicide nation. Organised populist loyalism was inherently flawed from its inception. Despite its immediate context, whole ranges of inducements were present, from the distributions of free beer at the burnings of Paine's effigy, to the arm-twisting from house to house, and work-place collections of signatures for the petitions. Most local associations had ceased to convene by 1794, as acknowledged above by Dr Eastwood; even the most persistent – confined to major democratic centres like Nottingham and Manchester – did not survive the serious disillusory developments of 1797. The distribution of loyalist literature was indeed massive, but it was orchestrated and financed from above, as Hannah More candidly acknowledged. There is no evidence that those targeted by the 'Penny Tracts', and their ilk, bought them. And, there were – as we shall see – dangers inherent in this literature's 'relentless demonstration that the poor exist to be saved by the upper classes'.[57]

The range of expressions of popular loyalism, from tradesmen's issue of

---

55 *The Argus*, 13 February 1796; *Cambridge Intelligencer*, 26 April 1794, 28 May 1796, 8 July 1797, 28 April 1798, 5 and 26 January 1799, 8 March, 3 May, 21 June, 2 August and 15 November 1800; Lady Taylor, and J. Newbolt, to Lady Strangeways, 3 March and 20 December 1797, in H. G. Mundy (ed.), *The Journal of Mary Frampton 1779–1846* (London, 1885), pp. 95–9; Revd J. Newton, *A Sermon for...a General Fast* (1794), pp. 21–2; Wells, *Insurrection*, pp. 184–6; *British Magazine* (August 1800), pp. 152–3; Reid, *Infidel Societies*, p. 50.

56 Historians making exaggerated claims include Clark, *English Society*, p. 263; E. Royle, 'The reception of Paine', *Bulletin of the Society for the Study of Labour History*, 52 (1987), p. 16; C. Jones (ed.), 'Introduction' to *Britain and Revolutionary France. Conflict, Subversion and Propaganda* (Exeter, 1983), p. 8; R. Dozier, *For King, Constitution, and Country: The English Loyalists and the French Revolution* (Lexington, Ky., 1983), p. 170.

57 Thale, *London Corresponding Society*, p. 63; Austin Mitchell, 'The association movement of 1792–3', *Historical Journal*, 4, 1 (1961), pp. 57, 62–6, 72–7; D. E. Ginter, 'The loyalist association movement of 1792–3 and British public opinion', *Historical Journal*, 9, 2 (1966), pp. 181–4, 187; David Eastwood, 'Patriotism and the English state in the 1790s' in ch. 7 of this volume: W. Roberts (ed.), *Memoirs of the Life and Correspondence of Hannah More*, 3rd edn, 4 vols. (London, 1835), vol. II, pp. 234, 384–7; Martha More, *Mendip Annals*, ed. A. Roberts (London, 1859), p. 7; Olivia Smith, *The Politics of Language, 1791–1819* (Oxford, 1984), pp. 76–8, 93.

token coinage, depicting British naval victories, to fears communicated over local perception that the King was inadequately guarded during his Weymouth retreats, is certainly impressive. 'It is not the wish of the Generality of Englishmen to Strive to Be upon an Equality', Earl Spencer was told by an anonymous character from Northampton in 1795, 'they which [wish] to have Superiours'. When crises loomed, many took heart if local grandees were in residence. Yet as the Northampton man made crystal clear, reciprocity was *the* condition; he stated that 'I take the Liberty of an English Subject to State my complaint to my Superiors', added that 'if We are not to Look up to Such Exalted caraters as your Lordship w[h]ere are we to Look for Redress', and expressed his sorrow 'that the complaints of the people are very Little regarded by those in power'.[58]

The main affect of organised loyalism was intimidatory; at times, and in places, this could be counterproductive, though rarely as extreme as at Nottingham in 1794, when rival celebrations of allied and French victories by loyalists and radicals respectively led to fierce fighting, and terminated in exchanges of gunfire. It is of the utmost significance that from the 1794–6 crisis, almost every display of mass loyalism required major efforts to orchestrate. The crisis which peaked in the first half of 1797 turned much articulate public sentiment against the war, and parliamentary moves to oust Pitt imposed themselves on government policy. In one cabinet minister's estimation, 'the times [are] so critical, that things hang together by a thread', while any ministerial change 'wou'd absolutely endanger the very existence of the Monarchy and the Country'. Pitt, who believed that financing the war necessitated an incomes' tax, calculated that 'nothing could be more necessary' to prepare public opinion for it, and his political survival, 'than an Attempt to obtain Peace'. While 'favorable terms of Peace for us, cou'd hardly be looked for', ministers feared that Malmesbury's resultant and much publicised peace mission might produce a situation in which 'the Country or Parliament, were to compel us to agree to such terms of Peace, as we did not think ... better for the Country than the continuance of the war', and the government would be forced to resign.[59] Malmesbury's mission, and his undiplomatic treatment at the hands of the French defused the crisis to a degree; from Birmingham it was reported that 'the majority of People' were 'warm in their wishes for Peace', and as they also believed in its 'near

[58] F. H. Arnold, 'Memoirs of Mrs Oldfield, by her son and notices of the neighbourhood of Oldfield Lawn, from 1785 to 1808', *Sussex Archaeological Collections*, 38 (1892), p. 98, n. 25; letters to Spencer, from Capt. Arnold, and J. Powys MP, 11 and 21 July 1794, 'T.A.' Northampton, 12 May 1795, and anon., 11 August 1798, BL, Alt, G.15, 17–18, 29.

[59] Wells, *Nottinghamshire*, pp. 12–13; letters to Lord Camden from Chatham, 5 June and 7 September, and Carrington (n.d. but) 1797, Kent County (C) RO, U840/C97; C102/3–4.

prospect ... seem[ed] perfectly satisfyed with the present Measures'. But it was Camperdown which ostensibly ended the prolonged invasion scare and *enabled* the orchestration of some renewed patriotism. The state poured huge psychological resources into victory celebrations; architects were employed to 'prepare St Paul's in readiness for the king's great service of national thanksgiving', and if the monarch himself was not insulted again in the streets, Pitt resorted to subterfuge to elude crowds baying for his blood on his departure from the cathedral, while his effigy was burnt in twenty of the metropolitan bonfires celebrating Admiral Duncan.[60]

If Pitt secured his incomes' tax, the voluntary contribution of that same year, 1798, in the face of renewed invasion fears, was not the unqualified success and symbol of unified patriotism so commonly assumed; the resistance is symbolised by one clergyman's resort to threatening all non-subscribers with taking their tithe in kind. But, despite the Irish Rebellion, which inevitably galvanised anti-Irish sentiment, loyalism's resurgence was ephemeral, and it soon continued to evaporate. Post-1795 Church and King activity was a rarity, requiring much local provocation, or conflict, including the frequency with which theatre audiences refused army officers' demands for renditions of 'God Save the King'.[61] This variety of obduracy, among much other evidence, confirms that 'mass and united patriotism' during the nineties (and indeed 1800s) was 'one of the enduring myths of English history'; patriotism was in fact 'not constantly evident', but 'for long years it was markedly absent', so much so that it is 'hard to claim that patriotism gave strength to government in more than one-quarter of the twenty-two years of war', principally when invasion scares peaked. The faintest echoes of Church and King in the final crisis of 1799–1801 occurred in orchestrated crowd actions against itinerant evangelical dissenting ministers when they penetrated closed villages. Loyalism's collapse was also revealed in one cynic calculating that Hadfield's royal assassination bid of May 1800 derived from secret-service attempts to revive monarchism itself.[62]

These structural weaknesses in loyalism were also reflected in the Volunteer Movement. This conscious creation of not simply a police

---

[60] J. Clark to Spencer, 7 July 1797, BL, Alt, G.25; Colley, 'George III', pp. 100, 126; Wells, *Insurrection*, p. 111.
[61] 'Clergyman of ... Kent', *A Sermon ... for Voluntary Contributions* (1798); *Anti-Jacobin Review* (December 1798), pp. 631–2; Wells, *Insurrection*, p. 173; *Cambridge Intelligencer*, 27 August, 3 September and 1 October 1796, 3 and 10 June 1797, and 24 March 1798. Cf. W. R. Ward, *Religion and Society in England, 1790–1850* (London, 1972), p. 25.
[62] Cunningham, 'Language of patriotism', pp. 13–15; Martin, 'Evangelical Dissenters', p. 180; John Rickman to Southey, 28 May 1800, in O. Williams, *Life and Letters of John Rickman* (London, 1911), pp. 30–1.

force, nor a last-ditch defence against a French invader, but of an armed party extolling patriotic virtues and political conservatism, was also a perfect mirror of a hierarchial society. A basic distinction must be drawn between the Volunteer infantry and Volunteer cavalry. The former were principally urban regiments, and their rank and file comprised largely artisans and labourers, while their officers were drawn from the middling and wealthy bourgeoisie; plebeian enrolment was facilitated by local subscription funds, and many joined, not simply from patriotic and political motives, but for social, economic and practical reasons. Their first real test occurred during the intense food rioting of 1795–6. Many corps reacted badly; minorities ignored the bugle call, and although there is little evidence of mutiny in the physical face of crowds, action against their own class, imposing 'moral economy' tenets which most plebeian Volunteers would have endorsed, generated a rash of subsequent resignations. Those who remained had to endure peer-group hostility, and the infantry's continued reliability was not taken for granted by those with first-hand knowledge. The unease extended to government, which from 1798 'discouraged the arming of the urban poor'. However, disbanding entire corps, as opposed to the expulsion of untrustworthy or insubordinate individuals, was never an option: essentially compromised and therefore suspect, urban-based infantry remained in being throughout the decade.[63]

The greatest strengths of the cavalry Volunteers lay in the countryside; there were urban-based corps, generally much smaller in size than their infantry counterparts, and in London cavalry regiments included the unique Light Horse Volunteers, whose deployment was personally controlled by the Home Secretary. Membership required affluence, and the rank and file were almost exclusively middle class, with farmers comprising the backbone of rural corps. However, with the major and portentous exception of the threats made by some cavalry corps from Midland towns to march into counties including Oxfordshire, Northamptonshire and Huntingdonshire, to release cereal stocks detained there in midsummer 1795 by the populace, commonly with the open support of the magistracy, the cavalry emerged triumphant from their oft-intensive policing duties in 1795–6. Yet there were problems even with corps comprising principally farmers. Members exhibited a parallel motivational miscellany. The rank and file did not simply enjoy the closer relationship

[63] J. R. Western, 'The Volunteer Movement as an anti-revolutionary force', *English Historical Review*, 71 (1956); J. Bohstedt, *Riots and Community Politics in England and Wales 1790–1810* (Cambridge, Mass., 1983), pp. 49–51; Wells, *Wretched Faces*, pp. 268–9; R. Glen, *Urban Workers in the Early Industrial Revolution* (London, 1984), pp. 51–2; Wells, *Dearth and Distress*, p. 31.

with the squires and grandees who officered them, but – as one Earl was informed – joined 'out of attachment to you & not to their country'.[64]

A multiplicity of strains and stresses can be detected ranging from jealousies over commissions and promotions, to demands for comparability with neighbouring Volunteers over uniforms and equipment. Even in the early days, a rich variety – including pressure from wives to time consumption – underlay resignations. Decisions to accept prosperous market-town tradesmen caused confusion and diluted regimental economic unities. Recurrent difficulties derived from the supply of ordnance and ammunition from the government. In certain grandee-controlled areas larger tenants were more or less compelled to enrol, and resented it. Conversely, a minority of the gentry remained aloof, thereby effectively preventing their tenants' enrolment; others were specifically excluded on grounds of age or health, for political and social reasons, thereby alienating men with local influence. The invasion scare of 1797–8 was followed in places by campaigns to oust Dissenters. Ironically, for many corps, relative inaction between 1797 and 1800, combined with a belief that the internal threat had declined, weakened morale and enthusiasm. Conversely, funds raised locally began to dry up, requiring injections of government monies early in 1798; at this critical moment, when invasion again threatened, many corps categorically stated their refusal to serve outside their counties, or even their boroughs.[65]

Discipline certainly became a problem even in grandee-dominated Northamptonshire. Non-attendance at field days and refusals to assemble for exercises extending over several days increased, with grave implications considering the rudimentary standard of military training achieved; thin turn-outs threatened to make corps 'the ridicule of the neighbourhood, particularly so, of the democratical part thereof', who, of course were the

---

[64] Glen, *Urban Workers*, p. 51; Wells, *Wretched Faces*, pp. 111–12. For several reasons, the following discussion draws heavily on Earl Spencer's papers recently deposited in the BL. First, Spencer, as CO of the Northamptonshire Yeomanry, assiduously preserved his correspondence, which was inflated by his almost permanent absence as a cabinet minister, 1794–1801. Secondly, they relate exclusively to a predominantly rural cavalry regiment, in a county unusually heavily dominated by grandees, which should have provided all the ingredients for a particularly enthusiastic and less troublesome regiment than others, details of whose unreliability have already appeared in print. Letters to Spencer from Cartwright, 17 April, 30 November and 5 December, and Carysfoot, 23 July 1794, BL, Alt, G.15.

[65] Letters to Spencer from Isted, 4 May; Cartwright, 14, 17, 22, 26 and 27 May; J. P. Hungerford, 25 May; Capt. Arnold, 22 June; A. E. Young, 18 April; J. Powys, 28 April; Watson, 11 May; J. Clark, 6, 7 and 25 May 1794, 16 and 17 July 1797 (and Spencer's endorsement on enclosed petitions); S. Stevens, 5 January 1795; J. Russell, 23 November 1796; Capt. Walcot, with enclosure, 24 September 1801; Spencer to Armourer's Agent, 20 March 1800; Leicestershire Yeomanry, printed rules, 28 April 1794, BL, Alt, G.15–17; 20; 24–5, 40, 44; *Anti-Jacobin Review* (August 1798), p. 210; Eastwood, 'Fading visions'.

principal focus of intimidation. The yeomanry had to stomach repeated ridicule from their neighbours, and endure provocation. Resistance to the payment of fines increased. Expulsions of delinquents were statistically not great, but those who were, usually suffered public disgrace. Resignation was embarrassing and commonly difficult.[66] The flow of replacements dried up to a degree after 1797–8, again even in Northamptonshire. In the main, such difficulties were kept from senior officers by junior officers, and even when they were passed on by juniors who tried to engineer disciplinary initiatives, senior commanders invariably advised caution, were very reluctant to risk driving matters to extremes, and equally unwilling to relate disciplinary problems to government. Nevertheless, prior to 1800, there were solid grounds for confidence in the cavalry, which contributed to the stances of loyalist campaigners, including W. H. Reid, who claimed that 'the safety of the sittings of the House of Commons was owing to the formation of the [Light Horse] Volunteers, while democracy raged in the metropolis'.[67]

VII

Historians have overestimated the stability of the vast English cornlands; in the nineties the eastern and southern countryside's role as the *ancien régime's* bedrock, should not be taken for granted. Marked resort to parliamentary enclosure galvanised more protest than orthodox interpretations allow, and its deadliest effect was the alienation of considerable majorities in the affected parishes.[68] Moreover, the adverse impact of enclosure on small farmers, dual-occupationists, village craftsmen and

---

[66] *Anti-Jacobin Review* (June 1799), p. 214; Wells, *Wretched Faces*, pp. 271–2; letters to Spencer from Clark, 5 April 1795, Russell, 30 January and 6 March 1797, T. Bosworth, 5 June 1799; R. Atterbury to Clark, 9 June 1799, BL, Alt, G.18; 28; 32; indictments, Hampshire CRO, QR/Epiphany 1799; *Cambridge Intelligencer*, 26 August and 2 September 1797; *Salisbury and Winchester Journal*, 24 December 1800 and 5 January 1801.

[67] Letters to Spencer from Russell (and reply), 30 and 31 December 1796, Thornton, 1 November 1798, and Cartwright, Clark, and Carysfoot, 1, 3, and 6 August 1802; returns, Peterborough troop, 1799, and comments thereon by their CO, Earl Fitzwilliam, and Spencer, BL, Alt, G.24; 31; 36; 45; Wells, *Wretched Faces*, p. 269; Reid, *Infidel Societies*, pp. 93–4.

[68] J. M. Neeson, 'The opponents of enclosure in eighteenth-century Northamptonshire', *Past and Present*, 105 (1984). Cf. M. E. Turner, 'Economic protest in rural society: opposition to parliamentary enclosure in Buckinghamshire', *Southern History*, 10 (1988). Turner's picture of almost mass apathy derives from the use of a narrow range of sources; the latter are explored in depth by J. M. Neeson, 'Common right and enclosure in eighteenth-century Northamptonshire', unpublished Ph.D. thesis (University of Warwick, 1978), pp. 363–72. For further examples of anti-enclosure protest see *Cambridge Intelligencer*, 1 and 15 November 1800; *Monthly Magazine*, 10 (October 1800), p. 282; W. R. Cartwright to Earl Spencer, 21 July 1799, BL, Alt, G.32.

labourers, had achieved a notoriety extending far beyond those communities which experienced it. Even estate consolidation by big landowners stimulated intense fears.[69] The greatly hated and widely publicised 'engrossing of farms' which benefited greater agrarian capitalists at the expense of lesser farmers, also destabilised villages, and was more widespread, and some said invidious, than even enclosure. Moreover, agrarian prosperity did not prevent all farmers' bitterness at the sheer scale of rent increases exacted by landlords.[70]

Trade unionism penetrated the countryside; if some journeymen craftsmen prised out wage increases, farm-workers' imitative attempts failed, some after fierce confrontations with the yeomanry, and ended in court. Farm- and other rural-workers certainly participated in food riots, and were primarily responsible for the blockade which virtually terminated grain shipments from the cornlands in the summer of 1795. Customary rights, notably gleaning, and traditional festivals, including St Andring, came under attack in many quarters. Nor was the countryside a passive source of men for the army; while many did enlist, a popular 'hatred of military service' remained. Ambiguities over militia recruitment led to serious disturbances in several counties, with the judiciary in the rising's epicentre 'intimidated into inaction', and the restoration of order required the deployment of regulars. If fears that these events presaged the non-implementation of the succeeding Supplementary Militia Act, were not realised, 1796 events reveal shadowy organisation with radical elements politicising the issue through the broad distribution of 'seditious handbills'. Distrust of the government was symbolised in Norfolk by the burning of Pitt and Windham's effigies. Official appeals to rural proletarians were useless, as many were 'so disposed to believe mischief & discard truth, that you may as well talk to a stone'.[71]

---

[69] 'As the principal part of the land in this Parish [North Creake, Norfolk] has lately fallen into one mans hands, it has and is likely, very much to Distress the small Tradesmen, and the small Landowners', wrote Robert Hawtry; his grievance derived from alterations to the roads, and the loss of roadside rough pasture, previously 'of very Great service' for men like him who kept 'Horses to do...business'. He concluded, 'we...be totally Deprived of Our antient Right, and privelege'; to T. Harrison, 9 December 1794; Harrison to Spencer, June 1796, BL, Alt, G.16, 33.

[70] Roger Wells, 'Social protest, class, conflict and consciousness, in the south-eastern countryside, 1700–1880' in M. Reed and Roger Wells (eds.), *Class, Conflict and Protest in the English Countryside 1700–1880*, (London, 1990), p. 124; J. H. Bettey, *Rural Life in Wessex 1500–1900* (Gloucester, 1987), p. 66; J. V. Beckett, 'Landownership and estate management' in Mingay, *Agrarian History*, pp. 620–2.

[71] Wells, 'Tolpuddle', p. 113 and n. 77; Wells, *Wretched Faces*, pp. 108–11; B. Bushaway, *By Rite. Custom, Ceremony and Community in England 1700–1800* (London, 1982), pp. 180–2; Neave, 'Anti-militia riots', pp. 25–7; J. R. Western, *The English Militia in the Eighteenth Century* (London, 1965), pp. 294–302; *Cambridge Intelligencer*, 13 August 1796. Harrison to Spencer, 17 November 1796, BL, Alt, G.23.

The collapse of farm-workers' real wages, and its corollary – the massive extension of Poor-Law operations – was the greatest source of social tension and protest in the rural districts. The relatively generous Speenhamland sliding scales were quickly replaced by niggardly static allowances-in-aid-of-wages to men with large families, supplemented by additional payments towards the costs of clothing, shoes, fuel and rents. It succeeded in turning Poor-Law administration into a gigantic theatre for conflict. Open protest included fierce lobbies extending on occasion to violent attacks by individuals, and groups of claimants, on parsimonious overseers and vestries. The transformation of the rural incendiary tradition from a mode of exacting private vengeance to expressing public protest, and the emergence of the 'unEnglish' crime of animal maiming, belong to the nineties. The farmers were primary targets, particularly those involved in Poor-Law administration, and also responsible for arbitrary sackings, inadequate wages and derisory relief payments.[72]

Poor-Law disputes set the smaller farmers and craftsmen against the grander farmers. Traditional conflicts between tithe-owning clergy and virtually entire rural communities were fuelled further when vestries imposed discriminatorily high rating increases on tithes, as poor rates soared. In contrast, tenants advanced the level of rates in negotiations over rents, as most landowners accepted the expense of rates, though they refused to consider wage levels. Additional antagonisms between ratepayers and landowners derived from the exercise of the latter's judicial role in overturning on appeal tight-fisted vestry decisions against relief claimants. Rural poverty was clearly behind the massive upturn in countryside crime, some of it clearly morally justified as a form of protest, together with an escalation in the operations of extensive criminal gangs.[73] Observer followed observer in the identification of a marked increase in tensions, ranging from Dissenter farmers 'caballing' against their Anglican neighbours, to multifaceted insubordination, on occasion tinged with expressions of political radicalism and class-consciousness. In Suffolk, by 1796, the Revd Thomas Howes typically identified 'a spirit of disaffection, and contempt of all civil authority and aristocratic power...gaining ground'. The Revd Davies's 1795 publication, *The Case of the Labourers in Husbandry*, was even put on a par with *The Rights of Man*, and the publication of its authentic evidence of the miseries of farm-workers had to be cleared by Pitt himself. There were even open

[72] Wells, *Wretched Faces*, pp. 290–302.
[73] M. Reed, 'The peasantry of nineteenth-century England: a neglected class?', *History Workshop Journal*, 12 (1984): and his 'Nineteenth-century rural England; a case for peasant studies', *Journal of Peasant Studies*, 14 (1986); Wells, 'Social protest', pp. 135–8; and his 'Rural rebels', pp. 27–9. R. Jambspur to J. Harrison, 14 April 1795, BL, Alt, G.19; *Cambridge Intelligencer*, 10 September 1796 and 25 February 1797.

suggestions that rural deference would have to be bought; implementation of militia laws, it was said, required half-guinea payments. 'Money is a great temptation to poor men as well as to the Dissolute & abandoned because of the Gratification it affords them.'[74]

VIII

The final crisis at the turn of the century, opened with the manifest failure of the 1799 harvest, rapidly rising food prices, and coincided with Pitt's tough, uncompromising rejection of Bonaparte's peace initiative at the end of that year. Instead of a diplomatic response, the government pressed ahead with the Second Coalition's 'strategy of overthrow', the next stage of which comprised the disastrous attempt to invade Holland. Ostensibly Pitt's commitment to war, which 'staggered some of his warmest supporters', remained unaltered. The government readopted and strengthened famine-containment policies first applied in 1795–6. The importation of every conceivable major foodstuff – including maize and rice – was underwritten by price guarantees for merchants. The cereal substitute programme was fortified; new legislation outlawed the sale of freshly baked bread, while local authorities were enjoined to use every means, especially manipulation of charities and the Poor Law, to diversify consumption away from wheaten and other cereal staples, to embrace all available sustenance, vegetables, potatoes, rice, maize and, above all, soups and gruels. This major official onslaught on customary food, reinforced the dietary revolution already dictated by market-place economics.[75]

Once food rioting assumed serious proportions from February 1800, the government insisted that traditional remedies for subsistence problems, embraced by the 'moral economy', caused public disorder, and were economically counterproductive. The ministry refused to investigate publicly the notorious May–June scandal, when metropolitan warehouses were crammed with imported foodstuffs, and the Thames clogged with cereal-laden merchantmen, while prices failed to stabilise, let alone decline. Instead, the cabinet put the regulars, militia and Volunteer armies on permanent alert, insisted that magistrates deployed them immediately against riots, and reinforced military by judicial repression. The

---

[74] *Annals of Agriculture*, 27 (1796), pp. 215–21; R. Sykes to Wilberforce, 27 January 1796, Humberside CRO, DD.SY. 101/54; W. M. Pitt to William Pitt, 5 May 1795, PRO.30/8/167, fos. 205–6; Clark, and Harrison, to Spencer, 9 and 17 November 1796, BL, Alt, G.21; 23; *Anti-Jacobin Review* (February 1799), p. 217.
[75] *Monthly Magazine*, 9 (March 1800), pp. 176–7; Wells, *Wretched Faces*, especially pp. 195–7, 214–18.

government sought, and obtained, full parliamentary endorsement of all the principal components of this strategy.[76]

Gloriously hot summer weather fuelled universal expectation among consumers of a superabundant 1800 harvest, with additional plentiful supplies from the unprecedented importation, an anticipation uncompromised by sudden torrential rain across the country in mid-August. The reality of seriously deficient cereal yields was apparent only to specialists, farmers, merchants and millers, and the grain supply to major centres of consumption collapsed spectacularly in September, while prices rocketed. Belief in a *pacte de famine*, embracing every element of the food trade, engrossed public opinion. September witnessed very serious and prolonged disturbances in most large, and many lesser towns, climaxed by food rioting's almost unprecedented extension to London. Many local authorities, including entire Corporations, individual magistrates and notably Anglican clergymen, supported the price-fixing fury of the crowds.[77]

Shaken, and with Parliament in recess until January 1801, ministers recondemned the 'moral economy', publicly rebuked local authorities who endorsed rather than opposed the crowds' objectives, and through a Royal Proclamation announced the King's commitment to whatever scale of military and judicial severity was necessary to extinguish disorder. The 'moral economy' was additionally deemed an unconstitutional infringement of the individual's absolute right to private property, and – even more disastrously – the Home Office arbitrarily declared, in the teeth of public opinion, that the harvest was substandard. Pitt's sole and very belated sop to public opinion, came with his capitulation to demands expressed in a burgeoning tide of petitions, framed in an increasingly insurrectionary climate, for the emergency recall of Parliament. It proved a transparent attempt to buy time, but public opinion believed that the 'moral economy' would be enacted in statutory form, with the embodiment of the people's paramount will – the imposition of maximum prices on all cereals. The government shielded itself behind Parliament while it manipulated much publicised parliamentary endorsement of its claim of harvest failure, stern advocacy of internal free trade, and re-embarked on established measures to use public funds to maximise food imports, stimulate the domestic fishing industry, and extend the cereal substitution and diversification programme. The Parochial Relief Act permitted poor relief to be given in substitute foods, and the attempted dietary revolution was climaxed by the Brown Bread Act, which illegalised the production of white wheaten bread; henceforth the primary staple had to contain a substantial proportion of bran. Although parliamentary

[76] *Ibid.*, especially pp. 86–7, 254–5.   [77] *Ibid.*, pp. 46–8, 79, 85–8, and ch. 8.

investigation of the components of the *pacte de famine* was pragmatically promised, this was deliberately delayed until much later in 1801, when to all intents and purposes the issue had been overtaken by events. Pitt's resignation was protracted and confused by the monarch's recurrent insanity, which also virtually paralysed Addington's ministry in its first two months. The new Prime Minister's diplomatic initiative was not public property until April; by that time, traumas deriving from famine and major industrial depression, and political instability at the core, were soon aggravated by Napoleon's intensifying invasion threat over the summer of 1801.[78]

The whole period from late 1799 to mid-1801 saw recurrent negations of the popular will by government, Parliament and the monarchy. These negations derived principally from the multifaceted issue of famine, and were accompanied by the rapid and cancerous development of war-weariness, with demands for peace at any price. Wyvill and his County Movement associates decided against petitioning for peace at the time of Pitt's rejection of Napoleon's peace initiative, confident that a fundamental 'Crisis of Public opinion' was on the immediate horizon. In February 1800, a narrow majority at an acrimonious London Common Hall petitioned for peace, but at this moment it proved possible to get a counterpetition expressing confidence in the government. By the autumn this was no longer the case once 'the whole Nation is dreadfully awake to the Sufferings of the Poor, who in a fainting voice are calling for Bread'. When the Middlesex freeholders convened in October, all speakers advocated peace as the sole remedy for the crisis as 'war is the cause', and they instructed county Members of Parliament to vote against it on every possible occasion. The most spectacular, and symbolic registration of public opinion over the war, occurred early in 1801, when previously unshakeable Pittite manufacturers and merchants in the West Riding petitioned for peace. Wyvill again decided against capitalising on these initiatives; it was symptomatic that he now feared that mobilising the Yorkshire freeholders alone might galvanise insurrection.[79]

From the autumn of 1800, a more covert operation was launched by Major Cartwright and the 'Town Associations'; his strategy was to orchestrate – with 'as much secrecy' as possible – petitions from London

[78] *Ibid.*, ch. 13, and especially pp. 236–48; Wells, *Insurrection*, ch. 9; Spencer to his mother, 23 and 27 February, and 15 May 1801, BL, Alt, G.22; Emsley, *British Society*, p. 91.

[79] Wyvill to Stanhope, 13 January, and to Fox, 22 October, 2 November, 26 December 1800, 8 January, 19, 24 and 25 February 1801, in Wyvill, *Political Papers*, vol. IV, pp. 78–82; vol. VI, pp. 66–8, 70–5, 83–92, 116–17, 119–21; William Lamb to Lady Melbourne, 6 and 14 January 1800, in L. C. Saunders (ed.), *Lord Melbourne's Papers* (London, 1889), pp. 7–8, 10–16; James Oriel, Battersea, to Spencer, 17 November 1800, BL, Alt, G.37; Wells, *Wretched Faces*, pp. 330–1; Wells, *Dearth and Distress*, pp. 10–11, 39–40; *Monthly Magazine*, 11 (April 1801), p. 282; *British Magazine* (February 1800), p. 187.

and industrial centres, demanding peace and political reform. He hoped that such a massive display of urban opinion would stimulate parallel movements among county freeholders, not to simply push principal Foxites into leading the movement, but to mould it into a new, broadly based 'National Association'. Precedents of 1795 and 1797 vintage proved that even liberal elements of the agricultural interest would hold back if peace *and* reform were inextricably linked; fears that any mobilisation of plebeians presaged revolution was the new 1800–1 ingredient. Cartwright recognised that only herculean efforts could rechannel unprecedented popular alienation away from widely anticipated revolutionary explosions, and into constitutional petitioning. The movement's failure can only have confirmed and fortified supporters' original alienation.[80]

Cartwright's perceptions were shared by many others who witnessed the scale of Jacobin sloganising which accompanied the Spring 1800 riots, and recurred with greater intensity in September. Some riots were provoked by radical elements, and the situation was exploited to publicise political causation and democratic political remedies. A doggerel, posted up at North Shields, opined that 'When King's neglect the peoples good...Ower Allegiance is...absolved'. Similar documents at Kidderminster typically linked together 'blood thirsty Farmers...monopolizers &...all Tyrants', and concluded that 'The Bishops Vicars Curates Parliament and Kings are not only Evils but worthless things'. In November, it was said – in the House of Lords – that 'the walls of the manufacturing towns throughout the kingdom were too small to contain the quantity of sedition that was written'; identical evidence derived from market-towns, and even country villages. Claims were repeatedly made that neither the regulars, nor militia, nor most Volunteers, would act against insurrection. Radical graffiti, handwritten and printed ephemera repeatedly used French precedents symbolised by the guillotine, and, moreover, again presented the French as saviours of an oppressed people, deliberately raising spectres of an invasion on the principles of the Decree of Fraternity.[81]

---

[80] Wyvill to Fox, 2 November 1800, 5 February and 29 April 1801; Cartwright to Wyvill, 31 December 1800, 14 January and 20 April 1801; Wyvill to Cartwright, 10 April 1801; editorial notes, 1804, in Wyvill, *Political Papers*, vol. VI, pp. 75–9, 102–5, 138–40, 226–30, 234–7, 247–50, 253–4.

[81] See especially ephemera and street literature enclosed with letters to Portland from Revd Mayrick, Ramsbury, 21 June, the Mayor of Portsmouth, 18 and 20 September, R. Laing, North Shields, 11 October, the Bailiff of Kidderminster, 17 December 1800, Mr Lloyd, Lenhan, Kent, 2 January, the Mayor of Rye, 14 February, W. A. Sandford, Wellington, Somerset, 23 March, Lt. Col. Rooke, Bristol, 20 April, Sir J. Wrottesley, Staffordshire, 2 June; J. A. White, Blackburn, to B. Markland JP, 6 July 1801, PRO, HO, 42/50–2, 55, 61–2; J. Bowles, *Reflections on the Conclusion of the War* (London, 1801), pp. 61, 179; Wells, *Wretched Faces*, pp. 144–5, 149–52.

The situation from the autumn of 1800 to the summer of 1801 is most confused. A *jacquerie* was confidently predicted in the west Midlands in October, a number of mass rallies were summoned, and several convened semi-clandestinely in Lancashire, south Yorkshire, and the east Midlands, before January 1801. By an oversight, the Seditious Meetings Act expired, and from February huge meetings were held on moorlands in Lancashire, Cheshire, Derbyshire and the West Riding. This powerful recrudescence of open politicisation proved short-lived, owing to the hurried re-enactment of the legislation, and intimidatory deployment of the regular army, but northern topography facilitated further secretive but well-attended meetings to continue into August 1801, notably in the West Riding. Cartwright claimed that these were manifestations of his petitioning strategy, and fell victim to the revamped legislation, but the context permitted a marked resurgence of the revolutionary United Englishmen, who recruited significantly in London, the Midlands and strongly in the north.[82] That miniscule minority of local authorities who maintained communications with Whitehall were unable to demarcate between these movements, or realistically assess a millenarian dimension inspired by several Southcottian converts and prophets, leading the New Jerusalemites, or Ezekielites, after their oath 'never to rest till the [essentially revolutionary] threats denounced in' Ezekiel 21 'are fulfilled'; this, it was caustically observed, 'does not breathe that humble Spirit that these wild Enthusiasts profess'.[83] Another sceptic noted that 'the spurgeous flimsy productions of the brain are every day more popular', and some dissenting ministers also took to preaching from Ezekiel. The sheer panic was promiscuously revealed, with one Methodist minister arrested for preaching from Isaiah, which referred to cursing the King, while Wesleyans kept their heads down, exemplified by Jabez Bunting's

[82] Wells, *Insurrection*, pp. 186–95, 198–201, 209–26; Portland to Wrottesley, 29 September 1800; Major Clayton, Blackburn, and Wrottesley (with enclosure), to Portland, 5 November 1800, and 2 June 1801, PRO, HO, 42/53, 62; 43/12, fos. 182–4; J. Westcomb Emmerton, Thrumpton, to his brother, 4 January 1801, Nottinghamshire CRO, DD.SY.284/6; Wells, *Nottinghamshire*, pp. 32–4; Thomas Grenville to Spencer, 24 April 1801, BL, Alt, G.43.

[83] Wells, *Insurrection*, pp. 208–19. Ezekiel 21 verses 25–7 comprised part of an oath, sworn by blindfolded converts on the Bible:
And thou profane wicked Prince of Israel whose day is come, when iniquity shall have an end, thus saith the Lord God, Remove the diadem, and take off the crown; this shall not be the same, exalt him that is low, and abuse him that is high. I will overturn, overturn, overturn it, and it shall be no more until he come whose right it is, and I shall give it him. Harrison, *Second Coming* pp. 67, 119–20.
Several Wesleyans, including at least one pastor, were converted; others, including Methodist choir-leader Wild of Sheffield, joined the United Englishmen. Letters to Portland from Coke, 16, 17, 19, 24 March and 4 April; Bancroft, 23 and 29 June; Revd W. Atkinson, 30 March; Fitzwilliam, with enclosure, 21 March 1801, PRO, HO, 42/61–2; L. Hird, Bradford, to Fitzwilliam, 19 March 1801, Sheffield City Library, Wentworth Woodhouse Muniments, F.45/8.

very careful selection of biblical texts at this juncture. In fact, Wesleyan pastors were nonplussed, seriously doubted whether their prayers for the nation 'did any good', were unnerved further by the 'wildness about some very pious people', and despaired as their confidence evaporated. In contrast, millenarian prophecies, notably with Southcott's paramount projection of famine, appeared to be on the brink of fulfillment.[84]

The degree of sheer disaffection among working- and middle-class people was universally evinced. Hadfield's May 1800 attempt to assassinate the King stimulated a tide of anti-monarchial sentiments in town and country, most evocatively by the London crowd which violently taunted the King as he left the theatre after Hadfield's bid. In November 1800, one magistrate claimed that the Potteries were 'more dangerous than at any period since the French revolution ... I have never apprehended half so much danger as now'. In the spring of 1801, further, but seriously under-reported, food rioting occurred in some of these politicised regions; it was said in Lancashire, where Assize judges had already acquired unprecedented military escorts, that 'we almost realize the Irish Rebellion'.[85] Simultaneously, the south-west was engulfed by a spectacular revolt of food protesters – again with a Jacobin dimension.[86] The regulars were sorely stretched by throwing cordon sanitaires round the south-west, the industrial Midlands, and the north. Maintaining military communications required strict new procedures, including a ban on all but paramount messages being despatched after dark.[87]

The state's worst enemy when invasion loomed over the summer was mass apathy inculcated by 'Sullen despair'. Populist responses to anticipated invasion were at considerable removes from every predecessor: 'all their armed men will be insufficient to repell an invading army of French republican veteran soldiers', opined Thomas Hardy in London. 'The people when speaking of invasion ... say what is it to us who come down'; it was impossible to 'be more ill-treated nor plundered more than we are by our own countrymen'. Among the scores of identical observations was that made by Arthur Young, from a very different

[84] *Gospel Magazine* (September 1801), p. 301; Densham to Eyre, 2 October 1800, DWL, NCM, 41/74; Pawson to Benson, 19 and 24 September 1799, 20 January 1801, JRL, MCA, PLP.82-15-8, 9; 82-17-2; Bunting diary, 1799–1801, JRL, MCA, diaries box.

[85] Wells, *Wretched Faces*, pp. 146–9; John Massey, Newcastle-under-Lyme, to Earl Gower, 5 November 1800, and T. B. Bayley, Hope, to Portland, 21 and 22 March 1801, PRO, HO, 42/53, 61; *Monthly Magazine*, 9 (May 1800), p. 403.

[86] Wells, 'South-west', where the scale of political sloganising was understated. GOC Simcoe reconsulted one standard authority on the Jacobin menace, namely Barruel's *Memoirs of Jacobinism*. Simcoe to Lord Lieutenant of Devon, Fortescue, 15 April 1801, Devon CRO; Fortescue Lieutenancy Papers, L.52.

[87] Circulars, GOC Grinfield, Lichfield, 23 March and 10 April 1801, BL, Alt, G.44.

location, the depths of rural Suffolk; he seriously expected 'to see men join an enemy in crowds'.[88]

All these developments were both causes and effects of a fundamental crisis of confidence between society and the existing state, wherein government comprised an 'active minority...liable to be deserted by high and low alike'. Desertions accelerated rapidly between 1799 and 1801, cumulatively constituting a multifaceted dissolution of the system of governance and with it, ultimately, 'the establishment' as previously defined. Every component was dysfunctional. One poignant testimony turned on the way the conflict between moral and *laissez-faire* economics played itself out. While government and Parliament insisted on free-market principles, the judges, led by the Lord Chief Justice, insisted that common law could be used to implement key components of the 'moral economy', and that the courts of Assize and Quarter Sessions were the forums. Hundreds of prosecutions for traditional marketing offences followed. A major ideological conflict developed between the government, backed by Parliament, and the professional judiciary, supported by a great proportion of the maids of all work, the Justices of the Peace, and a burgeoning number of Anglican clergymen. All aspects of the dietary policy were ignored, or resisted, by those responsible for its local implementation, magistrates, vestries, corporate and parish officers. A parallel fate befell the government's central law and order policy. The fact that some Pittite loyalists, in most regions, continued to try to enforce dietary reform, uphold *laissez-faire* principles, and acted aggressively on the public order front, served to aggravate disputes within local systems of governance, and between local and central government.[89]

In this climate society started to dissolve with traditional alliances and relationships, coming apart at the seams. In many industrial and urban locations, Poor-Law ratepayers were unable to meet demands; the social-security system began inwardly to collapse, and in places ratepayers commenced collective refusals to pay. Charity subscriptions plummetted, with contributors too impoverished to pay, or advancing political reasons for refusals. The resultant dramas were played out within corporate bodies, vestries, courts of law and on the streets, with the doors of ratepayers and the philanthropic slammed in collectors' faces. At another level, especially in the countryside where multidimensional conflict sharpened in the critical arena of public aid, vicars openly and privately rebuked farmers for exploiting poor and middling consumers; pulpits

[88] Adam Clarke to the Revd Bogis, 26 March 1801, JRL, MCA, PLP, 25-2-5; Hardy to Cartwright, 24 January 1801, BL, Add, MSS 27818, fos. 16–19; Wells, *Insurrection*, p. 262.

[89] Western, 'Volunteer movement', p. 603; Wells, *Wretched Faces*, chs. 5 and 13, pp. 230–48, 260–5; Knight, 'Letters to William Frend', p. 48.

resonated with denunciations, and acerbic exchanges wrecked social relationships.[90] Fierce antagonisms developed everywhere and people in all types of positions of authority, and from all social categories, reexamined their position, and revised permutations speedily developed.[91] While Anglican vicars castigated the entire food industry, and by implication government policies over subsistence, they remained by and large stirling supporters of the war. Many urban middle-class people supported food rioters as the means of 'over-awing the farmers... the great oppressors in the land'.[92]

Early in 1800, many Volunteer regiments, notably but not exclusively infantry, expressed serious misgivings at their role as the state's primary weapon against populist impositions of 'moral economy'. There were many resignations, not least through organised pressure, including the expulsion of working-class soldiers from their friendly societies; some entire corps formally dissolved themselves before the summer of 1800. Desertions, including collective mutinies, accompanied the September hypercrisis, and thereafter few retained any confidence in the infantry; even the yeomanry, especially urban-based corps, were sickened by their role. The scale of the transformation was symbolised by the many Volunteers, including officers, who led scores of crowds mobilised during the revolt of the south-west in the spring of 1801.[93] By then, even the Home Secretary's personalised London Light Horse Volunteers were in crisis, as absenteeism undermined their reliability. The political reasons behind their desertion were symbolised by two major expressions; diminutive numbers mustered when the regiment was ordered against the London Corresponding Society's attempt to hold mass rallies in November 1800, and again to guard Parliament while it sat during the autumn.[94] In Leicestershire and elsewhere, Volunteers now said that the

[90] Wells, *Wretched Faces*, pp. 307–14; *Salisbury and Winchester Journal*, 5 February 1801; *Evangelical Magazine* (December 1800), p. 540; Ayres, *Paupers and Pig Killers*, pp. 43, 47–8, 51; Mayor of Bideford to Portland, with enclosures, 8 January 1801, PRO, HO, 42/61.

[91] It took many forms. An Irish soldier, sentenced to hang for robbing a clergyman, escaped from the condemned cell at Leicester, and was 'pursued into a corn field' still chained, but 'instead of bringing him back', his irons were broken, clothes exchanged, food given, and he made a complete getaway; *British Magazine* (September 1800), p. 205.

[92] Wells, *Dearth and Distress*, p. 40; 'Clericus' to the *Gospel Magazine*, 5 (1801), pp. 31–5; the farmers and merchants 'are guilty of robbing the community and stand [as] criminal before God... as those who plunder on the highway'.

[93] Wells, 'South-west', pp. 724–5; Wells, *Wretched Faces*, pp. 267–73.

[94] During the September riots many 'either paid no attention to the summons, or chose to judge for themselves the urgency, a maxim subversive of all discipline'; on the state opening of Parliament, 'the LHV never mustered so few upon duty', and had to be replaced by the suspect Guards; General Meeting of Corps, 17 December 1800; Portland to the Duke of York, 9 November 1800, PRO, HO, 44/44, fos. 80–3; 50/10, fo. 571; Wells, *Wretched Faces*, pp. 270–1.

war was 'not...just and necessary'. Finally, at the height of the invasion scare, dissent broke out in some yeomanry regiments, even in grandee-dominated Northamptonshire, where men – instantly dubbed 'secessionists' – resigned in small bodies in response to government demands for maximum training. This additionally indicates that the government's position – on all fronts – was no longer backed even by agrarian capitalists, precisely that sector of the population whose apparently solid support for the status quo determined the Wyvillites against attempting to mobilise them. Now, at least, sectors revealed an aversion to the prospect of fighting the French invader.[95]

While confidence in the Volunteers evaporated, many entertained serious and certainly not paranoid fears, over the continued reliability of the regulars. Some regiments, including the Guards, were notoriously disaffected, and there were multiple indications that other regiments were not prepared to function unconditionally as a police force. Another, and perhaps the most serious form of desertion, the abdication of the Bench, actually occurred during the revolt of the south-west, and there were parallel responses especially in those regions on the brink of politically motivated insurrection. The west-Midland Bench was in a torpor from the autumn of 1800; simultaneously, Nottinghamshire Justices of the Peace virtually abandoned communications with Whitehall, and some spent energies fortifying their houses. In Lancashire and Yorkshire, resistance to the renewed popular democratic offensive, devolved on a tiny minority of magistrates. Collectively, the Lancashire County Bench sought legal guidance on whether Justices' personal presence with the regulars was necessary.[96] Ironically, the government independently effectively tore up the Riot Act, by promising to support Commanding Officers who mobilised their men against crowds without reference to the judiciary. It was a telling testimony to desertion; so too, at another level, were the animated private discussions in the highest political circles, when the King was expected to die early in 1801, over how the Prince of Wales's appalling public image could be purified to ensure a successful succession to the throne. Shoring up confidence extended to dragging the King from his

[95] *Monthly Magazine*, 10 (December 1800), p. 475; Circular, War Office, to Lord Lieutenants, 23 July; letters to Spencer, from Earl Camden, 26 July, J. Bedingfield, Navy Pay Office, 1 August and 8 September, and Walcot, 24 September 1801, BL, Alt, G.42, 44.

[96] 'Secret Information' from Richard Ford, 21 May 1800, PRO, PC, 1/3490; Wells, *Insurrection*, pp. 80, 105, 169, and ch. 10; P. Mackesy, *War without Victory: The Downfall of Pitt, 1799–1802* (Oxford, 1984), p. 164; Wells, 'South-west', pp. 724–30, 743; General Nicholls, Stafford, to Brownrigg, 16 November 1800, PRO, HO, 50/10; Lancashire Quarter Sessions' minute, 21 January 1801, Lancashire CRO, QSO/2/170, p. 198; Wells, *Nottinghamshire*, pp. 32–4.

sick-bed to the Privy Council on one occasion. In the words of one resigning cabinet minister, 'the situation of things is as bad as possible': 'What is to become of us I know not.'[97]

This last crisis, coming so speedily after its several predecessors, was characterised by multifarious, social, economic and political dysfunction and disintegration. At bottom, it comprised the most serious crisis centred on that long-standing and deepening, fundamental conflict of interests in eighteenth-century England, between what can be described as the agricultural and manufacturing interests. In 1799–1801, there were major elements of a radical conflict between town and country. But neither principal interest, however conceptualised or defined, was united. The urban middle class contained a significant sector of capitalists concerned with the food trade, and were, therefore, identifiable with the agricultural, not the manufacturing, or dominant urban economic interest. There were equally fundamental divisions within industrial capital, aggravated at least regionally, by the structural reorganisation of industry partially germinated by technological innovation. Similarly, the agricultural interest, was not united, not least because economic change spawned conflict between, for example, greater and lesser capitalist farmers. In both principal sectors of the economy, divisions on class lines rapidly emerged. In the countryside, the strongest expressions derived from the fiercest theatre of conflict, the social-security system. Industrial relations in manufacturing were clearly becoming tense in general, and increasingly liable to disputes – often involving violence – in particular. The state, through its legislative response, and its commitment of considerable resources to the maintenance of public order, categorically revealed its support for capital, and especially innovative capitalism, be it for enclosure, or new technology, against labour. The state's support for Anglicanism threatened to erode cherished religious freedoms, and it acted decisively on occasion against Millenarianism, further solid proof that it was as determined to repress popular religion, as it was popular politics, and with the attack on moral economy, popular economics as well. Famine, aggravated by other economic variables, including those deriving directly from the war, and the state's overall response, proved it to be the issue over which the system of government, and with it the ruling elite, lost its remaining vestiges of legitimacy. It was no accident that every element, be it hunger, disease, inadequate public aid, enclosure or technological innovation, was directly attributed to the establishment. As one bill put it,

will you suffer yourself to be...impos'd upon by a Majority of Mercenary

---

[97] Wells, *Wretched Faces*, pp. 256–7; Thomas Grenville to Spencer, 23, 24, 27 and 28 April; Spencer to his mother, 23 and 27 February, and 15 May 1801, BL, Alt, F.22; G.42.

Hirelings, Government Pimps, Corn-dealers, Place Men, Pentioners, Paracites etc and yourselves starving for Bread.

Perhaps this is best symbolised by that Yorkshire unit of the United Englishmen which decided, that on the revolution, 'the first thing that they should take... they should pull down all the Machinery which would restore the Manufacturing business to its old Channel'.[98]

Every agency's efficiency was severely compromised; elements had collapsed, and more threatened to follow. The Channel Fleet mutinies of 1797, 1798 and 1800 had seriously compromised faith in the navy,[99] and despite Nelson's victory over the Danish fleet in April 1801, these fears remained if an invasion was attempted by the French. By this time, the British state was on the brink of revolution from internal forces. Many, including Malthus, feared all along that an English revolution would start, as the French Revolution ostensibly had, with a famine. As another incisive commentator said, 'the wheels of government begin to fail; and the throne itself stands tottering at the danger'. And, he continued, in anticipation of an invasion, to

suspect there are persons who make loud professions of loyalty, and are on every occasion ready to calumnate those that may see objects through a different medium, a sycophantic tribe, who would be looking out for personal, rather than national security.[100]

This is perceivable. As an interest group, the farmers were the most hated of all; some had already began to hedge their bets when Napoleon threatened, through deserting the Volunteers, determined not to be the first internal victims of a revolution. For the introduction of the ultimate external force, an invading French army in these circumstances, as testified by people as fundamentally different as Hardy and Young, could have been the final ingredient, opinions endorsed at cabinet level. This constituted the scenario in which organised revolutionaries, with their allies on the periphery, including the critical Irish theatre, operated. At the time Addington succeeded Pitt, Portland remained at the crucially important Home Office. He orchestrated military deployments and political intelligence collection and revamped new repressive legislation with such drive that there was something of a counter-revolutionary thrust during the first six months of 1801. Nevertheless, non-revolution cannot be attributed simply to this; Napoleon did not invade, and the final testimony to the ultimate threat of insurrection and revolution came from

[98] Cited in Wells, *Dearth and Distress*, p. 41.
[99] For the mutinies of 1797 and 1798, see Wells, *Insurrection*, ch. 5 and pp. 145–51.
[100] *Gospel Magazine* (April 1798), pp. 157–8.

Addington himself, namely the derisory terms on which he achieved peace in the autumn of 1801 and subsequent ratification.[101]

[101] Camden to Spencer, 9 October 1801, BL, Alt, G.42; Roger Wells, 'Britain's avoidance of revolution in the 1790s revisited', *Bulletin of the Society for the Study of Labour History*, 54, 3 (1989).

Index

Printed in the United Kingdom
by Lightning Source UK Ltd.
102228UKS00002B/199-216